"Chock full of real-life and timely e

sured in scope, this altogether stu

learning—and learning well—the

the right note. An ideal choice for an introductory logic course, it can serve
as at least a partial antidote to a cultural moment rife with strong emotion
and unbridled passion but too often conspicuously deficient in intellectual
rigor. Baird would make John Wesley proud! Warmly recommended."

David Baggett, professor of philosophy and director of the Center for Moral
Apologetics at Houston Baptist University

"*How Do We Reason?* is an informative, accessible, practical, and lucid guide
to logical reasoning—a fresh and insightful resource for a new generation
of thoughtful Christians."

Paul Copan, Pledger Family Chair of Philosophy and Ethics, Palm Beach Atlantic
University, and coauthor of *An Introduction to Biblical Ethics*

QUESTIONS
IN CHRISTIAN
PHILOSOPHY

HOW DO
WE REASON?

—

AN
INTRODUCTION
TO LOGIC

—

FORREST E. BAIRD

ivp
Academic
An imprint of InterVarsity Press
Downers Grove, Illinois

InterVarsity Press
P.O. Box 1400, Downers Grove, IL 60515-1426
ivpress.com
email@ivpress.com

InterVarsity Press® is the book-publishing division of InterVarsity Christian Fellowship/USA®, a movement of students and faculty active on campus at hundreds of universities, colleges, and schools of nursing in the United States of America, and a member movement of the International Fellowship of Evangelical Students. For information about local and regional activities, visit intervarsity.org.

Cover design and image composite: David Fassett
Interior design: Jeanna Wiggins
Image: black and white op art: © Dimitris66 / DigitalVision Vectors / Getty Images

ISBN 978-0-8308-5515-5 (print)
ISBN 978-0-8308-5516-2 (digital)

Printed inPrinted in the United States of America ♾

InterVarsity Press is committed to ecological stewardship and to the conservation of natural resources in all our operations. This book was printed using sustainably sourced paper.

Library of Congress Cataloging-in-Publication Data
A catalog record for this book is available from the Library of Congress.

P   26   25   24   23   22   21   20   19   18   17   16   15   14   13   12   11   10   9   8   7   6   5   4   3   2   1

Y   43   42   41   40   39   38   37   36   35   34   33   32   31   30   29   28   27   26   25   24   23   22   21

CONTENTS

Am I a tolerable master of the sciences? Have I gone through the very gate of them, logic? If not, I am not likely to go much farther, when I stumble at the threshold. Do I understand it so as to be ever the better for it [and] to have it always ready for use; so as to apply every rule of it, when occasion is, almost as naturally as I turn my hand? Do I understand it at all? . . . Rather, have not my stupid indolence and laziness made me very ready to believe, what the little wits and pretty gentlemen affirm, "that logic is good for nothing?" It is good for this at least, (wherever it is understood,) to make people talk less; by showing them both what is, and what is not, to the point; and how extremely hard it is to prove anything.

JOHN WESLEY (1703–1791)
"ADDRESS TO THE CLERGY"

QUESTIONS IN CHRISTIAN PHILOSOPHY

JAMES K. DEW JR.
AND
W. PAUL FRANKS

C. S. Lewis once remarked that, "Good philosophy must exist, if for no other reason, because bad philosophy must be answered."[1] About that he is surely right. Unfortunately, many today are in the same position as those Americans Alexis de Tocqueville described in 1835: "They possess, without ever having taken the trouble to define its rules, a certain philosophic method which is common to all of them."[2] That is, many people today have embraced, often without even realizing it, an approach to knowing reality that undermines their ever coming to truly understand it. They draw inferences about everyday life, theorize about major events and developments in the world, and do all of this while blindly utilizing philosophical categories and tools. In other words, they've embraced a "philosophic method" that generates "bad philosophy." The cure is not to reject philosophical discourse altogether but to embrace good philosophy.

Thankfully there is more to good philosophy than simply answering bad philosophy. It also enables one to entertain questions that are central to one's worldview—questions related to the nature of truth, the nature of goodness,

---

[1]C. S. Lewis, "Learning in War-Time," in *The Weight of Glory* (New York: HarperCollins, [1949] 2001), 58.

[2]Alexis de Tocqueville, *Democracy in America: Historical-Critical Edition of De la démocratie en Amérique*, vol. 3, ed. Eduardo Nolla, trans. James T. Schleifer (Indianapolis: Liberty Fund, 2010), 699.

and the nature of beauty. However, finding examples of those doing philosophy well can be difficult. And yet, given the importance of questions we are interested in, doing philosophy well is critical.

For this reason, a contemporary introductory series to the major questions in philosophy is incredibly valuable. IVP Academic's Questions in Christian Philosophy series seeks to meet that need. It provides introductory volumes on the various branches of philosophy for students with little or no background in the discipline. Our authors have written their volumes with their students in mind. They don't presume prior philosophical training but instead provide careful definitions of terms and illustrate key concepts in ways that make philosophy tangible and useful for those who need it most. After all, it is not just professional philosophers who seek answers to philosophical questions—anyone attempting to love God with their mind will find themselves asking questions about the world God has created and seeking answers to them.

The authors have also approached their volumes in a way that takes seriously the claim that all truth, goodness, and beauty is found in God. That is, in undertaking Questions in *Christian* Philosophy, the authors are not merely engaging in these philosophical pursuits and then adding Jesus to the mix when they're done. Instead, they are pursuing these questions out of a love and devotion to Jesus that not only guides the questions asked but also motivates attempts to answer them.

It is our hope that each volume in this series will not only help readers become acquainted with various approaches to important topics but will also encourage people in their devotion to our Lord.

PREFACE

Is it possible to be a rational, logical person of faith? Many would say no. Consider the following claims:

> Faith is the enemy of reason. The one thing every single one of us here must be united in despising is faith. It's the barren refuge of the vacuous, the fearful, the frauds, and the obstacles to accomplishment.[1]

> Faith is the great cop-out, the great excuse to evade the need to think and evaluate evidence. Faith is belief in spite of, even perhaps because of, the lack of evidence.[2]

Or more simply,

> Faith is believing what you know ain't so.[3]

What these assertions have in common is the claim that faith, by its very nature, is without evidence and exists apart from or in opposition to reason. The listener is presented with a stark dichotomy. On the one hand, there is irrational faith, and on the other, reasonable unbelief. Look at the comments under an online article that touches on religion or go to one of the many atheist websites, and you will find this dichotomy repeated again and again:

> Christians are Christians because, to put it as nicely as possible, [they] are just plain stupid. They might have successful careers, but anyone who believes their

---

[1] P. Z. Myers, Reason Rally speech, National Mall, Washington, DC, March 24, 2012.

[2] Richard Dawkins, speech at the Edinburgh International Science Festival, April 4, 1992.

[3] Twain himself is not actually making this assertion (though it is consistent with other claims he made). Instead it appears here: "There are those who scoff at the school boy, calling him frivolous and shallow. Yet it was the schoolboy who said, 'Faith is believing what you know ain't so.'" Mark Twain, "Pudd'nhead Wilson's New Calendar," in *Following the Equator: A Journey Around the World* (Stilwell, KA; Digireads.com, 2008), 64.

moronic fantasies has a terrible mental illness which is almost always incurable. What a waste of a life. These cowardly feeble-minded people are pathetic.[4]

If believers accept this dichotomy, they are faced with a hard choice. They must choose between being unthinking, gullible believers or intelligent, logical atheists.

"IRRATIONAL FAITH"

Some Christians accept this dilemma and embrace the nonrational side of faith. They wear their lack of logical reasoning or engagement with secular thinking as a badge of honor. Other Christians are not as extreme in their denial of critical thinking but still shy away from engaging with reason and arguments. In some cases there is a fear that if we were to tackle the arguments of atheists and lose, we might lose our faith. Better to just stay away and ignore the onslaughts from the secular world. In other cases, it is simply lazy thinking. It is easier to claim discrimination on the basis of faith or to retreat to like-minded communities than to do the hard work of developing counter-arguments to attacks on faith.

"REASONABLE UNBELIEF"

Those who set up the dilemma and hold to "reasonable unbelief" frequently make two arguments: one concerning knowledge (epistemology) and one about reality (metaphysics). The epistemological argument focuses on the need for evidence and runs something like this:

> Premise 1: It is irrational to hold any belief without sufficient evidence
> Premise 2: There is not sufficient evidence to support belief in God
> Conclusion 1: Therefore, it is irrational to believe in God[5]

This argument is certainly valid—that is, the conclusion follows with certainty from the premises. But is it sound? To be sound, an argument must be valid *and* have true premises. Philosophers Peter van Inwagen and Alvin Plantinga have argued that at least one of these premises is false and hence the conclusion is unsupported. Van Inwagen asks what counts as "sufficient evidence."[6]

---

[4]BobC, comment on Ben Love, "If There Was a God," ExChristian.net, October 18, 2015, http://new.exchristian.net/2015/10/if-there-was-god.html.
[5]The classic statement of evidentialism is William K. Clifford, "The Ethics of Belief" (1877) (reprinted Pantianos Classics, 2017), 90: "It is wrong, always, everywhere, and for anyone to believe anything upon insufficient evidence."
[6]For more on his critique of evidentialism, see Peter van Inwagen, "Quam Dilecta," in *God and*

If we give a narrow view of evidence and include only that which will convince all rational people, then premise one is extremely implausible. What evidence, for example, could I give that would convince all rational people that I have a headache, that Michelangelo's *David* is beautiful, or that murder is wrong? For that matter, what evidence could I give that would convince everyone that the material world is real?

On the other hand, if we give a broader view of evidence that includes intuitions and private insights, then premise two is implausible. Why couldn't my experience of God's grace, my experience of love and beauty, or my sense of wonder at the vastness of the universe count as "sufficient evidence" of God's existence? As Van Inwagen concludes, "I perceive a widespread double standard in writings about the relation of religious belief to evidence and argument. This double standard consists in setting religious belief a test it could not possibly pass, and in studiously ignoring the fact that almost none of our beliefs on any subject could possibly pass this test."[7]

Plantinga goes even further and claims that both the premises above are demonstrably false. What reason would a person have for believing premise one to be true? That is, what is the sufficient evidence to believe that one should only believe that for which one has sufficient evidence? And—if one *could* give an answer to that question—what would be the sufficient reason for believing *that*? And so on and so on. The fact is, some beliefs are just properly basic—without evidence—and form the basis for other inferred beliefs. So the beliefs "I actually have a hand in front of me" or "I have a headache" are properly basic beliefs, though they are not really based on "evidence." According to Plantinga, "properly basic beliefs" are beliefs that are rationally held but do not depend on other beliefs for their rational status. He goes on to argue that belief in God can be properly basic.[8]

As for premise two, there are whole families of arguments that claim to provide sufficient evidence to support belief in God. There are cosmological arguments such as those based on contingency or the famed "kalam" argument. There are design (teleological) arguments based on analogy, or the inference to the best explanation, or the fine-tuning of the universe. There are

---

the *Philosophers: The Reconciliation of Faith and Reason*, ed. Thomas V. Morris (Oxford: Oxford University Press, 1994), 31-60.

[7]Van Inwagen, "Quam Dilecta," 46.

[8]For a simplified version of Alvin Plantinga's argument, see Alvin Plantinga, *Knowledge and Christian Belief* (Grand Rapids, MI: Eerdmans, 2015).

moral arguments based on objective moral truths, or the conscience, or the rational status of morality. There are ontological arguments—both the classical version from Anselm and more recent modal versions. There are arguments from mind based on free will, on properties such as flavors and colors, and on the relationship between ideas and reality.[9] And for Christians, of course, Jesus provides the best evidence to believe in God. Perhaps every one of these arguments is wrong, but at the least premise two is not obviously true.

While the evidentialist argument attacks faith epistemologically, the materialist argument attacks it metaphysically. A materialist is someone who believes there is only the material world and nothing else exists. There are many variations, but the essence of the argument has not really changed since Epicurus (341–270 BC) and runs like this:

> Premise 3: There is nothing but material things
> Premise 4: God is not a material thing
> Conclusion 2: There is no God[10]

Again the structure of the argument is valid and premise four seems obvious. But what about premise three? In the first place, contrary to what is often claimed, this is not a scientific statement but a metaphysical one. That is, this claim is a presupposition, not based on "evidence" at all. But more importantly, how many people really believe this claim is true? Does love really mean just hormone secretion? Is goodness just whatever behavior enhances reproduction of a species? Is knowledge just a survival-enhancing mechanism without any reference to truth or the external world? One often reads materialists who claim premise one to be true yet turn around and make claims that go well beyond the material world. If this premise is true, what do words like *truth*, *goodness*, and *beauty* really mean? Why would we talk about the *tragedy* of a debilitating illness or how oppression is *wrong* if, as Richard Dawkins claims, "the universe we observe has . . . no design, no purpose, no evil and no good, nothing but blind pitiless indifference"?[11] It is only when we assume

---

[9]See, for example, Alvin Plantinga, "Two Dozen (or So) Theistic Arguments," in *Alvin Plantinga*, ed. Deane-Peter Baker, Contemporary Philosophy in Focus (Cambridge: Cambridge University Press, 2007), 203-28; or Richard Swinburne, *The Existence of God* (Oxford: Oxford University Press, 1979).

[10]The classic presentation of materialism is Epicurus, *Letter to Herodotus*. A contemporary popular version is found in Sam Harris, *Free Will* (New York: Free Press, 2012).

[11]Richard Dawkins, *River out of Eden: A Darwinian View of Life* (New York: Basic Books, 1995), 133.

that things should be *better*, that life has *meaning*, that we have a reason to do anything—and that seems to require something beyond matter.[12]

REASONABLE FAITH

But are irrational belief or reasonable unbelief the only choices? Could there, perhaps, be a third option? Could there be such a thing as reasonable faith? The great thinkers of Christian history thought so. Figures like Saint Thomas Aquinas and Saint Augustine considered Christian belief to be rational—though they disagreed on the exact relationship between reason and faith. It is true that some Christian thinkers were skeptical of the value of reason in *coming* to faith—thinkers like Saint Teresa of Avila or John Calvin. But even these skeptics believed that reason had a role to play in developing *mature* faith. The notion that faith and reason stand in direct opposition to each other is based on modernist philosophy. Though many people today consider this dichotomy to be some kind of timeless truth, it is actually a recent invention in Western philosophy. As Dallas Willard explains,

> It is one of the curiosities of Western intellectual history that, during the last century or so, those with no serious involvement with practical Christianity—maybe totally ignorant of it or even hostile to it—have been allowed, under the guise of "scholarship" or innovative thought, to define what religion is and to reinterpret Christian teachings in light of their own biased definitions and purposes.[13]

Many today have reinterpreted Christian teachings and concluded that faith and reason are incompatible. Unfortunately, some Christians have accepted this distortion as well. These Christians have then urged fellow believers to avoid the study of logic or philosophy. But are faith and reason really so opposite? Perhaps "believing what you know ain't so" is no more acceptable for Christians than for atheists. As C. S. Lewis put it, "I am not asking anyone to accept Christianity if his best reasoning tells him that the weight of the evidence is against it. That is not the point at which Faith comes in. Faith, in the sense in which I am here using the word, is the art of holding onto things your

---

[12]For more on the problems of materialism, see Stewart Goetz and Charles Taliaferro, *Naturalism (Interventions)* (Grand Rapids, MI: Eerdmans, 2008).

[13]Dallas Willard, *Knowing Christ Today: Why We Can Trust Spiritual Knowledge* (New York: HarperCollins, 2009), 8-9.

reason has once accepted, in spite of your changing moods."[14] Reason, with its arguments and counterarguments, is important for Christian faith for at least four reasons. First, reason can be used to support faith. For example, the various proofs for God's existence attempt to give positive reasons for belief. Second, arguments, and the ability to assess arguments well, can remove obstacles to faith. The brief discussion of the evidentialist and materialist objections to faith given above shows how logic can be a tool for believers. As the work of Van Inwagen and Plantinga makes clear, many critiques of faith are badly argued—or not really argued at all, but just asserted loudly. By identifying the problems with these critiques, one can show that belief need not be irrational. Third, careful reasoning is needed to articulate the fundamental doctrines of belief. What are the essential dogmas, and what is secondary or even tertiary? But most importantly, Scripture calls Christians to "always be prepared to give an answer to everyone who asks you to give the reason for the hope that you have" (1 Pet 3:15). Clear thinking is essential for Christians— and one of the best ways to develop clear thinking is to study logic.

Finally, learning to think clearly is essential to us as citizens, as consumers, and as human beings created by God. Most of what follows will not be specifically "Christian" in the sense of arguments about faith issues. Instead, this book will focus on the basics of logic that are applicable to everyone. In this book you will learn how to analyze arguments and find the assumptions behind the claims. You will learn how language works in conveying arguments— and the ways in which it is abused. You will see how advertising and political campaigning can rely on shoddy reasoning. You will learn to see the structure of good arguments and some of the problems with bad ones. In short, this book can help you use the God-given power of reason more effectively.

HOW TO USE THIS BOOK

Following a brief introduction, this book is divided into three interchangeable sections. The first section introduces ordinary language and the many ways sentences are used—and misused. Next, we examine one particular kind of argument: the categorical syllogism. In this section, we use a very stylized way of constructing sentences that allows us to build clear arguments. Finally, we will move away from everyday language altogether and use symbols to identify

---

[14]C. S. Lewis, *Mere Christianity* (London: Geoffrey Bles, 1952), 123.

the logical arrangement of arguments. If we think of the "body" of an argument, this book starts with the outer skin and moves inward to find the "bones," or underlying structure of arguments.

While this is the standard approach in teaching logic, some may find it better to tackle the symbolic material first and get clear on the structure of arguments before moving back to ordinary language. If you want to try this approach, begin with chapter one, then go directly to unit three and then on to units two and, finally, one. I have taught this material both ways, and there are good reasons for each approach. However, if you are working through this book on your own—and not using it in a classroom setting—I would recommend taking it in the order given here. It is often hard to see the value of symbolic logic until one has struggled with the vagueness of language.

Regardless of which order one uses, the most important part of learning logic is to do the assignments. Reading about sentences, syllogisms, and symbols is important. But without the practice of identifying arguments, recognizing fallacies, or analyzing syllogisms, one simply cannot learn logic. Accordingly, there is at least one set of assignments after each section. The solution to every third problem (marked with an asterisk) may be found in the back of the book. It would be easy to just flip to the back and find the answer—don't do it. Instead, try hard to get the answer yourself and *then* check to see whether your answer matches. The best way to learn logic is to *do* logic, so don't shortcut that process.

Generally, there are fifteen problems in each assignment. For those using this book in a classroom setting, the assumption is that the first five of these will be done in class as examples, and the remaining ten assigned as homework. Accordingly, the first five problems include a range of difficulties so that they can be worked on in class.

ACKNOWLEDGMENTS

I am deeply indebted to Irving M. Copi, whose book *Introduction to Logic* first taught me to think logically. His approach to the subject has been the standard for generations of philosophers and has provided the basic blueprint for many logic textbooks—including this one. I am also grateful to three decades of students in PH201: Logic who raised questions and helped me find examples. I would especially like to thank my many teaching assistants—in particular Katie Vincent and Gabe Carter, who both made detailed corrections in the manuscripts. Much of the content for the preface came from a lecture by my colleague Nathan King, who has enthusiastically encouraged this project. A special thanks goes to David McNutt, my editor at InterVarsity Press, for his assistance with the nuances of a text filled with symbols and diagrams. My daughter, Whitney (Baird) Edwards, read and made helpful corrections on the entire manuscript. My other colleagues Joshue Orozco, Carol Simon, and Keith Wyma, and my other children, Sydney Baird Childers and Soren Baird, have all been immensely supportive. Finally, I would like to dedicate this book to my wife, Joy Lynn (Fulton) Baird, who has helped me think logically for over fifty years.

1

INTRODUCING LOGIC

What is logic? In the broad sense, it is the study of the correct method of reasoning. But in a narrow sense, it is the study of the correct form of *arguments*. As a subject, logic is not nearly as difficult as many people think—and most people use it all the time. The problem is that language is so vague and serves so many functions that it is often difficult to find the form of an argument embedded within it. One of the chief tasks of logic is to find that form, examine it closely, and determine whether the argument is properly structured.

This book will begin by defining arguments: the parts of arguments, the kinds of arguments, and what makes for a good argument. After this brief introduction, we will look at "full-bodied" language as expressed in everyday sentences and the many ways it is used. We will examine the difference between form and function, between denotation and connotation, and learn to find the arguments embedded within the common uses of language. We will also take time to look at a number of common "informal fallacies."

Next, we will start to look below the surface of everyday language by examining one very formal way of arguing: categorical syllogisms. These formal arguments will begin to show us the underlying logical structure of arguments as expressed in language. We will also learn how to determine whether these stylized arguments are correct, and we will learn to take ordinary language and turn it into these formal arguments.

In the final unit, we will examine the underlying form of arguments by using symbols. We will develop a set of rules for constructing a logic of sentences and find ways to evaluate these arguments. This will give us the skeleton, as it were, of the argument. We will conclude by going back to arguments in language and translating them into symbols to see how well they are constructed.

1.1 TERMS

Arguments. So what is an argument? In a famous Monty Python skit, Michael Palin goes into an "Argument Clinic." There, he pays John Cleese to have an argument with him. After some typical Monty Python silliness, the two men get down to arguing:

> Palin: I came here for a good argument.
>
> Cleese: No you didn't; no, you came here for an argument.
>
> Palin: An argument isn't just contradiction.
>
> Cleese: It can be.
>
> Palin: No it can't. *An argument is a connected series of statements to establish a proposition.*
>
> Cleese: No it isn't.
>
> Palin: Yes it is! It's not just contradiction.
>
> Cleese: Look, if I argue with you, I must take up a contrary position.
>
> Palin: Yes, but that's not just saying "No it isn't."
>
> Cleese: Yes it is!
>
> Palin: No it isn't! An argument is an intellectual process. Contradiction is just the automatic gainsaying of any statement the other person makes.
>
> Cleese: No it isn't.
>
> Palin: It is.
>
> Cleese: Not at all.[1]

In the middle of this short excerpt from the interminable exchange, Palin gives a very good definition of an argument: "a connected series of statements to establish a proposition." Notice there are three parts to this definition:

1. "statements"

These statements that are given as a reason to accept a certain proposition are called "premises." All arguments have at least one premise or reason given for why one should accept something else.

2. "a proposition"

The proposition that the argument is attempting to establish is called the "conclusion." This is what the speaker wants to prove.

3. "a connected series . . . to establish"

---

[1]"The Money Programme," *Monty Python's Flying Circus*, first broadcast November 2, 1972. Emphasis added. This video can easily be found on the internet. As of September 7, 2020, it was available on YouTube, "Argument," uploaded by user "Andy Quick" August 9, 2015, www.youtube.com/watch?v=xpAvcGcEc0k.

It is not enough to just have statements and propositions in order to have an argument—they must be *connected* in a certain way. Consider the following:

P₁ I am hungry

P₂ This is a pen

C Tomorrow is Tuesday[2]

While we have two statements and a proposition, this is clearly *not* an argument. What is missing? There is no *connection* here to *establish* the proposition "Tomorrow is Tuesday" on the basis of the previous two statements. The "connected series . . . to establish" is the part that makes an argument work. In fact, it is this third point that is the key to logic. Logic is not primarily concerned with the statements and propositions that make up an argument. (Are they true? False? Would most people accept them?) Instead logic is about the connections between these constituent parts of an argument. This connection is called *inference*, and it is what we will be trying to isolate and test throughout this book.

Propositions, statements, and sentences. The Monty Python skit uses different words for premises and conclusions: statements and propositions. But this is misleading. Both premises and conclusions are made from propositions. Further, statements are just one particular instance of a proposition expressed in a sentence. Let's unpack this a little to get our definitions straight. What exactly is a proposition?

A *proposition* is an idea that is true or false.

Now a *proposition* is conveyed by a statement, but it is not exactly the same thing as a statement. For example, the statement

S1: "Abraham Lincoln is the president of the United States"

was true in 1864, but the same statement is false today. Statements, then, are bound by time, but propositions are not. When statement S1 was expressed in 1864, it was expressing the proposition "Abraham Lincoln is the president of the United States in 1864," which is still true today. Similarly, the statement

S2: "This country has a president"

---

[2]P₁, P₂, etc. are typically used to designate *premises*. The line under the last of the premises indicates that what follows is the conclusion. The line can be "read" as *therefore*.

is true if you are in the United States, but false if you are visiting England. So statements are bound by place as well as time, but propositions are not. The proposition "The United States has a president" is true even if I happen to be in England.

So, strictly speaking,

A *statement* is a particular formulation of a proposition.

Now statements (and hence, propositions) are expressed in sentences. But neither a proposition nor a statement is the same thing as a sentence. In the first place, many perfectly good sentences are neither true nor false. For example, consider the sentence "Do you think logic is worth studying?" This is a perfectly grammatical sentence, but it is a question—and questions are not true or false. One could give the command "Study logic" or exclaim "Logic, yeah!" and again not have asserted anything that was true or false. In fact, sentences can do all sorts of things, as we will see in chapter two. One of those things is to express a statement (which, again, is a particular formulation of a proposition), but that is not the only function of sentences.

A sentence is not the same thing as a proposition for a second reason: many different sentences can express the same proposition. Consider the following sentences:

Ray loves Ginger.

Ray: "I love my wife, Ginger."

Ginger is loved by Ray.

Ray liebt Ginger. (German)

There exists an x and a y such that x has the function of loving y where x is Ray and y is Ginger.

These five different sentences all express the same proposition. It might be best to think of a proposition as some sort of Platonic ideal[3] and all sentences as attempts to express that ideal. Shown as a diagram it would look something like this:

---

[3]Plato believed that ideas such as justice and beauty actually existed in another world: the world of "forms." It is not necessary to actually believe Plato's theory of forms, but considering propositions as if they "existed" apart from individual statements and the sentences that express those statements is a helpful heuristic device.

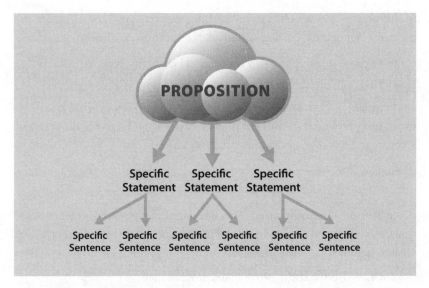

Consider these specific sentences:

1: Chicago is the second largest city in the United States.
    and
2: The largest metropolis in America outside of New York City is Chicago.

Both sentences express the statement that "Chicago is number two in population in the United States," which prior to 1982 expressed the true *proposition* that Chicago was the "Second City." However, if that specific *statement*, "Chicago is number two in population in the United States" (using any *specific sentence* to express it), is used today, it would express a false proposition (since Los Angeles is now larger).

Recognizing arguments. Arguments are often hard to find. Since premises and conclusions are both made up of statements expressing propositions, it can be difficult to tell which is which. What is a premise in one context may be a conclusion in another. There is no one rule that will allow a person to find the premises and conclusion of an argument. The order of the statements is no help, because conclusions can come at the beginning, the middle, or the end of an argument. For example, here is an argument with the conclusion coming first:

All fire trucks are red because red is easy to see and we always want to see when a fire truck is coming.[4]

---

[4]The fact that the conclusion here is false is irrelevant to finding the argument.

In this argument, the conclusion, "All fire trucks are red," comes before the premises. But in the following argument, the conclusion comes in the middle:

> Pine trees grow quickly so they make a good renewable resource, since fast growing plants are easy to reproduce.

The conclusion, "[Pine trees] make a good renewable resource," is placed between two premises. Of course, it is much easier to find the conclusion when it comes at the end of an argument as it does here:

> Running a marathon takes a lot of training, and I have not trained at all. Therefore, I am not going to run a marathon.

Given that the order does not tell us what are the premises and what is the conclusion, how are we to find them? The key to uncovering the structure of an argument is to ask two questions:

   1. Of what is the speaker trying to convince me?

The answer to that question will be the *conclusion*. Then one should ask:

   2. What reason or reasons is the speaker giving me in order to convince me of that conclusion?

This will identify the *premise(s)*.

   Often, though not always, there are words in an argument that help to identify premises and conclusions. Premises are often identified by such words as the following:

- for
- because
- inasmuch as
- on the basis of
- given that
- since
- as shown by

These words are *premise indicators* and let the reader or listener know that what follows are the statements that are used as reasons to establish a conclusion.

   Conclusions are often identified by such words as the following:

- therefore
- so

- it follows that

- as a result

- thus

- consequently

- which implies that

- hence

These words are *conclusion indicators* and let the reader or listener know that what follows is the proposition the speaker is trying to establish. There is one general rule that will follow throughout all of logic: *find the conclusion first.* Until you know what the speaker is trying to prove, you really cannot analyze the argument at all.

Premises or conclusions that do not appear to be propositions. Occasionally, the premises or the conclusion will not appear to be statements. For example, a rhetorical question does not *appear* to express a proposition. After all, questions are neither true nor false and so could not be premises or conclusions. However, a *rhetorical* question is not really a question at all; it is actually a statement that *is* conveying a proposition. For example, when a delegation from Parliament requested that Queen Elizabeth I (1533–1603) get married soon—and only to an Englishman—she responded,

> Was I not born in the realm? Were my parents born in any foreign country? Is not my kingdom here? Whom have I oppressed? Whom have I enriched to other's harm? What turmoil have I made in this commonwealth that I should be suspected to have no regard to the same? . . . I am your anointed Queen . . . [and] I will never be by violence constrained to do anything.[5]

Now this argument uses six rhetorical questions as premises for the conclusion "I will do what I want." But they are not really questions; they are expressing propositions: "I was born in the realm," "My parents were born here," and so on. Or consider the following argument by Mark Antony before the citizens of Rome:

> I thrice presented him [Caesar] a kingly crown,
> Which he did thrice refuse: was this ambition?[6]

---

[5]Queen Elizabeth I, Response to Parliamentary Delegation on Her Marriage, 1566.
[6]William Shakespeare, *Julius Caesar*, act 3, scene 2.

Clearly Mark Antony is arguing for the conclusion that Caesar was not ambitious, though it is never stated. Instead Mark Antony leaves the listener with a question—but one that he expects to be answered with a no. And he gives a reason why the listener should conclude that Caesar was not ambitious: he refused the crown three times.

Missing premise(s) or conclusion(s). This last example makes an important point. In ordinary language, it is common to leave out a premise or even the conclusion and expect the reader or hearer to supply the missing piece. Such arguments are called *enthymemes*, and we will discuss them more thoroughly in chapter six. Consider the following argument from Aristotle:

> The law does not expressly permit suicide, and what it does not expressly permit it forbids.[7]

In this argument the conclusion, "Suicide is prohibited by law," is only implied—it is not stated explicitly. An enthymeme draws the listener in by forcing him or her to participate in the argument.

Assignment 1.1. Find the premise(s) and the conclusion in the following arguments. (The solution to questions with an asterisk are found in the back of the book. Try to answer them *before* going to the back to check your answer.)

Example: "The nature of man is intricate; the objects of society are of the greatest possible complexity: and therefore no simple disposition or direction of power can be suitable either to man's nature or to the quality of his affairs" (Edmund Burke, *Reflections on the Revolution in France*).

Solution: Premise 1: The nature of man is intricate.

Premise 2: The objects of society are of the greatest possible complexity.

Conclusion: No simple disposition or direction of power can be suitable either to man's nature or to the quality of his affairs.

1. You really should not wear that outfit. It doesn't fit and it needs to be washed.

2. Musical theater performers are more talented than regular actors because they can sing, dance, *and* act.

---

[7]Aristotle, *Nichomachean Ethics*, trans. W. D. Ross, 1138a7 (Book V, Chapter 11).

*3. Kids who go to preschool are more likely to go to college. We want more people to go to college, so we should have public preschool for everyone.

4. Going off to school is traumatizing, and when people are traumatized, they are often not at their best. So we should probably give some slack to obnoxious frosh.

5. "At the present time, when women are beginning to take part in the affairs of the world, it is still a world that belongs to men—they have no doubt of it at all and women have scarcely any. To decline to be the Other, to refuse to be a party to the deal—this would be for women to renounce all the advantages conferred upon them by their alliance with the superior caste. Man-the-sovereign will provide woman-the-liege with material protection and will undertake the moral justification of her existence; thus she can evade at once both economic risk and the metaphysical risk of a liberty in which ends and aims must be contrived without assistance" (Simone de Beauvoir, *The Second Sex*).

*6. "From this equality of ability, arises equality of hope in the attaining of our ends. And therefore if any two men desire the same thing, which nevertheless they cannot both enjoy, they become enemies" (Thomas Hobbes, *Leviathan*).

7. "The social order is a sacred right which is the basis of all other rights. Nevertheless, this right does not come from nature, and must therefore be founded on conventions" (Jean-Jacques Rousseau, *The Social Contract*).

8. "It is admitted that moderation and the mean are best, and therefore it will clearly be best to possess the gifts of fortune in moderation" (Aristotle, *Politics*).

*9. "Now, can we say that people sometimes are thirsty, and yet do not wish to drink? Then we shall have reasonable grounds for assuming that these are two principles [in the soul] distinct one from the other" (Plato, *Republic*).

10. "Since there are evidently more than one end, and we choose some of these (e.g. wealth, flutes, and in general instruments) for the sake of something else, clearly not all ends are final ends" (Aristotle, *Nichomachean Ethics*).

11. "I desire what is good. Therefore, everyone who does not agree with me is a traitor" (George III of England).

*12. "*Thought.*—All the dignity of man consists in thought. Thought is therefore by its nature a wonderful and incomparable thing" (Blaise Pascal, *Pensées*).

13. "It is an article of faith that God exists. But what is of faith cannot be demonstrated, because a demonstration produces scientific knowledge; whereas faith is of the unseen (Heb. 11:1). Therefore it cannot be demonstrated that God exists" (Thomas Aquinas, *Summa theologiae*).[8]

14. "The existence of God and other like truths about God, which can be known by natural reason, are not articles of faith, but are preambles to the articles; for faith presupposes natural knowledge" (Thomas Aquinas, *Summa theologiae*).

*15. "It should be understood that [God's] presence is not felt so fully, I mean so clearly, as when revealed the first time or at other times when God grants the soul this gift. For if the presence were felt so clearly, the soul would find it impossible to be engaged in anything else or even to live among people" (Teresa of Avila, *Interior Castle*).

1.2 TYPES OF ARGUMENTS

Every argument claims there is some connection between certain propositions such that one or more propositions are claimed to follow from the others. But what sort of connection is being made? There are two basic kinds of arguments: deductive and inductive.[9]

Deductive arguments. Folks often claim that deductive arguments reason from the universal to the particular while inductive arguments reason from the particular to the universal—and this is frequently correct. It is also possible, however, to argue from universals to particulars, particulars to universals, universals to universals, and particulars to particulars in *both* an inductive and deductive manner. The key difference between deductive and inductive arguments is not the direction of the argument but the claim about necessity that is

---

[8]This is an argument with which Thomas Aquinas *disagrees.* The argument in number 14 is his response.

[9]Some logicians would add a third category: abductive. Sometimes these kinds of arguments are called "retroductive" or "inference to the best explanation." For more on abductive reasoning, see Douglas Walton, *Abductive Reasoning* (Tuscaloosa: University of Alabama Press, 2005); Peter Lipton, *Inference to the Best Explanation*, 2nd ed. (Abingdon, UK: Routledge, 2004); or Atocha Aliseda, *Abductive Reasoning: Logical Investigations into Discovery and Explanation* (Dordrecht, Netherlands: Springer, 2006).

being made. *In a deductive argument, the claim is made that the conclusion necessarily follows from the premise(s).* Here is a deductive argument:

P₁ All persons are mortal

P₂ Socrates is a person

C Socrates is mortal

There is no way the premises could be true and the conclusion false—it follows *with necessity* from the premises. Now the premises might be false, and in that case we don't know whether the conclusion is true. But *if* the premises here are true, then the conclusion *must* be true—the conclusion is not 99 percent or "very likely" to be true, it is absolutely necessary.

Inductive arguments. An inductive argument is not claiming that the conclusion follows with necessity, but only with probability. It may be a very high probability, but it is still not a certainty. So *in an inductive argument, the claim is made that the conclusion follows with probability—but not with necessity—from the premise(s).* Here is a sample inductive argument:

P₁ Socrates was an Athenian

P₂ Most Athenians ate fish

C Socrates ate fish

It is possible for the premises here to be true while the conclusion is false—perhaps Socrates was that rare Athenian who never touched fish.[10] The key question to ask in order to decide whether an argument is deductive or inductive is this:

> Is there anything I could add to the premise(s) that would make the conclusion more or less likely to be true?[11]

If the answer is no, then the argument is deductive. If the answer is yes, then it is inductive. Consider this argument:

P₁ Stephen watches Fox News four hours a day

P₂ Most people who watch Fox News
  four hours a day are political conservatives

C Stephen is a political conservative

---

[10]Note also that even if the word "most" in the second premise were missing, it is implied and hence the argument would still be inductive.

[11]Other than something that contradicts the premise(s), of course.

Now, is there anything you could add to the premises here (without contradicting them) that would make this conclusion more or less likely? Well, if you added the premise

P_3 Stephen is a member of the NRA

that would make the conclusion more likely. On the other hand, if you added the premise

P_4 Stephen watches Fox News to get material to mock on his TV show *The Late Show with Stephen Colbert*

the conclusion would be much less likely. Note that neither of these possible additional premises contradicts the original premises. Those original premises could be true, but if P_3 or P_4 was also true, Stephen's being a political conservative would be more or less likely.

So in summary:

	Deductive	Inductive
Premises claimed to:	Provide definitive conclusion	Provide tentative conclusion
Conclusion claimed to:	Follow with necessity	Follow with high probability

Assignment 1.2. For the following arguments, state the conclusion and determine whether they are deductive or inductive arguments.

Example: "As many more individuals of each species are born than can possibly survive; and as, consequently, there is a frequently recurring struggle for existence, it follows that any being, if it vary however slightly in any manner profitable to itself, under the complex and sometimes varying conditions of life, will have a better chance of surviving, and thus be naturally selected" (Charles Darwin, *The Origin of Species*).

Solution: The conclusion is, "Any being, if it vary however slightly in any manner profitable to itself, under the complex and sometimes varying conditions of life, will have a better chance of surviving, and thus be naturally selected." It is an inductive argument as it is arguing to a likely conclusion.

1. All life on earth is dependent on water, so if we find life on other planets, there will be water there as well.

2. It rarely snows in Seattle, so if you move there, don't bother taking a snow shovel.

*3. The swans on the Thames River are all white, the swans on Boston Common are all white, the swans at the San Diego Zoo are all white, so all swans are white.

4. It could not have been Miss Scarlett in the kitchen with the wrench or Colonel Mustard in the ballroom with the rope, and all other possibilities have been tried, so it must have been Professor Plum in the dining room with the candlestick.

5. Eleanor is wearing a pink tutu over her shorts. Yesterday she wore the pink tutu over her sweatpants. So the pink tutu must be her favorite.

*6. "NASA's newest Mars rover, Curiosity, has snapped photos of rocky outcroppings that jut out from the alien soil, and scientists say they look like the remnants of an ancient stream bed where water once flowed on the surface of the red planet. . . . Scientists looked at all this and came to this conclusion: 'This is a rock that was formed in the presence of water,' says John Grotzinger, project scientist at the Cal. Tech" (Nell Greenfieldboyce, "NASA's Curiosity Finds Water Once Flowed On Mars").

7. "Socrates: So when I went away, I thought to myself, 'I am wiser than this man: neither of us knows anything that is really worth knowing, but he thinks that he has knowledge when he has not, while I, having no knowledge, do not think that I have. I seem, at any rate, to be a little wiser than he is on this point: I do not think that I know what I do not know'" (Plato, *Apology*).

8. "Now in all states there are three elements: one class is very rich, another very poor, and a third in a mean. It is admitted that moderation and the mean are best, and therefore it will clearly be best to possess the gifts of fortune in moderation; for in that condition of life men are most ready to follow rational principle" (Aristotle, *Politics*).

*9. "[Jesus] either was (and is) just what He said, or else a lunatic, or something worse. Now it seems to me obvious that He was neither a lunatic nor a fiend: and consequently, however strange or terrifying or unlikely it may seem, I have to accept the view that He was and is God" (C. S. Lewis, *Mere Christianity*).

10. "If God exists, there is no pointless suffering. But there is pointless suffering. Therefore, God does not exist" (Bruce Russell, "Why Doesn't God Intervene to Prevent Evil?").

11. "For when the will abandons what is above itself, and turns to what is lower, it becomes evil—not because that is evil to which it turns, but the turning itself is wicked. Therefore it is not an inferior thing which has made the will evil, but it is itself which has become so by wickedly and inordinately desiring an inferior thing" (Augustine, *City of God*).

*12. "And must we not allow, that when I or any one, looking at any object, observes that the thing which he sees aims at being some other thing, but falls short of, and cannot be, that other thing, but is inferior, he who makes this observation must have had a previous knowledge of that to which the other, although similar, was inferior?[12] . . . And has not this been our own case in the matter of equals and of absolute equality? . . . Then we must have known equality previously to the time when we first saw the material equals, and reflected that all these apparent equals strive to attain absolute equality, but fall short of it" (Plato, *Phaedo*).

13. "All men by nature desire to know. An indication of this is the delight we take in our senses; for even apart from their usefulness they are loved for themselves; and above all others the sense of sight" (Aristotle, *Metaphysics*).

14. "There are deep similarities between the situation of woman and that of the Negro. Both are being emancipated today from a like paternalism, and the former master class wishes to 'keep them in their place'—that is, the place chosen for them. In both cases the former masters lavish more or less sincere eulogies, either on the virtues of 'the good Negro' with his dormant, childish, merry soul—the submissive Negro—or on the merits of the woman who is 'truly feminine'—that is, frivolous, infantile, irresponsible—the submissive woman" (Simone de Beauvoir, *The Second Sex*).

---

[12]That is, if we realize that something falls short of a standard, then we must already have known the standard to which it compares unfavorably.

*15. "A pure democracy, by which I mean a society consisting of a small number of citizens, who assemble and administer the government in person, can admit of no cure for the mischiefs of faction. A common passion or interest will, in almost every case, be felt by a majority of the whole; a communication and concert result from the form of government itself; and there is nothing to check the inducements to sacrifice the weaker party or an obnoxious individual. Hence it is that such democracies have ever been spectacles of turbulence and contention; have ever been found incompatible with personal security or the rights of property; and have in general been as short in their lives as they have been violent in their deaths" (James Madison, *The Federalist Papers* 10).

1.3 CHARACTERISTICS OF A DEDUCTIVE ARGUMENT

Validity. For the rest of this book, we will be focusing on deductive arguments alone.[13] Remember that in a deductive argument, the claim is made that the conclusion follows necessarily from the premise(s). However, *claiming* that the conclusion is necessary and proving that the conclusion *actually* follows with necessity are two different things. When an argument is arranged in such a way that the conclusion does, in fact, necessarily follow, that argument is *valid*. Put more formally, *in a deductive argument, if the conclusion follows with logical necessity from the premise(s), then the argument is valid.* Notice that even if the conclusion follows with really, really high probability from the premise(s), that is not sufficient. In a deductive argument, there is either necessity or nothing. Any deductive argument where the conclusion does not necessarily follow from the premise(s) is invalid.

In a deductive argument it is the *structure* that is valid or invalid. For example, the following argument is obviously valid:

P$_1$ All whales are mammals

P$_2$ All mammals are animals

C All whales are animals

---

[13]There is simply not enough space to include inductive arguments here. For introductions to inductive reasoning see Ian Hacking, *An Introduction to Probability and Inductive Logic* (Cambridge: Cambridge University Press, 2001); Brian Skyrms, *Choice and Chance: An Introduction to Inductive Logic*, 4th ed. (Belmont, CA: Wadsworth, 2000); or Aidan Feeney and Evan Heit, *Inductive Reasoning: Experimental, Developmental and Computational Approaches* (Cambridge: Cambridge University Press, 2007).

But this argument is valid as well:

P₁ All spiders are six-legged bugs

P₂ All six-legged bugs creep me out
_____
C All spiders creep me out

Both arguments have the same formal structure:

P₁ All A is B

P₂ All B is C
_____
C All A is C

It is this *structure* that is valid. But there is something very different about these two arguments. In the first argument, the premises are true, so we know the conclusion must be true.

In the second argument, however, the first premise is clearly false and the second premise depends on my personal response to six-legged bugs, which may or may not be true. So what about the conclusion—is that true? You don't know. Perhaps spiders creep me out, perhaps they don't. But there is one thing about which you can be sure: *If* spiders have six legs and *if* six-legged bugs creep me out, then spiders creep me out. This is true because of the *structure* of the argument.

Truth and validity. In our postmodern world, there are many questions about the nature of truth. What does it mean for a proposition to be "true"? How can we know whether it is true? Who gets to decide whether it is true? For our purposes as logicians, these important questions are irrelevant. Odd though it may sound, we are not really concerned about truth. What we want to know is what does or does not follow *if* a proposition is true. We will leave it up to others to decide whether, in fact, it *is* true.

There are eight different ways truth and validity might be combined in an argument: four that are valid and four that are invalid. We can formulate valid arguments with false premises and a true conclusion, invalid arguments with true premises and a false conclusion, and so on. All but one of these is possible. The one combination that simply cannot happen is a valid argument with true premises and a false conclusion. This means that the truth or falsity of a conclusion or premise tells us nothing about the validity of an argument. Even the fact that an argument is valid does not ensure that its conclusion is true. Nor does the fact that an argument contains all true propositions tell us that it is valid.

Sometimes because a person already believes so strongly in the truth of the conclusion and premises, they think the argument that puts them together must be valid. This happens often with proofs for and against God's existence: the believers or nonbelievers are so convinced of their conclusions that they fail to recognize that they do not actually follow from the premises given.

Soundness. The problem with the earlier argument about six-legged bugs and spiders is that it is *valid* but it is not *sound*. While its validity means that the conclusion must be true *if* the premise(s) are true, at least one of the premises here is false, so we don't know about the conclusion. If the premises of a valid argument are true, however, we can be certain that the conclusion is also true. *A sound argument is one in which (1) the argument is valid and (2) the premise(s) are true, which means the conclusion* must *be true.* Notice again that we are not just saying that in a sound argument the conclusion *is* true, but it *must be* true.

We often make this point in our discussions with friends. When someone is trying to convince you of something, she will often say, "Will you grant me this . . . ? Will you grant me this . . . ?" and then conclude by saying, "Then you must admit that. . . ." If you do not like the conclusion to which you have been led, you have two options. First you could say, "Wait a minute! I am not sure I should have granted you that premise." In other words, you can deny that one or more of the premises are true. Or you could say, "Even if what I granted you was true, it does not lead to your conclusion!" In other words, you could claim that the argument is invalid. What you can *not* claim (at least if you want to be rational) is that the premises you "granted" or accepted are true and the reasoning is correct, but you think the conclusion is false.[14] If the premises are true and the argument is valid, the conclusion *must* follow—regardless of how disagreeable it might be.

Persuasive. Many people think that validity and soundness are all there is to say about the inference of deductive arguments. But some logicians add another category of "persuasive." Unlike "valid" and "sound," there are many definitions for "persuasive." For our purposes, we will define a *persuasive argument* as one that *is both sound and convincing*—convincing in that most people (or at least the person being addressed) would accept the truth of the premises.

---

[14]This is assuming that the person was giving you a deductive argument. If your friend were giving an *inductive* argument, you could come up with additional premises that would make the conclusion less likely and still accept their premises as true and the reasoning as correct (but not "valid"). But you would still be able to say, "Even if what I granted you was true, it does not *necessarily* lead to your conclusion!"

A persuasive argument is one in which (1) the argument is valid, (2) the premise(s) are true, and (3) nearly everyone (or at least the people to whom the argument is addressed) would accept the truth of the premises. In that case the conclusion must be true and should be accepted by any rational person (or at least the person to whom it is addressed).

Notice that this definition is not as clean or precise as the definitions for "valid" and "sound." Instead we have to be attentive to what "nearly everyone"—or at least the person to whom we are presenting the argument—believes to be true. But while this definition may be messy, this is in fact what we do all the time. When we present an argument by asking, "Will you grant me this . . . ?," we are acknowledging that the listener must accept the truth of the premises for the argument to work.

To understand better what we mean by "persuasive," consider the following argument:

P_1 The sun is cold or God exists

P_2 It is not true that the sun is cold

C God exists[15]

Now this argument form is clearly valid—in fact it is so common, it has an official name: "disjunctive syllogism" (more on that later). In ordinary language, the first premise is just saying it is this or that, the second premise says it is not this, so, the conclusion says, it must be that.

But is this argument sound? Well, the second premise is obviously true. But what about the first premise? If either half of a disjunctive proposition (an "or" proposition) is true, then the entire proposition is true. If a person believes that God exists, she would hold that any disjunctive proposition that had "God exists" as one half would be true. So for that person "The sun is cold or God exists" is true because the second half of the "or" is true. But in that case, the truth of the conclusion is already assumed in the premise. While it might be formally valid, a person would only agree that the first premise is true if he also agreed that "God exists" is true—which is what the argument is trying to prove. So while the argument is valid—and perhaps it is sound as well—it is not persuasive.

Assignment 1.3. For the following arguments, determine whether they are valid or invalid, and—if valid—whether they are sound or unsound, and—if sound—indicate whether you find them to be persuasive.

---

[15]This sort of example is discussed in George Mavrodes, *Belief in God: A Study in the Epistemology of Religion* (New York: Random House, 1970), chap. 2.

Example: P₁ Snow is red

P₂ Anything red is beautiful
___

C Therefore, snow is beautiful

Solution: Valid, but not sound or persuasive. (This conclusion necessarily follows from the premises, so it *is* valid. But the first
premise is clearly false and the second premise is debatable
at best, so it *is not* sound or persuasive.)

1. P₁ All whales are mammals

P₂ All mammals have lungs
___

C Therefore, all whales have lungs

2. P₁ All whales are fish

P₂ All fish are animals
___

C Therefore, all whales are animals

*3. P₁ Snow is cold

P₂ No hot things are white
___

C Therefore, snow is white

4. P₁ I am happy and content
___

C Therefore, I am content

5. P₁ The Pacific Northwest is a lovely place to live

P₂ Lovely places to live are places to which people move
___

C Therefore, the Pacific Northwest is a place to which people move

*6. P₁ I have a bad feeling about this class

P₂ Whenever I have a bad feeling about something, my hands shake

P₃ Whenever my hands shake, I drop things
___

C Therefore, I am dropping things

7. P₁ All spiders are green

P₂ All bugs are spiders
___

C Therefore, all bugs are green

8. P₁ All birds have wings

   P₂ All doves have wings
   _____
   C Therefore, all doves are birds

*9. P₁ I exist
   _____
   C Therefore, I exist

10. P₁ If I owned 50 percent of Google, I would be wealthy

    P₂ I do not own 50 percent of Google
    _____
    C Therefore, I am not wealthy

11. P₁ If I stay out in the sun, I will turn red

    P₂ I turned red
    _____
    C Therefore, I stayed out in the sun

*12. P₁ If I stay out in the sun, I will turn red

    P₂ I did not turn red
    _____
    C Therefore, I did not stay out in the sun

13. P₁ If God loves all of humanity, then our lives have meaning

    P₂ God loves all of humanity
    _____
    C Therefore, our lives have meaning

14. P₁ No dogs are cats

    P₂ No canines are felines
    _____
    C Therefore, no dogs are felines

*15. P₁ If I tell her I love her, then she will run away from me
    _____
    C Therefore, if she doesn't run away from me, then I did not tell her I love her

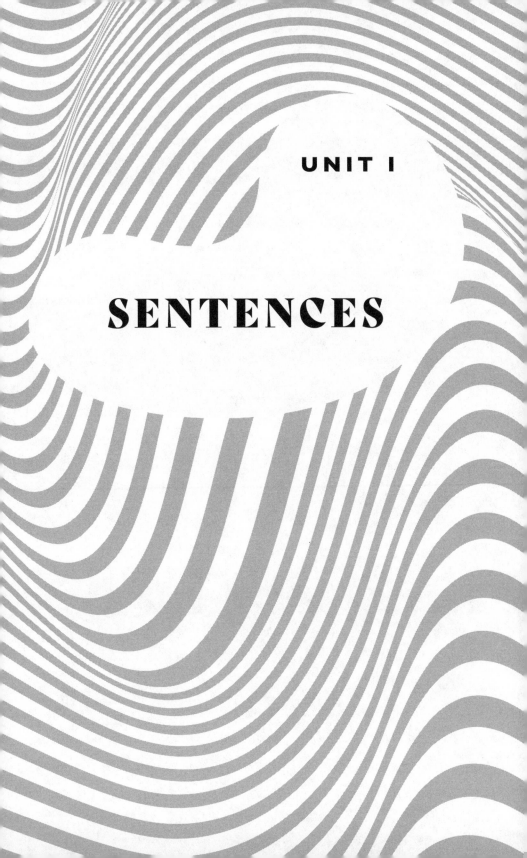

UNIT I

SENTENCES

2

THE FUNCTIONS
OF LANGUAGE

When we form arguments, we use propositions to make up the premise(s) and the conclusion. As we saw before, those propositions are communicated using sentences. But sentences do a lot more than just convey propositions. In *Philosophical Investigations*, the philosopher Ludwig Wittgenstein talks about the many uses of language. He points out that we play many "games" with language using language to accomplish many diverse tasks. Each of these "language games" has its own set of rules. There is no one rule that applies to all language games. So if we want to find out what a sentence *means*, we must first find out how it is being *used*.

For example, imagine you are walking across campus with friends. As you pass another student you say, "Hello, Amy, how are you?" It is doubtful that you are using this sentence as anything more than a greeting. It is an acknowledgment of Amy's presence. If Amy responded by saying, "Well, actually I am not doing very well. I did not get much sleep last night because my back is killing me and. . . ." Amy would be misunderstanding the use of your language. The context of passing on the way to class, the casual tone, the fact that you are walking with friends, and so on should be clues. Most people would understand that your question was not actually a question at all. Essentially, all you are really communicating is, *I acknowledge your existence.*[1]

---

[1] Have you ever had an exchange like this? "Good morning!"—"Fine and you?" Absurd as it looks, it is not uncommon. Since "Good morning!" and "Hi, how are you?" are both really saying "I acknowledge your existence," we might mix up the standard responses to having our existence acknowledged.

According to Wittgenstein, problems in the use of language arise when we use the rules of one language game in a completely different language game. For example, imagine Bill says, "Don't forget, swim practice begins at sunrise tomorrow," and you counter, "The sun doesn't 'rise.' The earth rotates on its axis and relative to us the sun does not move at all." Bill would probably respond, "Oh, thanks nerd. You know what I meant!" In this case you would be mistakenly applying the rules of the language game of science to the language game of everyday conversation that Bill was using.

On the other hand, imagine you and Bill were working for the Jet Propulsion Laboratory discussing the launch of a probe to Mars and the rocket needed to blast off on an initial trajectory toward the sun. In that case if Bill said, "Well, the sun will rise tomorrow and we can aim at it," and you countered, "No it won't . . . the sun only *appears* to rise . . . the earth rotates on its axis and relative to us the sun does not move at all," *Bill* would be the one who was mistaken. In this latter setting Bill would need to use the language game of science.

According to Wittgenstein there are "countless different kinds of use of what we call 'symbols,' 'words,' 'sentences.'" Among these many different language games are the following:

Giving orders, and obeying them—

Describing the appearance of an object, or giving its measurements—

Constructing an object from a description (a drawing)—

Reporting an event—

Speculating about an event—

Forming and testing a hypothesis—

Presenting the results of an experiment in tables and diagrams—

Making up a story; and reading it—

Play-acting—

Singing catches—

Guessing riddles—

Making a joke; telling it—

Solving a problem in practical arithmetic—

Translating from one language into another—

Asking, thanking, cursing, greeting, praying.[2]

But while there are many, many uses of language, we can group most of them into three major—and two minor—categories. Note that only one of them communicates propositions by making assertions.

2.1 USES AND FUNCTIONS OF LANGUAGE

Informative use of language and assertions. When language is used to communicate a proposition, we say that we are using language in an *informative* way. That is, we are using language to communicate information: propositions that are true or false.

For example, "René Descartes lived from 1596 to 1650" is giving us information about Descartes. It is communicating the true proposition about the dates of Descartes's life. "Whales are fish, not mammals" is also giving us information (though in this case it is communicating a false proposition). In logic we say these sentences have a "truth value"—that is, they communicate true or false propositions. In grammatical terms we say sentences performing this function are *assertions*. This is the language we will be most concerned about for the rest of this book.

Expressive use of language and exclamations. Though propositions are the logician's primary concern, language can be used for many other purposes. For example, while watching a basketball game, Joy might shout, "Go Spurs!" Now that sentence is not true or false. Of course, you could say, "Joy is a San Antonio Spurs fan" based on her sentence. In that case you would be using informative language, communicating a proposition. But Joy's use of language was *expressive*, expressing how she feels about her favorite team. Another example is poetry. Poetry is expressive in nature, though it may also communicate some information. For example, consider this sonnet:

If I should think of love
I'd think of you, your arms uplifted,

---

[2]Ludwig Wittgenstein, *Philosophical Investigations*, 3rd ed., trans. G. E. M. Anscombe (London: Blackwell, 1973), ¶23.

Tying your hair in plaits above,
The lyre shape of your arms and shoulders,
The soft curve of your winding head.
No melody is sweeter, nor could Orpheus
So have bewitched. I think of this,
And all my universe becomes perfection.
But were you in my arms, dear love,
The happiness would take my breath away,
No thought could match that ecstasy,
No song encompass it, no other worlds.
If I should think of love,
I'd think of you.

Essentially, the communication here is "You're hot and I wish I was holding you." This poem reports *some* information about how lovely this person is and how much the speaker wants the beloved. But primarily, the poem is not communicating *information*. The anonymous author's concern is with the feelings and expression of love. The goal here is to vent the speaker's emotions and, perhaps, to arouse the emotions of the listener.

Expressive language can be strictly personal, or it can be intended for an audience. In the case of private expression, a person might pray alone and express his or her feelings of awe in the presence of God's creation. In this case, the person is not communicating information, but expressing emotions or attitudes. Or, alone in her living room, Joy might shout "No!" at the TV if she sees the Spurs make a bad play. These are strictly personal uses of expressive language.

On the other hand, a person may use expressive language to attempt to evoke feelings, emotions, or attitudes in the listener.[3] When a preacher uses expressive language in a sermon or public prayer, the goal is to arouse those emotions in the listeners. If someone sends his wife an expressive love poem, he is probably hoping to arouse similar emotions in her. Often expressive language does both. For example, if Joy cheers at a Spurs game she is both expressing her love for the team and trying to evoke a similar emotion in the rest of the crowd. While not all expressive uses of language are *exclamations*, any sentence that functions as an exclamation is using language expressively.

---

[3]In some ways this might be considered a *directive* use of language because we are attempting to direct a change in attitude. But unless the language is intended to lead to an *overt action* based on the emotions evoked, we will consider it as primarily an *expressive* use of language.

Directive use of language and commands. A third major use of language is *directive*. In this case, the goal is to cause or prevent an overt action. For example, a teacher might say, "For homework, do numbers six through fifteen." This sentence is neither true nor false, nor is it expressing an emotion or attitude. It is being used to direct you to do something. Or a mother might say, "Stop hitting your sister!" In this case, she is using language to prevent an action. Whether either command is obeyed or disobeyed has nothing to do with the truth value of the sentence, because a command does not have a truth value. The command might be an inappropriate request or an unreasonable request, but a command is neither true nor false.

Of course, most directive use of language is hardly as blatant as "Do this" or "Don't do that." In fact, your teacher might say, "For homework, how about you do numbers six through fifteen?" Now it may look like he is asking a question, but if you responded, "How about we don't?" he would probably say you did not get his point. Your teacher was not actually asking anything; rather, he was directing you to do something. In grammatical terms we say sentences performing this function are *commands*.

Two minor uses of language.

a. Ceremonial. While most language is used in the broad categories of informative, expressive, and directive, there are at least two minor uses of language. They are minor in the sense that they are not used as often as the former. One of these is the *ceremonial* use of language. When you say to a friend, "Hello Amy, how are you?" and she responds, "Well, and you?" you are performing a little greeting ceremony. You are not really communicating information, nor are you expressing emotions or trying to direct behavior. You and Amy are really just acknowledging the presence of each other.

b. Performative. Another less common use of language is the *performative*. British philosopher J. L. Austin (1911–1960) noticed that some speech acts involve doing something, not just describing or directing. Such a "performative utterance [is] not, or not merely, saying something but doing something, and is not a true or false report of something." Instead, uttering (or writing) such a sentence "is, or is a part of, the doing of an action." So the words, "'I name this ship the *Queen Elizabeth*'—. . . when smashing the bottle against the stern," is not describing anything.[4] The saying *is* the doing. By

---

[4]J. L. Austin, *How to Do Things with Words*, ed. J. O. Urmson and Marina Sbisà (Cambridge, MA: Harvard University Press, 1962), 5.

speaking the sentence, we are doing the thing we are speaking.[5] This sounds complicated, but it is really pretty straightforward. In baseball, if the umpire says, "Yerr outta there!" then you are out. Now, he may have blown the call (that is, the proposition, "You did an action that constitutes an out," is false), but his saying you are out makes you out. Or if your teacher says, "I congratulate you for a good job on your exam," those words *are* the congratulation. The sentence is neither true nor false, it is not expressing an emotion (or at least it need not), and it is not directing you to any particular behavior. If you say (or write), "I apologize for my comments," that *is* the apology. If you say, "I promise to meet you for dinner at six," that sentence *is* the promise.

Of course in most contexts, we use language in multiple ways (as we will discuss below in 2.3). It is important to recognize the different functions of language because only one of these uses makes up arguments: the *informative*. There may be other uses for language, but for our purposes, these three major and two minor will suffice.

Informative Use of Language:	**Communicates propositions which are true or false**
Expressive Use of Language:	**Expresses feelings or attitudes**
Directive Use of Language:	**Intended to cause specific actions**
Ceremonial Use of Language:	*Used as part of a ceremony*
Performative Use of Language:	*Language where the saying is the doing*

Assignment 2.1. For the following passages, which language function is the primary one being used?

Example: "Enter amount from Form 1040, line 38" (IRS, Schedule A, line 2).

Solution: Directive

1. I hold it true, whate'er befall;
   I feel it when I sorrow most;
   'Tis better to have loved and lost
   Than never to have loved at all. (Lord Alfred Tennyson)

---

[5]French philosopher Jacques Derrida (1930–2004) argues in "Signature, Event, Context" (in *Limited Inc*, trans. by Jeffrey Mehlman and Samuel Weber [Evanston, IL: Northwestern University Press, 1988]) that in one sense *all* language is performative—an interesting idea that is beyond the scope of this book.

2. "If I speak in the tongues of men or of angels, but do not have love, I am only a resounding gong or a clanging cymbal" (1 Cor 13:1 NIV).

*3. "Dear Mr. Governor: I hereby resign effective November 16, 2008 from the United States Senate in order to prepare for my duties as President of the United States" (Senator Barack Obama, in a letter to the governor of Illinois).

4. Brazil is the largest country in South America.

5. "The history of the American Negro is the history of . . . this longing to attain self-conscious manhood, to merge his double self into a better and truer self" (W. E. B. DuBois, *The Souls of Black Folks*).

*6. "What traveler among the ruins of Carthage, of Palmyra, Persepolis, or Rome, has not been stimulated to reflections on the transiency of kingdoms and men, and to sadness at the thought of a vigorous and rich life now departed?" (G. W. F. Hegel, *Lectures on the Philosophy of History*, 1823).

7. Leave me alone!

8. "Can't sing. Can't act. Dances a little" (Anonymous talent scout describing famed actor-dancer Fred Astaire).

*9. Pastor: He is risen!
Congregation: He is risen indeed!

10. No trespassing!

11. "Your time is limited, so don't waste it living someone else's life" (Steve Jobs, Stanford University commencement address, 2005).

*12. "The horse is here to stay, but the automobile is only a novelty—a fad" (president of Michigan Savings Bank in 1903).

13. "Everything that can be invented has been invented" (Charles H. Duvell, US Commissioner of patents, 1899).

14. Amazing grace! How sweet the sound,
That saved a wretch like me!
I once was lost, but now am found;
Was blind, but now I see. (John Newton, 1779)

*15. Honey, what do you say when someone gives you a cookie?

2.2 FINDING PROPOSITIONS

The four basic forms of sentences. We have just seen how sentences are used. Now let's look at how sentences may be structured. In English, we have four basic forms of sentences: declarative, interrogative, exclamatory, and imperative. These four are characterized entirely by their formal structure, not by their use. A *declarative sentence* is one that ends with a period, and the subject, verb, and any other components are arranged in a certain way—typically the subject precedes the verb. For example, "The store is now open" is a declarative sentence. An *interrogative sentence* is easy to find because it always ends with a question mark. In an interrogative sentence the verb typically precedes the subject: for example, "Are you going to the store?" An *exclamatory sentence* is one that ends with an exclamation point. It is often missing some of the typical elements of a sentence, such as a subject or a verb. For example, "Great store!" is an exclamatory sentence that does not have a verb at all. Finally, an *imperative sentence* ends with a period, but it typically has a different order than a declarative sentence. In an imperative sentence, the subject is often assumed to be the listener. For example, "Go to the store" implies "*You* go to the store."

The four basic functions of sentences. In the previous section, we saw that there are three major (along with two minor) uses for language: informative, expressive, and directive. And these three major uses yield three kinds of sentences: assertions, exclamations, and commands. If we add *questions*—a request for an answer—we have four sentence *functions*,[6] which appear to match up with the four basic *forms*. A declarative sentence form uses language informatively to produce an assertion. An interrogative sentence form uses language to produce a question. An exclamatory sentence form uses language expressively to produce an exclamation. And an imperative sentence form uses language directively to produce a command.

Grammatical Form	Function (Use)	Example
Declarative ⟶	Assertion (Informative)	"The stove is hot."
Interrogative ⟶	Question	"Is the stove hot?"
Exclamatory ⟶	Exclamation (Expressive)	"Ouch!"
Imperative ⟶	Command (Directive)	"Don't touch the stove."

---

[6]Some grammarians would add the conditional (or "if . . . then") form. We will consider this grammatical form as a type of the declarative form of sentences. For more on conditionals, see chap. 7.

Only assertions (using the informative use of language) can communicate propositions. That is, only assertions are true or false—not questions or exclamations or commands. So assertions are the only kind of sentences that can be used to form arguments, and hence are the only kind of sentences that concern us as logicians.

Since the *function* of assertions corresponds to the declarative grammatical *form*, to find an argument we need only look for these kinds of sentences. Sentences structured so that they end with a question mark or exclamation point or have the words arranged in an imperative form are irrelevant to us as logicians. We are trying to find the sentences that express propositions. We can ignore these other forms as they are incapable of doing so. If we want to find an argument in a passage of writing or in a speech, we can ignore all the sentences that are not in the declarative form. Right?

Form versus function. Ah, if only it was that easy. It would be so much easier if the relationships in the chart above were the only possibilities. But in fact, the grammatical *form* of a sentence does not actually tell us about the *function* of the sentence at all. For example, imagine your mother comes in your room and says, "This room is a mess." Now that sentence is declarative in form, but it is highly unlikely your mother was just trying to assert some information about the state of your room. And if you answered, "Why yes, Mother, your sentence asserts a true proposition," you would likely get some additional chores that day. Or imagine your mother says, "Why is this room such a mess?" Is she really asking a question where an appropriate response from you would be, "Because I never pick anything up and just throw everything on the floor"? Or how about if your mother utters the exclamation, "What a mess!" In all three of these examples, your mother is actually giving you a command: "Clean up this mess." In this case, the table showing the relationship between grammatical form and function looks like this:

Grammatical Form	Function (Use)	Example
Declarative		"This room is a mess."
Interrogative		"Why is this room such a mess?"
Exclamatory		"What a mess!"
Imperative	Command (Directive)	"Clean up this mess."

Sometimes the interrogative form is used to make an assertion—as in a rhetorical question: "Are you aware that the current administration is spending trillions of dollars that we don't have?" This question is not really asking anything—it is making an assertion that is either true or false.[7] The interrogative form can be used expressively and even function as an exclamation. So after LeBron James makes an impressive dunk, your friend might say, "Did you see that?" What she is doing is expressing her admiration for his basketball ability, not asking a question about your eyesight.

Exclamatory sentences can be used to make assertions, imperative sentences can be used to express feelings, and so on. The fact is, language is very messy, and any one of the grammatical forms can be used for just about any of the sentence functions. Since our goal is to find arguments that are made up of premises and conclusions, we must look for sentences that communicate propositions. This means *regardless of the grammatical form, our concern is with assertions.* Our chart really looks something like this:

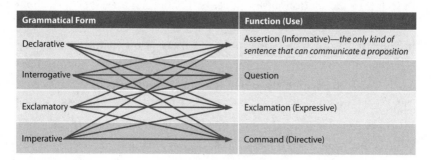

Grammatical Form	Function (Use)
Declarative	Assertion (Informative)—*the only kind of sentence that can communicate a proposition*
Interrogative	Question
Exclamatory	Exclamation (Expressive)
Imperative	Command (Directive)

So knowing the form of a sentence does not tell us its function—and our interest is in sentences that function as assertions (and so communicate propositions). To find those assertions, we will have to look at all the different forms, and we will have to discover the function or use of a sentence before we can begin analyzing any arguments.

Assignment 2.2. For the following sentences, state the grammatical form and give the most likely *function.* Then reword the sentence to make the form explicitly reflect the function.

---

[7]If it really *was* functioning as a question, the answer would presumably be either, "Yes, I was aware of that," or "No, I was not aware of that."

Example: Why do I always have to do the dishes?

Solution: Form: Interrogative.

Most likely function: Directive.

Reworded: You take a turn doing the dishes.

1. Did you know that René Descartes was born in 1596?

2. Watch out, the stove is hot.

*3. Honey, the lawn has not been watered in two days.

4. This is great!

5. If you want one of these cupcakes, what's the magic word?

*6. At sea level water freezes at 32° F (0° C).

7. What is the answer to homework number 7?

8. Why are you such a whiner?

*9. Did you know that former vice president Al Gore and actor Tommy Lee Jones were freshman roommates at Harvard?

10. You have not told me how you got here.

11. How did I get so lucky as to have someone like you love me?

*12. When asked for your PIN, you will enter the numbers 3356.

13. This plate is hot!

14. Paris is the capital of Norway.

*15. "I'm the map, I'm the map, I'm the map, I'm the map . . . I'm the Map!" (The Map, *Dora the Explorer*).

2.3 THE MULTIPLE FUNCTIONS OF LANGUAGE

While it is important to be able to tease out the *primary* function of a particular sentence or an entire passage, most ordinary language has multiple functions. For example, if someone says, "That law will ruin our health-care system," he is doing much more than simply making an assertion. That is because this sentence has multiple functions:

1. The *informative* use of this sentence: A claim that the law will ruin our health-care system.

2. The *expressive* use of this sentence: I don't like that law.

3. The *directive* use of this sentence: You should be against that law.

Notice that the *informative* use here is true or false—that is, it communicates a proposition. The *expressive* and *directive* uses do not. To fully understand what a sentence or passage is communicating, we need to look for all three of these basic uses of language. While our interest as logicians is with the *informative* use of language, we would miss the entire point of the passage if we did not acknowledge the other uses as well. In fact, when we examine informal fallacies in the next chapter, we will often find that an argument "feels right" because of these other uses of language—even when the reasoning is fallacious. Here is another sample:

> Blessed is the one
>> who does not walk in step with the wicked
> or stand in the way that sinners take
>> or sit in the company of mockers,
> but whose delight is in the law of the Lord,
>> and who meditates on his law day and night. (Ps 1:1-2 NIV)

This passage is used *informatively* to tell us what sort of persons will be blessed. This information is either true or false. This passage is also *expressing* King David's admiration for those who keep away from bad folk and meditate on God's law. However, this passage is probably primarily used *directively*: to encourage the listener not to hang out with wicked people, but instead to delight in the law of the Lord.

Assignment 2.3. What are the likely *informative*, *expressive*, and *directive* uses of each of the following passages?

Example: "A holy war is a contradiction in terms. War dehumanizes, war diminishes, war debases all those who wage it" (Elie Wiesel).

Solution: Informative: War is never "holy."
             Expressive: Evoking strong feelings of animosity toward those who claim to be fighting a "holy war."
             Directive: Don't fight wars.

1. "There never was a good war, or a bad peace" (Benjamin Franklin, *Poor Richard's Almanac*).

2. "In Italy, for thirty years under the Borgias, they had warfare, terror, murder and bloodshed, but they produced Michelangelo, Leonardo da Vinci, and the Renaissance. In Switzerland they had brotherly love, they had five hundred years of democracy and peace, what did they produce? The cuckoo clock" (Orson Welles).

*3. "For those regarded as warriors, when engaged in combat the vanquishing of thine enemy can be the warrior's only concern. Suppress all human emotion and compassion. Kill whoever stands in thy way, even if that be Lord God, or Buddha himself. This truth lies at the heart of the art of combat" (Hattori Hanzô, *Kill Bill: Vol. 1*).

4. "If in fact you weren't washing your hair, as I suspect you weren't because your curls are still intact, wouldn't you have heard the gunshot, and if in fact you had heard the gunshot Brooke Windham wouldn't have had time to hide the gun before you got downstairs, which means you would have had to find Brooke Windham with a gun in her hand to make your story plausible, isn't that right?" (Elle Woods, questioning a witness in *Legally Blonde*).

5. "Hello, ladies, look at your man, now back to me, now back at your man, now back to me. Sadly, he isn't me, but if he stopped using ladies scented body wash and switched to Old Spice, he could smell like he's me" (*The Man Your Man Could Smell Like*, Old Spice TV commercial).

*6. "The city which is composed of middle-class citizens is necessarily best constituted in respect of the elements of which we say the fabric of the state naturally consists" (Aristotle, *Politics*).

7. "Since the greatness of God is without limits, His works are too. Who will finish telling of His mercies and grandeurs? To do so is impossible, and thus do not be surprised at what was said, and will be said, because it is but a naught in comparison to what there is to tell of God" (Teresa of Avila, *Interior Castle*).

8. "He [Benjamin Disraeli] is a self-made man, and worships his creator" (John Bright, British MP).

*9. "If Gladstone fell into the Thames, that would be a misfortune, and if anybody pulled him out, that, I suppose, would be a calamity" (Benjamin Disraeli, prime minister of the United Kingdom).

10. "Suppose you were an idiot. And suppose you were a member of Congress. But I repeat myself" (Mark Twain).

11. "Where you have the most armed citizens in America, you have the lowest violent crime rate. Where you have the worst gun control, you have the highest crime rate" (Ted Nugent, musician).

*12. "The absence of fully programming to these enlisted manpower requirements without a concomitant reduction in either ship capability requirements or endurance parameters forms a dichotomy between our stated mission/objectives and the individual unit's ability to carry out the stated mission in a peacetime environment" (Excerpt from US Navy briefing).

13. "If we don't get gun-control laws in this country, we are full of beans. To have the National Rifle Association rule the United States is pathetic" (Harvey Weinstein, film producer).

14. "Humanity is male and man defines woman not in herself but as relative to him; she is not regarded as an autonomous being" (Simone de Beauvoir, *The Second Sex*).

*15. "The Christian hypothesis contradicts a lot of evidence, makes numerous failed predictions, is not the best explanation of the universe we find ourselves in, and fails to find sufficient evidence in its own support. Therefore, I believe Christianity is false" (Richard C. Carrier, "Why I Am Not a Christian," 2006).

2.4 EMOTIVE USE OF LANGUAGE

Denotation versus connotation. To this point we have been talking about sentences and passages, but individual words and phrases are also used in multiple ways. Each word or phrase has a literal meaning—that which it *denotes*. In this case, the word or phrase is like a label that attaches to something. This denotative, literal meaning may be hard to find because individual words can have multiple literal meanings. So, for example, among the meanings for the word *jack* are: a kind of rabbit, a kind of cheese, a mechanism that lifts a car, a rank of playing card, and the act of stealing something. So the first thing we have to do is be clear on which denotative, literal meaning we have in mind when we are using a word.

Beyond establishing the correct denotative meaning for a word or phrase, we also need to be aware of the emotional suggestiveness or emotional "weight" that these words and phrases carry. Put another way, words not only have a denotative meaning but also *connote* certain feelings, attitudes, and emotions. For example, "public servant" and "bureaucrat" both denote someone who is employed by the government. These two terms, however, have very different connotations.

In *Sports Illustrated* Rick Reilly made fun of the way fans will describe their own sports team in terms with a positive connotation while bashing their opponent's team—even when the denotative meaning is the same:

> Your team sucks.
> My team is in the first year of its annual five-year rebuilding program.
>
> Your team is full of thugs, criminals and perverts.
> My team is colorful.
>
> Your college coach wouldn't suspend his star players even if they stored the stolen stereos under his desk.
> My college coach believes in due process.
>
> Your quarterback is dumber than a bottle of peroxide. He wouldn't know the playbook if Elmo read it to him.
> My quarterback relies on his athletic instincts. . . .
>
> Your coach is a bloodthirsty, chair-heaving madman who ought to be handcuffed for emotionally and physically bullying his players and staff.
> My coach is old school.
>
> Your draft choice is a complete bust.
> My draft choice is still getting comfortable with the intricacies of the system.

Of course the joke here is that every pairing literally means the same thing. That is, they are *denoting* the same thing but using words and phrases with very different *connotations*.

Sometimes changes are made to words and phrases to discourage what most of us would consider an appropriate emotional response. When the *Challenger* space shuttle blew up, killing the entire crew on January 28, 1986, NASA released a statement. They called the accident an "anomaly," the bodies of the astronauts were, "recovered components," and the astronauts' coffins became "crew transfer containers." In this case NASA was trying to minimize the horror people experienced because of the accident. Likewise, the Department of Defense sometimes uses phrases like "manually powered fastener-driver impact device" or "hexiform rotatable surface compression unit" when they just spent $435 on a hammer and $2,403 on a nut.[8] In these cases the denotation stays the same, but the connotation is either sanitized or "fancified" to change the natural emotional response associated with the horror of death or the outrage at wasteful spending. Consider the following deliberately obfuscatory verbiage (i.e., confusing words):

entry system = door

environmentally operable panel = window

high-velocity multipurpose air circulator = fan

previously owned parts = junk

resilient vinyl flooring = linoleum

unlawful or arbitrary deprivation of life = murder

hydro blast force cup = toilet plunger

aerodynamic personnel decelerator = parachute

interlocking slide fastener = zipper

adverse mortality experience = death

To illustrate the ways in which we often use connotation to our advantage, British philosopher Bertrand Russell made a little joke where he "conjugated" an "irregular verb." An irregular verb, of course, is one where the first, second, and third person do not follow the normal pattern. For example, "I *am*," "you *are*," and "he/she/it *is*." But Russell's joke was that while the verb denotes the same thing in all three persons, the connotation changes from positive to neutral to negative:

I am firm.

You are obstinate.

He is a pig-headed fool.

---

[8]It may be that the DOD did not actually pay this much *per item*. They were bundled into a complete billing. You can read about it here: James Fairhall, "The Case for the $435 Hammer," *Washington Monthly*, January 1, 1987, http://www.thefreelibrary.com/The+case+for+the+$435+hammer.-a04619906.

Now all three of these "irregular verbs" denote someone who does not easily change his or her mind. But the connotation of the first person is very positive, the connotation of the second person is more neutral, and the connotation of the third person is completely negative. Here are some other examples:

I am enjoying my independence.

You are single.

He is hard-up for a date.

I share my concerns for others.

You talk about people's problems.

She is a gossip.

In each of these cases, the denotation is the same while the connotation changes dramatically. So, in summary

Denotation: What a word or phrase literally means (what it denotes).

Connotation: All the feelings and attitudes that are connoted by that word or phrase.

Emotionally charged words and phrases. In logic, we are interested in the propositions that lie behind the sentences used in arguments. When we encounter emotionally charged words or phrases, we are often blinded to the actual meaning or swayed by emotion. For that reason, as logicians we need to focus on the denotation of words so that we can discover what proposition they are being used to communicate. Logicians, therefore, are highly suspicious of the expressive use of language and of emotionally charged wording. The key question the logician always wants to ask is, What proposition is being communicated here, and what properly follows from it? Insofar as emotionally colored words and phrases obscure this, the logician wants to get past them.

In politics we frequently find candidates using emotionally charged words and phrases to sway their constituents. For example, in the abortion debate you may hear one side calling itself "pro-choice" and their opponents "anti-choice." At the same time, the other side calls themselves "pro-life" and dismisses their opponents as "anti-life."

In general we as logicians should try to avoid—or at least look past—emotionally charged language. There are exceptions, however. In some cases, the emotion that is connoted by words or phrases is appropriate—as noted above with the example of NASA and the department of defense. In poetry, for instance, the point is not just to communicate propositions but to evoke a response by using beautiful words. British psychologist Robert Thouless argued that

> in poetry [emotionally toned words] have a perfectly proper place, because in poetry (as in some kinds of prose) the arousing of suitable emotions is an important part of the purpose for which the words are used. In *The Eve of St. Agnes* [John] Keats has written:
>
> > *Full on this casement shone the wintry moon,*
> > *And threw warm gules on Madeline's fair breast.*
>
> These are beautiful lines. Let us notice how much of their beauty follows from the proper choice of emotionally coloured words and how completely it is lost if these words are replaced by neutral ones. The words with strikingly emotional meanings are *casement, gules, Madeline, fair,* and *breast.* . . .
>
> Let us now try the experiment of keeping these two lines in a metrical form, but replacing all the emotionally coloured words by neutral ones, while making as few other changes as possible. We may write:
>
> > *Full on this window shone the wintry moon,*
> > *Making red marks on Jane's uncoloured chest.*
>
> No one will doubt that all of its poetic value has been knocked out of the passage by these changes. Yet the lines still mean the same in external fact; they still have the same factual meaning. It is only the emotional meaning which has been destroyed.[9]

A former student performed a similar "emotive-ectomy" on a famous Bible passage:

> Like an apple tree among the trees of the forest
> > is my lover among the young men.
> I delight to sit in his shade,
> > and his fruit is sweet to my taste.
> He has taken me to the banquet hall,
> > and let his banner over me be love.
> Strengthen me with raisins,
> > refresh me with apples,

---

[9]Robert H. Thouless, *Straight and Crooked Thinking* (London: Pan Books, 1953), 7.

> for I am faint with love.
> His left arm is under my head,
>   and his right arm embraces me.
> Daughters of Jerusalem, I charge you
>   by the gazelles and by the does of the field:
> Do not arouse or awaken love
>   until it so desires. (Song 2:3-7)

Rewritten without the emotion, but communicating the same basic information:

> My man is better than the other men.
>   I'm happy next to him and he turns me on;
> He's nuts about me too.
>   Better get me some eats 'cuz I'm weak from excitement.
> He hugs me.
>   A piece of advice for you women of Jerusalem:
> Play it cool with men. When the time is right, move in.

Clearly something has been lost.

Assignment 2.4a. Make up three examples of "irregular verbs"—that is, verbs that have the same denotation, but the first person has a positive connotation, the second person has a neutral connotation, and the third person has a negative connotation. Be sure the denotation does not change.

Example: I am petite.
                 You are short.
                 She is a shrimp.

Assignment 2.4b. Find a piece of poetry and perform an "emotive-ectomy" by rewording it without the emotive elements (while keeping the denotative meaning the same).

2.5 TYPES OF DISAGREEMENTS

Since language does more than just communicate propositions, when people disagree they may be disagreeing on several different levels. Frequently people will have a disagreement in *belief about the facts* in a given case. That is, they may disagree about what is the true state of affairs. In such cases, they are disagreeing about which proposition properly applies to the situation. For example, consider the following pair of statements:

Example 1:

A: The Affordable Care Act (ACA) is horrible and will cost the United States trillions of dollars.

B: The ACA is great and will save the United States trillions of dollars.

To resolve a dispute like this, each side would gather facts about the revenue streams and costs of the ACA. Both A and B would try to show that the facts support their position.

But sometimes when people disagree they actually have the same belief about the facts. Instead, their disagreement may stem from their *attitude toward the facts*. For example, consider these statements:

Example 2:

A: The ACA sticks job creators with punitive taxes.

B: The ACA is partially funded by a slight increase in taxes on those who can most easily afford it.

Now both sides would presumably acknowledge that the ACA is partially funded by a 3.8 percent tax on unearned income for joint filers who make $250,000 or more. But A would say, "Yes, and it's terrible!" while B would say, "Yes, and it is fair!" There is no disagreement about these facts, but rather about the *attitude* toward those facts.

In example one above, there was a disagreement in both *belief about the facts* and *attitude toward the facts*. That is, even if A and B could agree on the costs of the ACA, they would still have different attitudes toward the legislation. But it is possible—though perhaps rare—for people to agree in *attitude toward the facts* while disagreeing in their *belief about the facts*. One sometimes sees this in politics when supporters will praise a politician for mutually exclusive traits:

Example 3:

A: When he was president, Obama stood by his promises and pushed through the ACA.

B: When he was president, Obama wisely responded to the needs of the country and changed his mind on Guantanamo prison and kept it open.

In this case, both A and B agree in their attitudes about the facts, but the facts are very different. A believes that Obama kept his campaign promises, while B thinks Obama abandoned a campaign promise—but both of them praise his leadership. These examples show the following kinds of agreement and disagreement:

		Belief About the Facts	
		Disagree	Agree
Attitude Toward the Facts	Disagree	Example 1	Example 2
	Agree	Example 3	*(no disagreement)*

The key question to ask here is, What would it take to convince the other person they are wrong? If the answer is that they need to accept the truth of certain facts, then there is a disagreement in *belief about the facts*. If the answer is that they need to change the value they are giving the facts, then there is a disagreement in *attitude toward the facts*. Of course, in many—if not most—cases of disagreement, you will find both. But it is possible to have one kind of disagreement without the other. If you want to resolve disagreements, you must first figure out exactly where the disagreement lies.

Assignment 2.5. Explain whether the following pairs agree or disagree in their belief about the facts and their attitude toward the facts.

Example: A. "The power to ban publications was held by the minister of the interior under the Publications and Entertainments Act of 1963. . . . Thousands of books, newspapers, and other publications were banned in South Africa from 1950 to 1990" (Beacon for Freedom of Expression).

B. "We do not have censorship. What we have is a limitation on what newspapers can report" (Louis Nel, former deputy minister of information for South Africa).

Solution: **Agreement** *in belief about the facts:* Both agree that publications were restricted.

Disagreement *in attitude toward the facts:* A implies this is bad; B does not.

1. A. Susan plays games creatively.
   B. Susan cheats.

2. A. Ms. Jones is a glutton.

   B. Ms. Jones eats like a bird.

*3. A. "Heavy Bombing by U.S. Continues in Cambodia" (*New York Times* headline).

   B. "You always write it's bombing, bombing, bombing. It's not bombing, it's air support" (US Air Force Colonel David Opfer speaking to the press).

4. A. "The moral worth of an action does not lie in the effect expected from it" (Immanuel Kant, *Critique of Practical Reason*).

   B. "The Greatest Happiness Principle holds that actions are right in proportion as they tend to promote happiness, wrong as they tend to produce the reverse of happiness" (John Stuart Mill, *Utilitarianism*).

5. A. "The only way to erect such a common power, as may be able to defend them from the invasion of foreigners, and the injuries of one another, and thereby to secure them in such sort . . . is, to confer all their power and strength upon one man, or upon one assembly of men, that may reduce all their wills, by plurality of voices, unto one will" (Thomas Hobbes, *Leviathan*).

   B. "It is evident that absolute monarchy, which by some men is counted the only government in the world, is indeed inconsistent with civil society, and so can be no form of civil government at all" (John Locke, *Second Treatise on Government*).

*6. A. "Women are preprogrammed [by evolution] to feel dependent on men" (Nick Neave, evolutionary psychologist).

   B. "A woman needs a man like a fish needs a bicycle" (Irina Dunn, writer and filmmaker).

7. A. "The walls we build around us to keep sadness out also keeps out the joy" (Jim Rohn, motivational speaker).

   B. "It's easy to cry when you realize that everyone you love will reject you or die" (Chuck Palahniuk, novelist).

8. A. Johnny is clueless about what he will do after graduation.

   B. Johnny is keeping his options open.

*9. A. Birds of a feather flock together.

   B. Opposites attract.

10. A. Nothing ventured, nothing gained.

    B. Look before you leap.

11. A. "Reason, therefore, by which man distinguishes between good and evil, by which he understands and judges, being a natural talent, could not be totally destroyed, but is partly debilitated, partly impaired, so that it exhibits nothing but deformity and ruin" (John Calvin, *Institutes of the Christian Religion*).

    B. [God speaking to Adam:] "Thou, like a judge appointed for being honorable, art the molder and maker of thyself; thou mayest sculpt thyself into whatever shape thou dost prefer. . . . Thou canst again grow upward from thy soul's reason into the higher natures which are divine" (Giovanni Pico della Mirandola, *Oration on the Dignity of Man*).

*12. A. "Men despise religion; they hate it, and fear it is true. To remedy this, we must begin by showing that religion is not contrary to reason; that it is venerable, to inspire respect for it; then we must make it lovable, to make good men hope it is true; finally, we must prove it is true" (Blaise Pascal, *Pensées*).

    B. "Monotheistic religion is a plagiarism of a plagiarism of a hearsay of a hearsay, of an illusion of an illusion, extending all the way back to a fabrication of a few nonevents" (Christopher Hitchens, *god Is Not Great: How Religion Poisons Everything*).

13. A. "Success is not the key to happiness. Happiness is the key to success" (Herman Cain, businessman, former Republican presidential candidate)

    B. "What do you take me for, an idiot?" (General Charles de Gaulle, when a journalist asked him if he was happy).

14. A. "The Steelworkers Union . . . guaranteed that the higher-paying, cleaner, and healthier jobs, offering opportunities for advancement into skilled classifications, were reserved exclusively for whites" (Herbert Hill, *Race and the Steelworkers Union: White Privilege and Black Struggles*).

    B. "It is just not accurate to believe that blacks were confined somehow to the lowest-paying jobs; rather, there was some tendency for blacks to be congregated in certain units which had a variety of characteristics including, in some instances, a somewhat lower average pay than some units where there might be a heavy concentration of white employees" (Ben Fisher, special assistant to the president of the United Steelworkers of America).

*15. A. "Education is the most powerful weapon which you can use to change the world" (Nelson Mandela).

B. "We don't need no education. We don't need no thought control" (Pink Floyd).

3

INFORMAL FALLACIES

3.1 FORMAL VERSUS INFORMAL FALLACIES

Sometimes when we want to say something is not true, we say it is a "fallacy." We might say, "It is a fallacy that we use only 10 percent of our brain," when what we are really claiming is that the statement is false. But in logic, we use the term *fallacy* to refer specifically to an error in reasoning or argumentation, not truth value. In other words, any error in reasoning is a fallacy. So the argument

Dogs are animals

Cats are animals
_____

Therefore, the sky is blue

is a fallacy. However, we usually reserve the word *fallacy* for arguments that have the *appearance* of validity—even though the inference is erroneous.

These errors in reasoning are categorized as formal or informal fallacies. *A formal fallacy is one in which the form or structure of the argument is incorrect.* Consider the following argument:

Senator Jones supports social security

Socialists support social security
_____

Therefore, Senator Jones is a socialist

The problem here is that the *form* of the argument is fallacious. It really does not matter what terms make up the argument. Nor does it matter whether the three propositions being conveyed here are true or false. The argument is fallacious because it infers that two things that share a quality must be the same thing. Any argument of the form

A has the quality C

B has the quality C

_____

Therefore, A is B

will be invalid. Such arguments will be invalid regardless of whether the individual propositions being conveyed are true or false. The problem is with the structure—not the beliefs about Senator Wilson, the value of Social Security, or who is a socialist.

One way to show the invalidity of the argument here is to construct another argument using the same *form* as the argument above where the premises are clearly true and the conclusion is patently false.[1] Since this combination is not possible in a valid argument, it would serve to highlight the fallacious reasoning here. This is called *refutation by analogy*, and it is something we do all the time in ordinary discourse. If we wanted to show the fallacious nature of the argument above, we could respond, "Well, you might as well argue that

Horses run fast

Cheetahs run fast

_____

Therefore, horses are cheetahs!"

Assignment 3.1. Refutation by analogy. For the following invalid deductive arguments, make up an argument with the same logical structure where the premises could easily be true and the conclusion false.

Example: We all know that if you study hard, you are more likely to get good grades. Since you got good grades, I can conclude that you studied hard.

Put formally:

If you study hard, you will get good grades

You got good grades

_____

You studied hard

Solution: That's like saying,

If you start in Spokane and run sixty miles a day for five days, you could be in Seattle by next week

_____

[1]In chaps. 5 and 8 I will present more formal ways of showing invalidity.

You are in Seattle next week
_____
You started in Spokane and ran sixty miles a day for five days

1. Some physicians are hospital employees since some doctors are hardworking and some hospital employees are hardworking.

2. All people who can think several steps ahead are good at chess, so some people who can plan ahead are nerds, since no nerds are good at chess.

*3. If you can't be seen, you can't be captured. Therefore, if you are seen you will be captured.

4. All socialists are people who believe taxes should be raised and government should regulate business. So all people who believe taxes should be raised are people who believe government should regulate business.

5. If you love someone, then you should treat them well. So if you hate someone, you should treat them badly.

*6. If you have ADHD, then you will have trouble focusing on academic work. Therefore all gamers have ADHD since all gamers have trouble focusing on academic work.

7. Some dogs are not large animals, so some pets are not dogs, since some pets are not large animals.

8. If I go to the store, then I will get something for dinner. But I did not go to the store, therefore I have nothing for dinner.

*9. No people afraid of heights are mountain climbers, but all mountain climbers are fit, so no people afraid of heights are fit.

10. Governor Jones is a good administrator because if you are a good administrator, then you would have a surplus in your budget at the end of the fiscal year and Governor Jones had a surplus.

3.2 INFORMAL FALLACIES OF AMBIGUITY

While formal fallacies have a problem with their structure, informal fallacies may or may not have such problems. For example, as we will see below, the fallacy of begging the question—where the conclusion is the same as the premise(s)—is formally valid. *Informal fallacies are arguments that might be psychologically persuasive but are erroneous in some way.* So in all informal fallacies there is some reasoning that is incorrect—even though it may appeal to us on a gut level.

In the sections that follow, we will look at sixteen typical informal fallacies (along with a few subdivisions). This is not an exhaustive list. In fact, while Aristotle listed thirteen fallacies, Irving Copi and Carl Cohen have eighteen, W. Ward Fearnside and William B. Holther found fifty-nine, and David Hackett Fischer described 112.[2] We will divide these sixteen into fallacies of ambiguity and fallacies of relevance.

FALLACIES OF AMBIGUITY

All of the fallacies of ambiguity turn on a misunderstanding in *language*. It may be that a specific word or phrase changes meaning halfway through the argument, or it may be that the grammar as a whole is ambiguous. Now a lack of clarity may be annoying, but it is not *by itself* a fallacy. The fallacy occurs when the lack of clarity is used to draw a conclusion that does not follow from the premises.

A1. Equivocation. As we discussed in chapter 1, individual words and phrases frequently have multiple meanings. *The fallacy of equivocation occurs when an argument uses a single word or phrase to signify two or more different meanings.* The fallacy here is that the equivocal terms introduced in the argument have no real connection of meaning with one another. For example, consider the following classical example of equivocation:

The end of a thing is its perfection

Death is the end of life

Therefore, death is the perfection of life

The word "end" in the first premise means the goal of something as in, "The end of a drive in football is to get a touchdown." But in the second premise, "end" does *not* mean the goal. Instead here "end" means the final event, as in, "By the end of the party everyone was drunk."[3] Thus by using the same word ("end") to signify two different things ("goal" vs. "finish"), the argument fails to establish the conclusion from its premises.

---

[2]Aristotle, *Sophistical Refutations*; Irving M. Copi and Carl Cohen, *Introduction to Logic*, 11th ed. (Upper Saddle River, NJ: Pearson, 2009); W. Ward Fearnside and William B. Holther, *Fallacy: The Counterfeit of Argument* (Englewood Cliffs, NJ: Prentice Hall, 1959); David Hackett Fischer, *Historian's Fallacies* (New York: Harper & Row, 1970).

[3]Now if the *goal* of your parties is to get drunk—and that is the last event of the evening—then there is no equivocation. But you need to go to better parties.

Sometimes these equivocations can be used as a joke:

God is love

Love is blind

Ray Charles is blind

Therefore, Ray Charles is God[4]

In order to discover the fallacy of equivocation, ask yourself, Does the meaning of any word or phrase change during the argument? Generally, the equivocal word or phrase will appear at least twice—but it may only be implied. For example, comedian Peter Kay once said, "I went to a restaurant that serves breakfast at any time. So I ordered 'French Toast during the Renaissance.'" The joke is based on an equivocation on the word "time"—even though it only appears once. "Time" clearly means "hour of the day" to the restaurant. But Kay humorously takes it to mean "historical era."

A special class of the fallacy of equivocation is based on "relative" terms like *tall*, *heavy*, and so on. The problem is that words like this may refer to drastically different things depending on the context. For example,

If you are over six feet, you are considered tall.

Bill is a tall jockey

Bill must be over six feet

A2. Amphiboly. Sometimes words and phrases maintain the same meaning throughout the argument, but a problem with the grammar leads to incorrect reasoning. This is called an amphiboly (from the Greek *amphiboles*, meaning "thrown on both sides"). Often an amphiboly is the result of a misplaced modifier. For example, the headline "The Farmer Blew Out His Brains After Taking Affectionate Farewell of His Family with a Shotgun" leaves us wondering about the body count. While all the individual words and phrases maintain the same meaning, grammatically the clause "with a shotgun" refers to *how* the farmer said farewell to his family. This would mean several people died. The phrase "with a shotgun" was undoubtedly meant to modify how the farmer "blew out his brains," leaving only one person dead.

Now a misplaced modifier—or other grammatical mistakes—may make for awkward writing, but it is not by itself a fallacy. It becomes a fallacy when

---

[4]Of course, equivocation on the word *blind* is not the only problem with this "argument."

someone draws an incorrect conclusion on the basis of this error. Take this example from the September 2013 issue of *Reader's Digest*:

> A wife asks her husband, "Could you please go shopping for me and buy one carton of milk and, if they have avocadoes, get six." A short time later, the husband returns with six cartons of milk. "Why did you buy six cartons of milk?" his wife asks. He replies, "They had avocados."

Grammatically, the wife's instructions were to get six cartons of milk in the event the store also carried avocadoes. But undoubtedly she *meant* that she wanted one carton of milk and six avocadoes—assuming the store carried avocadoes. Hence the fallacy of amphiboly.

A3. *Begging the question* (petitio principii). In one sense, the fallacy of begging the question is fairly easy to spot: it is when someone simply assumes the conclusion of an argument as a premise. Quite simply it is of the form,

A
—
A

Strictly speaking, this is a valid argument. That is, if the premise is true, then the conclusion must also be true—*because they are exactly the same.*

Now the obvious question is, Why would anyone fall for such a ridiculous argument? If I said to you, "Musical theater is wonderful because musical theater is wonderful," you would laugh at the absurdity of such an "argument." So why would anyone find begging the question to be psychologically persuasive? Because in an argument that begs the question, a proposition is repeated in a subtly different way. Remember how multiple sentences can express the same proposition? By switching between those sentences an argument may *appear* to infer something significant when it is really just saying "A because A." Consider the following argument:

> To allow every man an unbounded freedom of speech must always be, on the whole, advantageous to the State, for it is highly conducive to the interests of the community that each individual should enjoy a liberty perfectly unlimited of expressing his sentiments.[5]

Put formally this becomes,

It is . . . conducive to the interests of the community that each individual should enjoy liberty of expression

---

C Therefore, freedom of speech must be . . . advantageous to the State

---

[5]Richard Whately, *Elements of Logic* (London: Longman, Green, and Co., 1875), 134.

The premise and the conclusion here are both expressing the same proposition: "Free speech is good for the community."

Sometimes begging the question involves a chain of arguments that we call "arguing in circles." For example, one could argue that Beethoven is the greatest composer of all time because people with good taste in music think so. When questioned about who the people are with good taste in music, one might say, "those who prefer Beethoven." Or consider this exchange between *Sports Illustrated* writer Michael Rosenberg and then NCAA head Myles Brand over the question of paying college athletes:

> [Brand:] "They can't be paid."
>
> [Rosenberg:] "Why?"
>
> [Brand:] "Because they're amateurs."
>
> [Rosenberg:] "What makes them amateurs?"
>
> [Brand:] "Well, they can't be paid."
>
> [Rosenberg:] "Why not?"
>
> [Brand:] "Because they're amateurs."[6]

This kind of circular reasoning is an example of assuming what you are trying to prove—that is, begging the question.

Equivocation, amphiboly, and begging the question all can be psychologically persuasive because of the relationship between sentences and propositions. In the case of equivocation and amphiboly, the same word or sentence is being used in expressing two different propositions (see fig. 3.1).

In the case of begging the question, two different words or sentences are being used to express the same proposition (see fig. 3.2).

One side note here. In recent years people have started to use the expression "begs the question" to mean something quite different. For example, a sports announcer might say at the end of a report on the flaws of Coach Smith, "All this begs the question, 'Why hasn't Coach Smith been fired?'" Now actually, it doesn't beg the question, it *raises* the question. If it was *begging* the question, it would be something like "Coach Smith has not been fired because he is still employed."[7]

---

[6]Michael Rosenberg, "Change Is Long Overdue: College Football Players Should Be Paid," *Sports Illustrated*, August 26, 2010, https://www.si.com/more-sports/2010/08/26/pay-college. (It seems clear in the article that Rosenberg is giving the gist of the conversation, not quoting Brand verbatim.)

[7]Of course, language is always changing and we would be committing the fallacy of begging the question if we said, "The term 'begging the question' should only be used in the correct logical manner defined here because to use it any other way shouldn't be done."

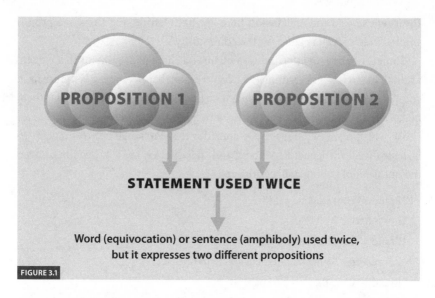

Word (equivocation) or sentence (amphiboly) used twice,
but it expresses two different propositions

FIGURE 3.1

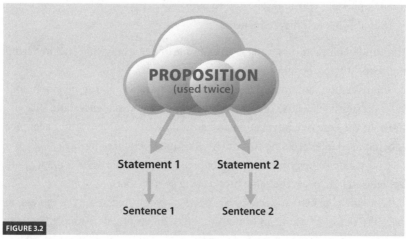

FIGURE 3.2

A4. Accent. The fallacy of accent, like equivocation and amphiboly, changes the meaning of a sentence and uses that sentence to express two different propositions. In the case of accent, it changes the meaning by highlighting part of a sentence to convey a completely different meaning. The most obvious case of the fallacy of accent is found in cases of quoting out of context. In politics, people will often quote their opponents in such a way that the opponent seems to be expressing a proposition that is different from what they actually believe.

For example, Shirley Sherrod was forced to resign from her position as Georgia state director of rural development for the United States Department of Agriculture in 2010. Earlier that year, she had given an address at an NAACP event where she was shown on video saying that as a Black woman she did not want to help a White farmer save his farm when so many Black farmers were losing farms. The video was trumpeted as a clear case of reverse discrimination, and she was strongly denounced by virtually everyone—even the NAACP. Later the *entire* video was discovered. It turned out that while she *had* said those words, they came in the middle of a story about how she came to realize that poverty affects everyone and that we must all move past our racial prejudices. She ended the story by saying, "Working with him made me see that it's really about those who have versus those who don't, you know. And they could be Black, and they could be White; they could be Hispanic. And it made me realize then that I needed to work to help poor people—those who don't have access the way others have."[8] By accenting one part of the speech and ignoring the context, her words were used to express a completely different proposition from the one she actually asserted.

The fallacy of accent also appears quite frequently in tabloids and clickbait websites. A headline will scream, "The Three Things Every Person Is Doing Wrong!" to get your attention. Then the article will talk about the need to brush your teeth and so on. The fallacy of accent also happens in a more subtle way when certain truths are brought to light—rather than others. Why is a newspaper or newscast covering *this* murder rather than another? Why is *this* political rally getting coverage and not another? Why does the *Washington Times* include stories that *Huffington Post* ignores—and vice versa?[9] By emphasizing one item over another, it is possible to commit the fallacy of accent even if everything being reported is true. For example, suppose you wrote a note to the dean saying, "Our logic teacher did not swear at any students today." Undoubtedly this is true, but it still commits the fallacy of accent: by accenting the teacher's lack of swearing today, you are implying that she usually swears and today was unusual.

---

[8]Shirley Sherrod, "Address at the Georgia NAACP 20th Annual Freedom Fund Banquet," American Rhetoric Online Speech Bank, March 27, 2010, www.americanrhetoric.com/speeches/shirley sherrodnaacpfreedom.htm, accessed June 12, 2016.

[9]It is interesting, when studying current events, to visit *both* sites or to watch Fox News *and* MSNBC, Al Jazeera America *and* BBC News.

A5 and A6. Division and composition. To understand this pair of fallacies, we must first make a distinction in how groups can be discussed. We talk about a group *collectively* when we talk about the properties of the group *taken as a whole*. So, if we say the Olympians at the Rio games in 2016 came from 206 countries, we are talking about the collection of athletes as a whole. But we talk about a group *distributively* when we talk about the properties of a group as *individual members of the group*. So when we say the Olympians at the Rio games consumed between two thousand and eight thousand calories a day, we are talking about each individual athlete—not the collection of athletes as a whole. After all, one to four calories per Olympian would not be enough to sustain them.

The *fallacy of division* occurs when an argument shifts from discussing the characteristics of a group as a whole to discussing the characteristics of a group as individuals—that is, from *collectively* to *distributively*. The *fallacy of division argues from the whole, taken as a whole, to the parts*. So, for example, someone might argue, "America has no problem with poverty because we are a rich nation." While it is true that America is a rich nation *taken as a whole*, that does not mean every American is wealthy.

The *fallacy of composition* is exactly the opposite. This fallacy occurs when an argument shifts from discussing the characteristics of a group as individuals to discussing the characteristics of a group as a whole—that is, from distributively to collectively. The *fallacy of composition argues from the parts to the whole, taken as a whole*. "Every part of this car weighs under two hundred pounds, therefore the car must weigh under two hundred pounds" would be an example. Since groups taken as a whole usually have properties that are different from the individual members of that group, it is a mistake to assume that the properties will be the same collectively as they are distributively. Sports fans often commit this fallacy: "The Kansas City Chiefs have the best player at every position, so they have to win the Super Bowl." While it may or may not be true that each individual member is the best at his position, it certainly does not follow that the team as a whole will be the best.

A7 and A8. Accident and hasty generalization (or converse accident). The *fallacy of accident* occurs when we take a general rule and apply it to unusual (or "accidental") circumstances—or at least circumstances different from those assumed in the general rule. For example, it is a rule that you need to have an appointment before you can see the doctor. If someone is bleeding profusely, however, and we said she could not see the doctor because she lacked an appointment, we would be committing the fallacy of accident. Notice, there is no confusion here between taking a group collectively or distributively—as there is in the fallacies of composition and division. Rather, one is taking the general rule *that applies to every member of the grouping distributively* and applying it to a case that does not fit.

The *fallacy of hasty generalization* (or *converse accident*[10]) does exactly the opposite of the fallacy of accident. In a hasty generalization, we take some unusual cases or examples of a group and draw a conclusion about every case or member of the group. Again, there is no switch from seeing the group collectively or distributively, but instead we take unusual cases and make a general rule about it.

Let's consider an example to make these two clear. One of the important features of a sailboat is the amount of room it has below deck for eating, sleeping, and relaxing. Often an ad for a sailboat will mention that it has "standing headroom." Now imagine that you go looking for a sailboat with your good friend Hall of Fame basketball player Kareem Abdul-Jabbar. If you two checked out a sailboat that listed "standing headroom" and you objected that the ad lied because there was only six feet five inches of clearance and Kareem could not stand up below deck, you would be committing the fallacy of accident. The general rule is that a person can stand up below deck, but you are trying to apply that rule to a very unusual circumstance: a person who is seven feet two inches tall. If you and Kareem checked out every sailboat in the boatyard and he was not able to stand up below deck on any of them and you concluded, "None of these boats have standing headroom," you would be committing the fallacy of hasty generalization. That is, you would be taking an unusual case (again, Kareem's height) and trying to make a general rule.

Clearly, there is a similarity between the fallacies of accident/hasty generalization and those of division/composition. In all four cases there is an illegitimate movement from parts or individual cases to or from the whole or rule.

---

[10]Some logicians would argue that the fallacies of hasty generalization and converse accident are actually slightly different. While there might be some subtle differences, we are looking at the ways in which they are generally the same.

The key difference between these two sets is whether we are talking about the collection taken as a whole (collectively). Put in diagrammatic form, we can see the key differences:

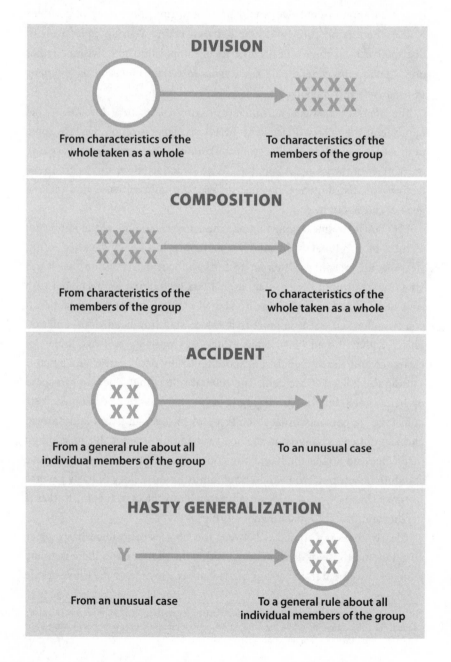

DIVISION

From characteristics of the whole taken as a whole

To characteristics of the members of the group

COMPOSITION

From characteristics of the members of the group

To characteristics of the whole taken as a whole

ACCIDENT

From a general rule about all individual members of the group

To an unusual case

HASTY GENERALIZATION

From an unusual case

To a general rule about all individual members of the group

Assignment 3.2. For the following passages, identify and explain the fallacy of ambiguity.

Example: Headline: "Woman with Dog's Head Taken to Hospital"
                    Jay Leno: "Well that's kind of mean!"

Solution: Amphiboly. Presumably the headline meant to say that a
                    woman who was holding the head of a dog was taken to the
                    hospital. But Leno takes it to mean an insult about the
                    woman's appearance—that is, that her head looks like a dog's.

1. Classified ad: Wanted—Smart young man for butcher. Able to cut, skewer, and serve customers.

2. Priest: The mass has ended.
   Congregation: Thanks be to God!

*3. Everything that runs has feet. The river runs. Therefore the river has feet.

4. The judge stayed awake during the hearing today.

5. Anyone who is really your friend helps you out when you are in trouble. So since you won't help me cheat on my logic exam, I guess you are not my friend.

*6. Headline: "Passenger Trains Hurt by Lack of Track"
    Jay Leno: "Uh-oh . . . look out. . . ."

7. Each of the professors who is on the teaching team for that course is great, so you know the class will be fantastic!

8. Miracles are impossible because they contradict the laws of nature and nothing can do that.

*9. When Bill had to go to the district playoffs with the team, the prof said it was okay for him to miss class, so the prof doesn't care whether we come.

10. Since all humans are mortal, the human race must someday come to an end.

11. For sale: Antique desk suitable for lady with carved legs and large drawers.

*12. There must be lots of jobs available in physical education because the dean said she will talk to graduating seniors about their employment opportunities in Graves Gym tonight.

13. Since there was a 20 percent drop in nationwide sales last month, our store must have taken a beating.

14. Professor Jones must be a good teacher since he is such a good person.

*15. Susan and Sarah are both bad at math. Clearly girls are terrible at math.

3.3 INFORMAL FALLACIES OF RELEVANCE

In the fallacies that follow there is not really a lack of clarity, but the premises are logically irrelevant to the conclusion. However, in each case there is something psychologically relevant—that is, something that *feels* like a connection. In some cases it is the expressive use of language that evokes a particular attitude. That attitude may seem connected to the premise(s) and conclusion. But in fact, the conclusion does not follow from the premises in a fallacy of relevance. We will look at these fallacies of ambiguity in roughly the order one should use in trying to find them.

R1. Argumentum *ad hominem* (or just ad hominem). A central tenet of philosophy is the belief that one can separate an idea from the person who asserted the idea. One might be a good person and assert a false proposition; one might be a bad person who sets forth a true proposition. While the characteristics of persons may give us reason to be suspicious of their claims, their characteristics tell us nothing about the truth or falsehood of their statements. Undoubtedly, Adolf Hitler said some things that were true—the fact that *he* said them does not make those propositions any less true. Conversely, Mother Teresa probably said some things that were false.

While we may acknowledge this separation between speaker and truth value, it is hard to make this distinction in practice. Let's face it: it is difficult for any of us to separate ideas from the person holding them. If you attack a friend's assertions, your friend will likely feel personally attacked. In the same way, we are inclined to disbelieve the assertions of persons we find obnoxious.

The fallacy of *ad hominem* is based on a denial of this distinction between person and assertion. This fallacy is so prevalent that its old Latin name has become part of our vocabulary. Literally, it means "to or against the person." So we define the fallacy of *ad hominem* as *arguing against the person and not his or her assertions.*

In middle school, you might observe a group trying to decide what to do. Someone low on the social-acceptance scale says, "Let's go to the mall," and everyone mutters, "That's stupid." Later in the discussion, a popular kid makes the same suggestion. Now, everyone agrees it is a terrific idea. When a proposition is dismissed based on who asserted it, that is the fallacy of *ad hominem*.

Abusive ad hominem. While *any* dismissal of a proposition based on the person who said it is an ad hominem, there are several subdivisions worth mentioning. The first and most obvious is the abusive *ad hominem*. In this fallacy one *simply abuses the speaker and ignores what they have to say.* "You're an idiot" is not really a logical response to the assertion of a proposition (though it is shocking how often it occurs as though it *were* a counterargument).

Circumstantial ad hominem. The circumstantial *ad hominem* is far less crude—though just as fallacious. The circumstantial version of *ad hominem* argues against the person based on the *circumstances* of that person. So, for example, one might reject a claim that tariffs hurt the global economy because it was asserted by a shipping-company executive. Now obviously, the shipping company has an interest in keeping tariffs low. One would be wise to examine their *argument* carefully. But to reject the argument simply because of who asserted it is a fallacy.

Another version of circumstantial *ad hominem* is to dismiss a person's argument because they do not live out the propositions they are asserting. It is hard to take advice from someone who tells us, "Do as I say, and not as I do." However, the advice may still be correct. The Latin term *tu quoque*, meaning "you also," is sometimes used to identify this particular type of circumstantial *ad hominem*. For example, when Osama bin Laden was asked by CNN in 1997 if he funded military training camps and supported international terrorism, he responded,

> Wherever we look, we find the U.S. as the leader of terrorism and crime in the world. The U.S. does not consider it a terrorist act to throw atomic bombs at nations thousands of miles away, when it would not be possible for those bombs to hit military troops only. These bombs were rather thrown at entire nations, including women, children and elderly people and up to this day the traces of those bombs remain in Japan. The U.S. does not consider it terrorism when hundreds of thousands of our sons and brothers in Iraq died for lack of food or medicine. So, there is no base for what the U.S. says and this saying does not affect us, because we, by the grace of God, are dependent on Him, Praise and Glory be to Him, getting help from Him against the U.S.[11]

---

[11]"CNN March 1997 Interview with Osama bin Laden," FindLaw.com.

Whether or not the United States has done all the things asserted here really has no bearing on the truth or falsehood of the proposition that Bin Laden supported terrorism.

Sometimes the fallacy of circumstantial *ad hominem* is taken to the level of dismissing all of a person's ideas entirely. This has been called "poisoning the well," because one is dismissing ("poisoning") the source ("well") of a person's beliefs. So one might say, "Well, he is a communist, so what can you expect from him?" or "She is an archconservative, so there is no point in even listening to her," or even "He is Osama bin Laden, so what he said above about the United States must be false." In this case one does not reject particular ideas based on who said them, but rejects all of a person's ideas en masse.

A side note on ad hominem, *inconsistency, and the proper role of the person.* While an argument that uses an *ad hominem* commits a fallacy, there may still be some value in connecting a person and their ideas. If a person who espouses a strict vegan lifestyle is wearing a mink coat, it may be hard to take her arguments for veganism seriously. If you know that a speaker talking compassion gave up his job on Wall Street to work full-time in a homeless shelter, you might be more inclined to listen. Now to dismiss the arguments of the first and accept the claims of the second because of what they do would be the fallacy of *ad hominem*. But it is hardly irrational to be on your guard when someone is being hypocritical or more receptive when listening to someone who "practices what they preach."

R2. Appeal to illegitimate authority. The fallacy of appeal to illegitimate authority is the mirror opposite of the fallacy of *ad hominem*. Where an *ad hominem* associated a person and their ideas negatively, the fallacy of appeal to illegitimate authority associates them positively. Now, there is nothing wrong with accepting a proposition because it was asserted by a *legitimate* authority. Life is much too complicated to test everything for ourselves. We must—and do—rely on authorities to inform us of facts. The problem comes because of what some people call the "halo effect." When a person is an expert in one area, we have a tendency to believe that they are an authority in many other areas—even if they are not. For example, Tiger Woods is certainly an expert on golf, but what reason do I have to accept his assertion that Buick is a great car? Now if he was telling me which golf club I ought to use, it would be wise to take his advice.[12] But if he tells me to buy a Buick, I might want to do some further fact-checking.

---

[12]Of course, given that he was being paid millions by Nike to say nice things about their products, we might have reason to raise some questions here as well. But we don't want to commit the fallacy of circumstantial *ad hominem* and assume that his endorsement was false.

Sometimes the legitimacy of authority is not so easy to determine. When a model advertises for the nutritional value of a breakfast cereal, there is no question we have a fallacy. But if she is advertising makeup, is she a legitimate or illegitimate authority? She may be beautiful, but does she really have any authority when it comes to types of makeup? (Does she even do her own makeup?) Or how about when Sigmund Freud tells us that "religious phenomena are only to be understood on the pattern of the individual neurotic symptoms familiar to us"?[13] Clearly he is a legitimate authority about neurotic symptoms. But does that make him a legitimate authority on "religious phenomena"? Now the model and Freud may be correct, but their authority in one area (looking good and psychoanalysis respectively) does not mean they are authorities in all areas. One should be on one's guard with all authorities. When a favorite actor makes a claim about a product, we might want to double-check the facts. When your pastor gives political advice, you might want to read some other opinions. And when your professors make assertions beyond their field of expertise. . . .

R3. Appeal to force. The fallacy of appeal to force is committed when the reason given to accept the conclusion is force or the threat of force. The phrase "might makes right" captures the essence of this fallacy. It may be that "might" has the power to force the hearer to accept a conclusion, but that does not mean the conclusion follows logically. We see this most clearly on the international scale, when a country threatens another country with force if it does not accept the conclusion demanded. A classic example of this fallacy is found in the Melian conference when the ancient Athenians threatened the islanders of Melos with ruin if they did not submit:

> For ourselves, we shall not trouble you with specious pretenses—either of how we have a right to our empire because we overthrew the [Persians], or are now attacking you because of wrong that you have done us—and make a long speech which would not be believed . . . since you know as well as we do that right, as the world goes, is only in question between equals in power, while the strong do what they can and the weak suffer what they must.[14]

The fallacy of appeal to force need not be such a blatant threat. If a supervisor asks a subordinate to support his proposal and adds, "It would be a

---

[13]Sigmund Freud, *Moses and Monotheism: Three Essays*, trans. Katherine Jones (London: Hogarth Press, 1939), 94.

[14]Thucydides, *The History of the Peloponnesian War*, trans. Richard Crawley (London: Longmans, Green, and Co., 1874), 397.

shame if this proposal does not get accepted. We would hate to have to re-organize your department," this is an appeal to force. If a lobbyist tells a legis-lator she should support a certain bill by reminding her how many people his lobby represents or how much money they donated to her campaign, that is an appeal to force.

R4. **Argumentum** *ad populum (or just* **ad** populum *or appeal to emotion).* The fallacy of *argumentum* ad populum makes an emotional appeal "to the people." Sometimes it is just called appeal to emotion, but we will use its old Latin name, *ad populum.* In this fallacy, the facts are ignored and the emotions are engaged. The orator frequently uses this fallacy to get the crowd on his side. Mark Antony's famous speech about Julius Caesar's death is a great example— as are Hitler's rallying speeches at Nuremberg. Advertisers use this fallacy in multiple ways to get customers to buy their products. In fact, modern adver-tisers have become masters at developing different versions of this fallacy— some of which are worth considering separately.

Bandwagon. The claim that a certain product should be purchased because "everyone else is buying it," or that a certain proposition should be accepted because "everyone thinks it," is the "bandwagon" version of the fallacy of *ad populum.*[15] When we are told we should buy a car because it is the bestselling brand, we are encountering the bandwagon *ad populum* fallacy. When we hear that we should support a certain candidate because she is likely going to win, we are encountering the bandwagon *ad populum* fallacy. The effects of this fallacy can be seen clearly in politics. For example, in 1980 third-party can-didate John B. Anderson was running for president of the United States. In all the polls leading up to the election, Anderson trailed far behind the two main candidates, Jimmy Carter and Ronald Reagan. However, when people were asked, "If you thought John B. Anderson had a chance to win, for whom would you vote?" he actually outpolled Carter and Reagan. Of course, no one thought he had a real chance to win, and he ended up with 6.6 percent of the popular vote and zero Electoral College votes.

Snob appeal. The flip side of the bandwagon effect is the snob appeal version of the fallacy of *ad populum.* In this version, the listener is invited to buy the product or accept the idea because "only the best" sort of people do. The

---

[15]In times long past, a candidate in an election would have a wagon with a musical band drive through town. People who wanted to show their support for the candidate would "jump on the bandwagon."

hidden assumption is that by doing the same, you too can become one of the best. When the US Marines advertise that they are "The few. The proud. The Marines." they are using snob appeal. The hidden push is for the hearer to join that proud few. When a product is advertised as "exclusive" or "of distinction," it is using snob appeal.

Lifestyle (or image) advertising. One of the most effective uses of the fallacy of *ad populum* is found in lifestyle or image advertising. Viewers are shown a setting that appeals to them, and it is implied that all that stands between them and this lifestyle is the product. It really doesn't matter what the lifestyle is—so long as it is one that appeals to the intended audience. So an ad for a brand of skateboards might include pictures of tattooed rebel-looking boys with baggy clothes having a great time boarding in an urban environment. An ad for Scotch will likely show several slim, beautiful women draped on the arm of a handsome young man holding a tumbler. What is being sold is the lifestyle that (supposedly) goes *with* the board, goes *with* the Scotch.

If you look at a couple on the cover of a magazine or paperback novel, you can usually tell the intended target audience simply by looking to see who is looking off in a bored way and who is looking at the other person with rapt attention. If the man is totally focused on the woman while she is gazing in the distance, it is a magazine or romance novel for women. A woman is enticed to buy this because *she* wants to be the woman in the picture. For men, the situation is simply reversed.

The powerful thing about lifestyle or image advertising is that it works even when we know what the advertiser is doing. As Virginia Stem Owens explains,

> My . . . parents often pointed out to me in my youth the insidiousness of [image] advertising. It was the favorite topic of my logic professor in college. I harangued my own students about its perils to clear, objective thinking. But the beauty part of image advertising is that the audience can be aware of the ruse yet still affected by it. Catching on to the gimmick does not make us immune to the infection. Despite our most rationally disapproving selves, we still lust after the image in the picture.[16]

We know that the conclusion, "I need this product," does not follow logically from the premise, "All these people with the life I want use this product," yet

---

[16]Virginia Stem Owens, *The Total Image: Or, Selling Jesus in the Modern Age* (Grand Rapids, MI: Eerdmans, 1980), 26.

it is so psychologically persuasive that we fall for it. Years ago, Sprite soft drink had a series of ads that poked fun at this phenomenon. They had famous athletes endorse Sprite while the corner of the screen showed a count of the money the athlete was getting from the endorsement. The commercial ended with the tagline "Image is nothing. Thirst is everything. Obey your thirst." Of course, if "image is nothing," why would they pay to have the famous athletes in the spot in the first place?

Humor. Another version of the fallacy of *ad populum* involves using humor. If an ad or a speaker can get the audience to laugh, they are more likely to accept what the ad is selling or the speaker is advocating. During Super Bowl XLV in 2011, the most popular commercial featured a six-year-old boy. Dressed as Darth Vader, the boy unsuccessfully tried to use "the Force" to start the washer and dryer, to wake the dog, and so on. He eventually goes outside and is stunned when he is able to use the Force to start his father's new Volkswagen Passat. Of course, the audience can see through a window that his father is actually using the remote-start function of the Passat. Very cute and very funny. But what does that have to do with value of the Passat as an auto-mobile—aside from showing that it has remote-start capability? In a similar vein, why do public speakers invariably start their talks with a joke? Yes, it puts folks at ease, but is it also used to encourage acceptance of the speaker's ideas?

While these are just a few of the subdivisions, any appeal to emotion as a reason to accept a conclusion is an example of the fallacy of *ad populum*.

One final note here: the fact that an argument includes emotion does *not* necessarily mean that it is committing a fallacy. Sometimes emotion is entirely appropriate as a part of an argument. But if emotion is being used to win assent to the truth of a conclusion in the absence of supporting propositions, then we have a fallacy.

R5. Appeal to pity. In the case of the fallacy of appeal to pity, the specific emotion of pity is used as the reason to accept a conclusion. In a court of law, a defense attorney may try to get a client acquitted on the basis of pity—even if the client is guilty as charged. Sometimes charities will use pictures of starving children or wounded animals to try to raise funds. A student may tell his professor about how hard his week has been or how many hours he spent trying to do his homework, but that is really not relevant when it comes to accepting late work.

Appealing to pity is in itself not a fallacy. But when the emotion of pity is used as the *reason* to accept a conclusion, then a fallacy has occurred. For example, in 1990, Congress was debating whether to approve a military response to the Iraqi invasion of Kuwait. A fifteen-year-old Kuwaiti girl gave the following testimony at a Congressional hearing: "Mr. Chairman and members of the committee, my name is Nayirah, and I just came out of Kuwait. While I was there, I saw the Iraqi soldiers come into the hospital with guns. They took the babies out of the incubators, took the incubators, and left the children to die on the cold floor."[17]

The first problem here is that the event never happened. Further, Nayirah was the Kuwaiti ambassador's daughter, and the entire hearing had been set up by a public-relations firm working for the Kuwait royal family. But *even if the story were true*, the conclusion "We should invade Iraq" does not follow from the premise "Those people were hurt." At the least some additional premises are needed.

R6. False cause. The fallacy of false cause occurs when one claims a cause-effect relationship that does not exist. Sometimes we use the Latin phrase *post hoc ergo propter hoc* (or just *post hoc* for short), which means "after this, therefore because of this." The basic idea here is that just because one thing follows another does not necessarily mean that the first caused the second. The aphorism "correlation does not prove causation" makes this point well.

For example, if you walk under a ladder and later in the day something bad happens to you, that does not mean the first event caused the second. Or, for a more serious example, politicians will sometimes claim that some bill they got passed is responsible for an improvement in the economy simply because passage preceded the upturn. Their opponents, of course, will point to whatever bad happened after that politician got elected and claim that they caused it. Many conspiracy theories are based on this fallacy. The theorist attributes a specific causality to a series of seemingly distinct events. Of course, causality is often hard to determine—and it may be possible to misuse the recognition of the fallacy of false cause. For example, the American Tobacco Institute used to publish papers arguing that no one had ever proved that smoking causes any health problems. If we take a very strict understanding of cause and effect, they were correct: no one has ever proved with certainty that smoking causes heart disease, lung cancer, emphysema, or anything else. In

---

[17] As quoted in Douglas Walton, "Appeal to Pity: A Case Study of the *Argumentum ad Misericordiam*," *Argumentation* 9 (1995): 769-84. This article includes a careful discussion of the proper and improper uses of pity in argumentation.

fact, if you look at the warning label on a cigarette pack, it says that smoking "could" cause cancer.[18] Perhaps there is some third factor—perhaps genetics— that causes both lung cancer and the desire to smoke. Still, if we take this fallacy too far, the entire field of science and the concept of inductive reasoning goes down the drain.[19]

R7. Appeal to ignorance. The fallacy of appeal to ignorance has a very definite structure. It either argues that something must be true because no one has proved it false or something must be false because no one has proved it true. Basically it is an argument that comes to a point of ignorance, but then instead of admitting the ignorance and stopping there, jumps to a conclusion. Diagrammatically:

For example, to say that UFOs must exist because no one has proved that they don't would be the fallacy of appeal to ignorance. Of course, to say that they *don't* exist because no one has proved that they *do* would be the exact same fallacy.

This brings up a point about what is sometimes called the "burden of proof." In a courtroom, we assume that a person is innocent if they are not proved guilty. Strictly speaking, this is an appeal to ignorance. But we accept this because we

---

[18]In 2009 the FDA tried to change the labels to read "smoking causes cancer" without the modifier "could" (along with eight other equally specific claims). After a suit by the major tobacco companies, the US Court of Appeals for the District of Columbia struck down the change. As of this writing, the case is still pending.

[19]This is essentially what philosopher David Hume (1711–1776) argued.

assume that the "burden of proof" rests with the prosecution. In a similar way, we would generally believe that the burden of proof rests with a person making a claim that is outside our usual experience. So we generally assume that in the absence of evidence for UFOs, it is reasonable to say they don't exist.

This question of burden of proof can itself be the subject of much debate. For example, with religious belief, who has the burden of proof? Should the default position be atheistic and it is up to the theist to prove there is a God? Or is it the other way around? When the evidence is inconclusive, to which conclusion should one rationally come?[20]

In everyday settings, we encounter this idea of burden of proof often enough. Imagine a friend told you there was an elephant running loose in a building. You then went in the building and found no evidence of an elephant. It would *not* be the fallacy of ignorance for you to conclude that your friend's assertion was false. That is because we would expect to find evidence of something as large as an elephant. Without piles of elephant dung, broken doorways, or screaming people, we can rationally conclude there is no elephant there.

R8. Straw man. The fallacy of the straw man is arguing against a poorly presented version of the opponent's argument and then concluding the actual argument has been defeated. The name comes from the idea that it is easier to argue against a man made of straw than a real man. So rather than presenting an opponent's argument in a robust way, one gives a poor or extreme version of that argument, which can then be easily dismissed. The speaker then implies that the opponent has been logically vanquished, when in fact the argument demolished was so weak that no one would reasonably hold it. For example, suppose you argued that we need to stop using drone strikes in the war on terror. You might make the claim "My opponents want to be able to blow up anybody, anywhere, for any reason!" Now, is that really what your opponent is advocating? Probably not. If it is not really what your opponent is advocating, then your argument against the "straw man" is actually irrelevant to the *real* argument your opponent is making. However, it is appealing enough that one sees it frequently in politics and informal debates.

Assignment 3.3. For the following passages, identify and explain the fallacy of relevance.

---

[20]This is what philosopher Blaise Pascal (1623–1662) had in mind when he developed his famous "wager" in *Pensées* 233. For a fascinating discussion of Pascal's wager, see Michael W. Rota, *Taking Pascal's Wager: Faith, Evidence and the Abundant Life* (Downers Grove, IL: IVP Academic, 2016).

Example: The *New York Times* has run a series of articles critical of the proposed F-35 Joint Strike Fighter Jet. Apparently the *Times* wants to leave our country defenseless!

Solution: Straw man. (Pointing out the problems with this plane is not arguing to "leave our country defenseless.")

1. If you don't agree that this merger is a good idea, you may find yourself in a price war.

2. I deserve a good grade because my mother took an extra job working nights to help put me through school and it would break her heart if I flunked out.

*3. Feminists want to treat men and women exactly the same.

4. Everybody loves Taylor Swift, so we need to buy her latest album!

5. Senator Jones said it, so it must be wrong.

*6. L'Oréal, because you're worth it!

7. Isn't it true that students who get all A's study hard? So if you want me to study hard, professor, the best way is to give me an A.

8. Karl Marx was not able to handle his own family's finances, so his economic theories must be wrong.

*9. There is no proof the secretary leaked the news to the papers, so it couldn't have been the secretary who did it.

10. No one has objected to the new campus parking policy, so everyone must agree with it.

11. Jared Fogle says the Subway diet is the best way to lose weight, so I am going to use it to lose weight.

*12. Jared Fogle turned out to be a pedophile, so anything he said about Subway must be wrong!

13. I make the rubric in this course. If you disagree with me, you are welcome to take an F.

14. Title 1 elementary schools have many more kids living in poverty, and so they should not have to take any standardized exams.

*15. More students are being taught sex ed in middle and high school than ever before in the history of our country. Fewer and fewer young people are remaining virgins until they are married. So to cut down on sexual promiscuity we must get rid of sex ed in the schools.

3.4 IDENTIFYING FALLACIES

Our goal as logicians is to avoid fallacies whenever possible. To avoid the fallacies of ambiguity, we must always be careful about the meanings of words and phrases. One way to do this is to rephrase arguments in our own words. In this way, equivocations and amphibolies will become clear. Then we may clarify what exactly we are saying, what the argument is trying to establish, and what is being used to back up that claim.

That latter point will also help with avoiding fallacies of relevance. By always looking to the conclusion to see what the argument is trying to prove, we can then ask ourselves if the reasons given for that conclusion apply.

Here is a list of questions to help guide you as you look for logical fallacies.[21] It is generally helpful to take the questions in this order.

FALLACIES OF AMBIGUITY	
Is the meaning of one sentence or word unclear or changed? Is one word used with different meanings?	→ Equivocation
Is one sentence grammatically unclear?	→ Amphiboly
Does the conclusion simply restate one of the premises?	→ Begging the question
Is a phrase taken out of context and/or emphasized?	→ Accent
Do the premises refer to something as a whole and the conclusion as the parts?	→ Division
Do the premises refer to a thing's parts and the conclusion to it as a whole?	→ Composition
Is a general rule being applied to a special case?	→ Accident
Is a general rule derived from a few atypical cases?	→ Hasty generalization
FALLACIES OF RELEVANCE	
Does a premise abuse a person or appeal to the characteristics of that person to argue against their idea?	→ *ad hominem*
Does a premise cite an authority outside their area of expertise?	→ Illegitimate authority
Does a premise threaten or appeal to power to prove a conclusion?	→ Force
Does a premise appeal to strong emotions or to popularity as a reason to accept the conclusion?	→ *ad populum*
Does a premise whine and/or plead to accept the conclusion?	→ Pity
Is a cause-effect relationship illegitimately claimed in the premises?	→ False cause
Is the conclusion claimed to be true because it cannot be disproven or to be false because it cannot be proven?	→ Ignorance
Is the position being attacked presented poorly?	→ Straw man

---

[21]I am indebted to Dr. Steve Dilley for this list.

Assignment 3.4. For the following passages, identify and explain the fallacy. (Remember, it may be any one of sixteen fallacies.)

Example: "When California governor Earl Warren testified before a congressional hearing [concerning the internment of Japanese-Americans at the beginning of the World War II] in San Francisco on February 21, 1942, a questioner pointed out that there had been no sabotage or any other type of espionage by the Japanese-Americans up to that time. Warren responded, 'I take the view that this lack [of subversive activity] is the most ominous sign in our whole situation. It convinces me more than perhaps any other factor that the sabotage we are to get, the Fifth Column activities are to get, are timed just like Pearl Harbor was timed. . . . I believe we are just being lulled into a false sense of security'" (Robyn Dawes, *Rational Choice in an Uncertain World*).

Solution: Warren is giving an argument from ignorance.

1. "If the parts of the Universe are not accidental, how can the whole Universe be considered as the result of chance? Therefore the existence of the Universe is not due to chance" (Moses Maimonides, *Guide for the Perplexed*).

2. Headline: "Missouri woman big winner at hog show"
   Jay Leno: "Uh, lady, I wouldn't brag about this too much" (Jay Leno, *Headlines III*).

*3. "A woman who set [a fire that burned 467 homes and scorched 469,000 acres] said Thursday that she had been lost in the wilderness for two nights and was desperate to get the attention of a passing TV helicopter. 'You can't blame me for saving my life,' she said" (Alisha Blackwood, "Woman Who Set Signal Fire Was Lost, Desperate," *East Valley Tribune*).

4. "For the benefit of those representatives who have not been here before this year, it may be useful to explain that the item before the General Assembly is that hardy perennial called the 'Soviet item.' It is purely a propaganda proposition, not introduced with a serious purpose of serious action, but solely as a peg on which to hang a number of speeches with the view to getting them into the press of the world. This is considered by some to be very clever politics. Others, among whom the present speaker wishes to be included, consider it an inadequate

response to the challenge of the hour" (Henry Cabot Lodge, speech to the United Nations General Assembly, November 30, 1953).

5. "The war-mongering character of all this flood of propaganda in the United States is admitted even by the American Press. Such provocative and slanderous aims clearly inspired today's speech by the United States representative, consisting only of impudent slander against the Soviet Union, to answer which would be beneath our dignity" (Baranovsky, speech to the United Nations General Assembly, November 30, 1953).

*6. This is why I'm hot:

I'm hot cause I'm fly. (MIMS, "This Is Why I'm Hot" [2009])

7. Ad: Amazing new weight-loss discovery has taken Europe by storm. . . . Can 14 million people be wrong?

8. "No, son, you lose. 'Cause this is a Smith & Wesson I'm holdin' here" (Canada Bill Jones [1840–1880], riverboat gambler).

*9. "[Defense attorney Ellis Rubin] hopes to use a defense of 'television intoxication' to prove that a fifteen-year-old boy charged with shooting an elderly woman to death was addicted to television crime shows. . . . 'Without the influence of television, there would not have been any crime,' Rubin argued. He claims [the boy's] constant exposure to TV crime shows such as 'Kojak' and 'Police Woman' and a television film depicting the Charles Manson mass murders was responsible for 'diseasing his mind and impairing his behavior controls'" (*Lakeland Ledger*).

10. In a recession it is appropriate for the federal government to increase spending and cut income by cutting taxes. So during a recession, your family should save less and spend more.

11. Headline: "When it comes to student achievement, how high is your high school?"

Jay Leno: "You don't want to know." (Jay Leno, ed., *More Headlines*)

*12. "I know that psychiatry is a pseudo-science" (Tom Cruise).

13. Officer, if you give me a ticket for speeding, it will be my fifth and I will lose my license. I have to drive to work and without my income my family will starve.

14. "I know children regress after vaccination because it happened to my own son" (Jenny McCarthy, actor, *The Huffington Post*).

*15. Movie review: "This is one of the worst movies ever made! Perhaps if it had a plot and some decent acting, it could have been a great movie" —Joe Hollywood.

Movie poster: ". . . A great movie!" —Joe Hollywood.

3.5 A WARNING ABOUT FALLACIES

Psychologist Abraham Maslow famously declared, "If the only tool you have is a hammer, you tend to see every problem as a nail."[22] So if Marxist ideology is the only tool one has to make sense of the news, one is likely to see all current events in terms of the struggle of the proletariat. If feminist theory is the only tool to understand social interactions, then everything one encounters will seem to be an example of patriarchy. If Fox News is the only source for making sense of politics, everything the Democrats do will seem treasonous. And if one has recently learned about fallacies, every argument will look to be fallacious. Logic students frequently report that they start finding fallacies everywhere (and tend to annoy their friends doing so).

But the fact that an argument mentions the circumstances of a person, describes emotions, or addresses power does not necessarily mean it has committed a fallacy. Take for example this biblical passage from Revelation: "I warn everyone who hears the words of the prophecy of this scroll: If anyone adds anything to them, God will add to that person the plagues described in this scroll" (Rev 22:18 NIV). Now one could argue that this passage commits the fallacy of appeal to force by arguing to the conclusion that one should not add to the book based on the premise that bad things will happen if one does. This seems pretty clearly to be a threat—and the resulting argument would be a fallacy. But what if it is just explaining what will happen if you add to the book, not giving an argument at all? If I warn you that you are likely to get hurt playing in the street, I have not committed a fallacy—I am just letting you know the possible consequences of your action. But is the passage above just explaining what will happen, or is it giving a reason why one should not add to the book based on an appeal to force? The answer to that question will be decided partly by what one believes about Scripture. But at any rate, it is not entirely clear whether this is a fallacy.

---

[22]Abraham Maslow, *The Psychology of Science* (1966; repr., Chapel Hill, NC: Maurice Bassett, 2004), 15.

Assignment 3.5a. For the following passages, either identify the fallacy committed or explain why you think there is not a fallacy.

Example: "Who did you pass on the road?" the King went on, holding out his hand to the Messenger for some more hay.

"Nobody," said the Messenger.

"Quite right," said the King: "this young lady saw him too. So of course Nobody walks slower than you." (Lewis Carroll, *Through the Looking Glass*)

Solution: Equivocation on the word "nobody." (The Messenger means he did not pass anyone, but the King takes "Nobody" to be the name of a person.)

1. "Our universe, however, did begin with the primordial explosion, since we can obtain no information about events that occurred before it" (*Scientific American*).

2. "Several years have now elapsed since I first became aware that I had accepted, even from my youth, many false opinions for true, and that consequently what I afterward based on such principles was highly doubtful; and from that time I was convinced of the necessity of undertaking once in my life to rid myself of all the opinions I had adopted" (René Descartes, *Meditations*).

*3. "Wolf partisans seem to have no regard for the feelings of the deer and elk the wolves feed on. Would you like to be stalked by killers night and day, the year round, finally to be pulled down and eaten? Better to be shot during hunting seasons than to suffer this way" (John Norman Constenius, letter to the editor, *Time*).

4. "One morning I shot an elephant in my pajamas. How he got in my pajamas, I don't know" (Groucho Marx, *Animal Crackers*).

5. "Death is nothing terrible, for if it were, it would have seemed so to Socrates" (Epictetus, *Handbook*).

*6. "There is no nation, however barbarous, which has not and will not recognize the existence of punishments and rewards. That reward and punishment exist is, then, a Common Notion, though there is the greatest difference of opinion as to their nature, quality, extent, and mode" (Lord Herbert of Cherbury, *De Veritate* [*On Truth*]).

7. "Why *do* people keep saying, 'God is in the details'? He isn't in ours, unless his yokel creationist fans wish to take credit for his clumsiness, failure, and incompetence" (Christopher Hitchens, *god Is Not Great: How Religion Poisons Everything*).

8. The Bible says "Thou shalt not kill." That is why you should not join the US Army.

*9. "No, no, no, no . . . it's not a *new* number, it's . . . it's . . . it's just a changed number. See? It's not different, it's the same . . . just . . . changed" (Elaine, *Seinfeld*, explaining to the telephone installer why she should not have an area code set up for new numbers).

10. "Every family in America has to balance their budget. Washington should too" (House Speaker John Boehner, 2013).

11. "Anytus: Socrates, it seems to me that you easily speak badly of people. Now I could give you some advice, if you're willing to be persuaded by me, to be careful: since it is perhaps easier to do harm to people than to benefit them in other cities too, and in this city that is certainly so. But I suppose you know that yourself" (Plato, *Meno*).

*12. The Village People are a very successful disco group, so if the "cop," Victor Willis, goes out on his own, he can be sure to have a great career as a soloist.

13. "There is a certain attitude in the world, by some, that says that it's a waste of time to try to promote free societies in parts of the world. I've heard that criticism. . . . I just strongly disagree with those who do not see the wisdom of trying to promote free societies around the world. If we are interested in protecting our country for the long-term, the best way to do so is to promote freedom and democracy" (President George W. Bush, post-election press conference, November 4, 2004, in response to a question about the American image in the Islamic world).

14. Bert: "Ernie . . . you still have that banana in your ear!"

Ernie: "Yeah, Bert, I know."

Bert: "You know?! Ernie, why is that banana still in your ear?"

Ernie: "Listen, Bert. I use this banana to keep the alligators away."

Bert: "Alligators?! There are no alligators on Sesame Street!"

Ernie: "Right! Doing a good job, isn't it Bert?" (*Sesame Street*, 1971)

*15. "Two hunters are out in the woods when one of them collapses. He's not breathing and his eyes are glazed, so his friend calls 911. 'My friend is dead! What should I do?' The operator replies, 'Calm down, sir. I can help. First make sure that he's dead.' There's a silence, then a loud bang. Back on the phone, the guy says, 'Ok, now what?'" (Scott Weems, *Ha! The Science of When We Laugh and Why*. A survey of one million people concluded this was the world's funniest joke.)

Assignment 3.5b. For the following passages, either identify the fallacy committed or explain why you think there is not a fallacy.

Example: "It was only a few persons having irresponsible views and perverted minds who denied [divinely ordained persons the truth of whose mission is evident from the miracles they performed]. But in serious discussions no importance can be attached to such persons; and no notice ought to be taken of them. And they must be branded with diabolical perversity and stupid contumacy, so that their example may be a deterrent" (al-Ghazālī, *The Incoherence of Philosophy*).

Solution: *Ad hominem* (abusive)

1. *Question:* If you could live forever, would you and why?

   Answer: I would not live forever, because we should not live forever, because if we were supposed to live forever, then we would live forever, but we cannot live forever, which is why I would not live forever. (Miss Alabama in the 1994 Miss USA Contest)

2. The story is told about Wendell Phillips, the abolitionist, who one day found himself on the same train with a group of Southern clergymen on their way to a conference. When the Southerners learned of Phillips's presence, they decided to have some fun at his expense. One of them approached and asked,

   "Are you Wendell Phillips, the abolitionist?"

   "Yes sir," came the reply.

   "Are you the one who makes speeches in Boston and New York against slavery?"

   "Yes, I am."

"Why don't you go to Kentucky and make speeches there?"

Phillips looked at his questioner for a moment and then asked,

"Are you a clergyman?"

"Yes, I am," replied the other.

"Are you trying to save souls from hell?"

"Yes."

"Well—why don't you go there?"

*3. "The clinching proof of my reasoning is that I will cut anyone who argues further into dogmeat" (Sir Geoffrey de Tourneville, Norman knight, ca. 1350).

4. "Beauty is love made real, and the spirit of love is God. And the state of beauty, love and God is happiness. A transcendent state of beauty, love and God is peace. Peace and love is a state of beauty, love and God. One is an active state of happiness and the other is a transcendent state. That's peace" (Imelda Marcos, campaigning for her husband, Ferdinand Marcos, the president of the Philippines who was indicted by a US grand jury for embezzling $100 million to buy property in New York City).

5. "Wrangler Advanced Comfort Jeans are the most comfortable jeans you'll ever wear, guaranteed" (Drew Brees, NFL quarterback, New Orleans Saints).

*6. When King Croesus asked the Oracle at Delphi what would happen if he went into battle against Cyrus the following day, the Oracle responded, "If you go into battle, a mighty nation will be destroyed." Liking this answer, Croesus went into battle and his army was decimated by Cyrus. Limping back to the Oracle, Croesus complained, "You said if I went into battle, a mighty nation would be destroyed!" "Yes," replied the Oracle, "and that is exactly what happened—your mighty nation was destroyed."

7. "When you test, you have a case. When you test, you find something is wrong with people. If we didn't do any testing, we would have very few cases" (President Donald Trump, press conference, May 14, 2020, in response to a question about testing for Covid-19).

8. After a testy encounter with Donald Trump at a press conference, Univision anchor Jorge Ramos found himself on the defensive, trying to explain how his self-proclaimed position as an advocate for immigration reform does not undercut his role as a journalist.

"In the aftermath of this incident, I was accused of being an activist," Ramos wrote in an online post Wednesday. "That's not the case—I'm simply a journalist who asks questions. And journalists have an obligation to take a stand when it comes to racism, discrimination, corruption, public lies, dictatorships and human rights violations" (*Los Angeles Times*).

*9. "All religions have based morality on obedience, that is to say, on voluntary slavery. That is why they have always been more pernicious than any political organization. For the latter makes use of violence, the former—of the corruption of the will" (Aleksandr Ivanovich Herzen [1812–1870], the "father of Russian socialism").

10. "Winfield goes back to the wall. He hits his head on the wall and it rolls off! It's rolling all the way back to second base! This is a terrible thing for the Padres!" (Jerry Coleman, San Diego Padres baseball announcer, describing a fly ball hit by a member of the opposing team).

11. "In his memoir, Lt. Calley (who was convicted of murdering 22 Vietnamese civilians in Mar., 1968) claims that the My Lai killings were an effort to 'destroy communism.' He claimed, 'If we're in Vietnam another 10 years, if your son is killed by those babies you'll cry at me, "Why didn't you kill those babies that day?"'"

*12. "It is the knowledge residing in its smallest class or section, that is to say, in the predominant and ruling body, which entitles a state, organized agreeably to nature, to be called wise as a whole" (Plato, *Republic*).

13. "Welders make more money than philosophers. We need more welders and less philosophers" (Marco Rubio, Republican presidential candidate).

14. Candidate: We cannot lower taxes until we cut back on government spending.

Rival Candidate: My opponent has gone on record stating that "we cannot lower taxes"!

*15. "Dear Abby: If GOING BALD doesn't have any signs of rash, or sores on her head, she should make a mixture of castor oil and sheep dung, and plaster it on her head every night. (Tell her to wear a shower cap so she won't mess up her pillow.) I started losing my hair after the birth of my child. My grandmother gave me this remedy and it worked."

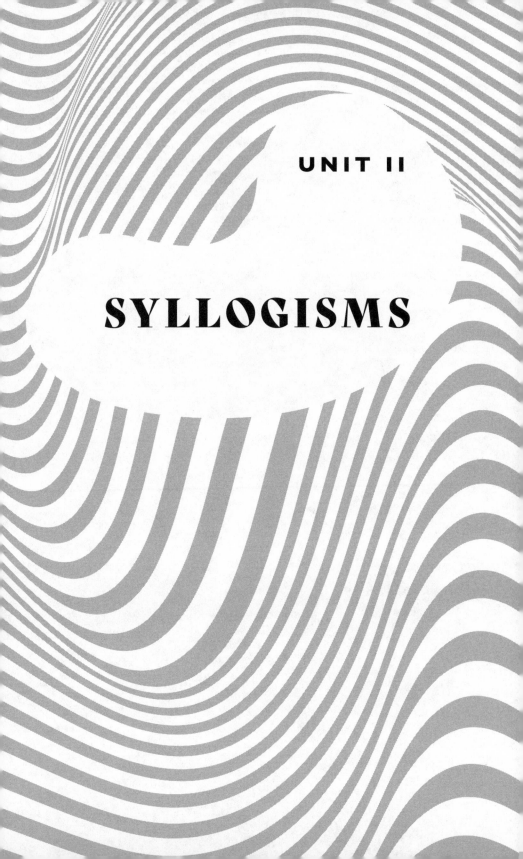

UNIT II

SYLLOGISMS

4

STANDARD-FORM
CATEGORICAL PROPOSITIONS

As we have seen, ordinary language can be very imprecise and has many functions. If we want to find the logical structure of arguments, we will need to dig below the surface of everyday sentences. Let's begin by considering one very specific type of sentence: the standard-form categorical proposition.

4.1 DEFINITION OF STANDARD-FORM
CATEGORICAL PROPOSITIONS

Remember that a proposition is the idea behind a statement that is true or false, and that a statement is expressed with a sentence. For the sake of simplicity, what follows will conflate *sentence* and *proposition*. That is, in this section, we are only going to consider those sentences that are specific instances of statements that express a proposition. For the time being, we will ignore all the other uses of sentences, and focus on this one important use.

Classes. In order to understand this particular type of proposition, we must first understand the concept of a class. Now in logic, a "class" refers to *any group that has a common characteristic.* So there is the class of students and the class of flowers; the class of just acts and the class of angry words. A class need not be something concrete—it is any grouping with a common characteristic. This means we can also speak about the class of unicorns and the class of round squares. In the first case, it is all those creatures with the characteristics of being a horse with a single long horn. So far as we know, this class has no members, but it is still a class. As for the class of round squares, unless we are equivocating in some way, we know that there could not be any members of this class. But, again, it is still a class: the class of all plane figures made up of four lines of equal length that meet at four points at ninety-degree angles (i.e., square) with each point on the lines equidistant from a central point (i.e., round). We will sometimes refer to a class as a "term" when talking about its use in a proposition.

Categorical propositions. A *categorical proposition is one that affirms or denies class inclusion.* That is, a categorical proposition is one that says the members of class A have some relationship to class B. Either they are members of class B, are *not* members of class B, some are members, or some are not. For example, "Dogs are animals" is a categorical proposition because it is claiming the members of the class dogs are also members of the class animals. Similarly, "Cats are not dogs" is denying that one class is included in the other. And "Many dogs are beagles" is claiming a partial class inclusion.

Standard-form. Now we want to consider a very specific type of categorical proposition: the *standard-form* categorical proposition. A standard-form categorical proposition will always have the following structure:

Quantifier—subject term—copula—predicate term

So what are each of these elements? The *quantifier* will tell *how many* members of one class belong or do not belong to another class. We will only use three quantifiers: *all*, *no*, and *some*. The first two are "universal"—that is, they tell us that every member of the subject-term class is or is not a member of the predicate-term class. For our purposes in logic, we will use *some* to mean "at least one." In ordinary language, when we say "Some S is P," we are usually implying that some S is *not* P. But this is not the case in logic. All we mean by "some" is at least one. This means the standard-form categorical proposition "Some dogs are animals" is true: at least one dog is an animal. Now we might want to say, "But *all* dogs are animals"—and that would also be true. But it does not negate the truth of "some dogs are animals."

The *copula* is always a version of the verb *to be.* This is what connects the subject term and the predicate term. This includes *is, are, was, were, will be,* and so on. However, we include the word *not* as a part of the copula when we want to deny that at least one member of a given class is a member of another given class. In that case, we will say, "Some S is not P." Here the copula is the words *is not.*

Finally, the *subject term (or class) is everything between the quantifier and the copula* and the *predicate term (or class) is everything after the copula.* This is *not* the way it works in ordinary English grammar. Consider the standard-form categorical proposition

All spotted dogs that run very fast are greyhounds that are bred.

Now grammatically the subject here is "dogs" and all the rest around it just modifies "dogs." Similarly, the predicate is just "greyhounds." But in logic, we count everything after the quantifier and before the copula as part of the subject. So the subject here is "spotted dogs that run very fast." Similarly, the predicate is everything after the copula—so in this case, "greyhounds that are bred." The word "All" is the quantifier, and the first instance of the word "are" is the copula.

Assignment 4.1. Give the quantifier, the copula, and the subject and predicate terms for each of the following standard-form categorical propositions.

Example: Some children in theaters are not children who should be allowed to see scary movies.

Solution: Quantifier: Some
                 Copula: are not
                 Subject: children in theaters
                 Predicate: children who should be allowed to see scary movies

1. All dogs are brown things.

2. No people who are afraid of the dark are people who should watch the movies in the *Halloween* franchise.

*3. All people who enjoy a great love story and quirky humor are people who should watch *Strictly Ballroom*.

4. Some movies like *John Carter* and *The Lone Ranger* were not profitable films.

5. No people who want to see realistic action sequences are people who should watch any of the *Fast and Furious* movies.

*6. Some members of the clergy are disreputable people.

7. "No men in civil society can be [persons] exempted from the laws of [civil society]" (John Locke, *Second Treatise on Government*).

8. Some iPhones are expensive items.

*9. All usable pens will be things we will need.

10. Some women were not persons who were willing to date him.

11. "All fixed, fast-frozen relations with their train of ancient and venerable prejudices and opinions are things swept away" (Karl Marx and Frederick Engels, *Communist Manifesto*).

*12. Some drugs are habit-forming things.

13. Some people who follow professional sports are fanatics.

14. No classes in philosophy are time-wasters.

*15. Some philosophical treatises are incredibly complicated and grammatically dense writings.

4.2 QUALITY, QUANTITY, NAMES, AND DISTRIBUTION

Using the letter S to stand for the subject term (however long or short that may be) and the letter P for the predicate term, there are only four different kinds of standard-form categorical propositions:

A: All S is P
E: No S is P
I: Some S is P
O: Some S is not P

Each of these four standard-form categorical propositions has a *quality* and a *quantity* as well as a letter that is used to name the type of proposition. The *qualities* are *affirmative (when the proposition affirms class inclusion)* and *negative (when the proposition denies class inclusion)*. The *quantity* refers to how many of the members of the subject class are being claimed to belong to the predicate class. *Universal propositions make a claim about every member of the subject class* while *particular propositions make a claim about at least one member of the subject class.* The letters A, E, I, and O are traditionally used to name the four kinds of standard-form categorical propositions.[1]

This brings us to a final, rather odd feature of standard-form categorical propositions: whether the terms are distributed. A term is distributed if the proposition is saying *anything* about every member of the class. In a universal, affirmative A proposition like "All dogs are animals," we are clearly saying

---

[1] These letters are based on the Latin words *AffIrmo* (I affirm) and *nEgO* (I deny).

something about every member of the class of dogs (namely, that they are animals). However, we are *not* saying anything about every animal. Accordingly, *in an A proposition the subject is distributed, but not the predicate.*

In a universal, negative E proposition like "No dogs are cats," we are saying something about every member of the class of dogs (that none of them are cats). But we are also saying something about every cat—namely, that they are not dogs. So *in an E proposition, both the subject and the predicate are distributed.*

In a particular, affirmative I proposition like "Some dogs are small animals," we are not saying anything about every dog, nor are we talking about every small animal. So *in an I proposition, nothing is distributed.*

The case of the particular, negative O proposition is a bit harder to see. Clearly when we say "Some dogs are not beagles" we are not saying anything about *all* dogs—and so the predicate term is not distributed. However, in an O proposition, we *are* saying something about every member of the predicate class. We are saying that every member of the predicate class is not the "at least one" subject that we were discussing. In the example above, we are saying that every single beagle is not one of those dogs we were discussing when we began "some [i.e., at least one] dogs." So *in an O proposition, the predicate is distributed, but not the subject.* If that is difficult to understand, just memorize the distribution rule that follows.

Whenever we write out a standard-form categorical proposition, we will underline any terms that are distributed so we don't forget. If we don't know what the classes are, we will use "S" for the subject term and "P" for the predicate term. Putting all this together we have the four standard-form categorical propositions:

		Quality	Quantity	Distributed
A	All S is P	Affirmative	Universal	S only
E	No S is P	Negative	Universal	S + P
I	Some S is P	Affirmative	Particular	— (neither)
O	Some S is not P	Negative	Particular	P only

Assignment 4.2. Give the quality, the quantity, the letter name, and underline any terms that are distributed for each of the following standard-form categorical propositions.

Example: Some choir members are not chemistry majors.

Solution: Quality: Negative
                 Quantity: Particular
                 Name: O
                 Distributed: "chemistry majors" (predicate)

1. All dogs are animals.

2. No computer printers are items that never malfunction.

*3. All people who take a logic class are people who care about thinking clearly.

4. Some drivers are very responsible persons.

5. Some students in this class are not philosophy majors.

*6. No buildings in downtown Lisbon are buildings that survived the earthquake of 1755.

7. No canal boats in England are vehicles wider than seven feet.

8. Some statues by Michelangelo are masterpieces.

*9. All philosophy classes are courses worth taking.

10. Some Parisians are not rude people.

11. All thermometers are things that have mercury inside.

*12. Some popes are deeply spiritual men.

13. Some maps are not things that keep you from getting lost.

14. No knights in shining armor are people coming to help you do your homework.

*15. Some archaeological sites in Turkey are places that allow you to freely roam without fences or guards.

4.3 VENN DIAGRAMS

Everything I have said so far about categorical propositions was developed by the Greek philosopher Aristotle in the fourth century BC. Aristotle laid out rules for arguments that stood for over two thousand years and dominated the thinking of Europe and the Middle East. Saint Thomas Aquinas (1225–1274), for example, used this form of arguing when developing his famous "Five Ways" for proving the existence of God.

But beginning in the nineteenth century, logicians first began to make changes to Aristotelian logic. They eventually developed an entirely new way of expressing arguments that allowed for more flexibility. In 1881, John Venn (1834–1923) updated Aristotelian logic by coming up with a visual way of representing standard-form categorical propositions. If we think of the inside of a circle representing all the members of a given class, we end up with diagrams like those in figure 4.1.

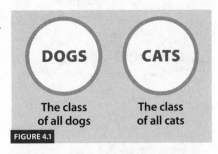

The class of all dogs   The class of all cats

FIGURE 4.1

In this case, these classes are completely separate—they share no members.

Diagram for an E standard-form categorical proposition. Now how about if we overlap these circles, but show that the overlapping part of the circles they *might* share actually is empty—that there are no members of both classes. We would say it, "No *dogs* are *cats*," and we would show it like figure 4.2 (where the shading means there is nothing there[2]):

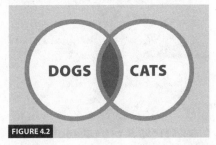

FIGURE 4.2

Of course, this would work for any case where we are universally denying class inclusion. So any E proposition ("No S̲ is P̲") would look like figure 4.3.

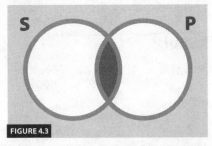

FIGURE 4.3

Diagram for an I standard-form categorical proposition. If we wanted to diagram the I proposition, "Some dogs are small animals," we could start with the overlap of the two classes, dogs and small animals (see figure 4.4).

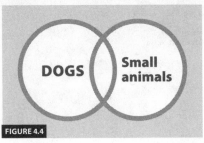

FIGURE 4.4

---

[2]This may be a bit confusing to mathematicians as shading in set theory usually means there *is* something in the class.

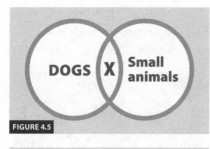

FIGURE 4.5

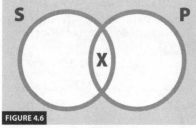

FIGURE 4.6

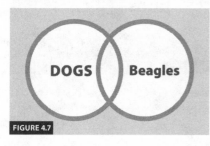

FIGURE 4.7

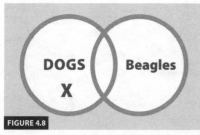

FIGURE 4.8

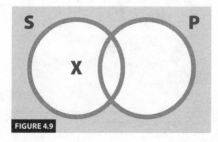

FIGURE 4.9

Now to show that "some"—that is, at least one—dogs are small animals, we could put an X in the part both circles share. This indicates that there is at least one member (signified by the X in fig. 4.5) that is both in the dogs class and the small-animals class.

This would work for any case where we are affirming particular class inclusion. So any I proposition ("Some S is P") would look like figure 4.6.

Diagram for an O standard-form categorical proposition. If we wanted to diagram the O proposition, "Some dogs are not <u>beagles</u>," we could again start with the overlap of the two classes, dogs and beagles (see fig. 4.7).

Now to show that some dogs—that is, at least one—are not beagles, we could put an X in the dog circle that is not also in the beagle circle. This indicates that there is at least one member (signified by the X in fig. 4.8) of the dog class that is not in the beagle class.

This would work for any case where we are denying particular class inclusion. So any O proposition ("Some S is not <u>P</u>") would look like figure 4.9.

Diagram for an A standard-form categorical proposition. I have saved the A proposition diagram for

last as it is not as intuitively obvious
as the other three. If we use the same
overlapping circles to diagram the A
proposition, "All <u>dogs</u> are animals,"
we would need to make it clear that
no dogs are not animals. We can do
that by using the overlapping circles
and shading out the part of the dog
circle that is outside the animal circle (see fig. 4.10).

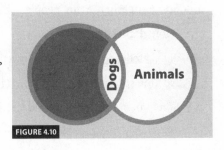

FIGURE 4.10

Now it may seem a bit odd to diagram a sentence that begins "All dogs . . ."
by crossing out three-quarters of the dog circle. But by saying that all dogs
belong to the animals class, we are saying that there are no dogs that are
outside the animal class—and so we
shade out that entire part of the diagram. Once again, this would work
for *any* case where we are affirming
universal class inclusion. So any A
proposition ("All <u>S</u> is P") would look
like figure 4.11.

FIGURE 4.11

Assignment 4.3. Diagram each of
the following standard-form categorical propositions, labeling each circle with
the appropriate term.

Example: All <u>football players</u> are athletes.

Solution:

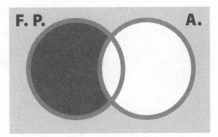

1. All <u>garbage trucks</u> are large vehicles.

2. No <u>self-addressed envelopes</u> will be <u>things accepted by the council</u>.

*3. All <u>picture frames</u> are expensive items.

   4. Some superheroes are people with secret identities.

   5. Some digital cameras are not <u>cheap toys</u>.

*6. No <u>skateboards</u> are <u>things allowed in this park</u>.

   7. No <u>glue sticks</u> are <u>things allowed in the library</u>.

   8. Some memo pads are free advertising gifts from merchants.

*9. All <u>pewter steins</u> are pencil holders.

 10. Some solar-powered calculators are things that work indoors.

 11. Some air vents are not <u>things left open in the summer</u>.

*12. Some shampoo bottles are containers in the shape of cartoon characters.

 13. All <u>reference books</u> are useless items now that we have the internet.

 14. No <u>timelines of history</u> are <u>records that are completely accurate</u>.

*15. Some mechanical pencils are hard-to-find items.

5

STANDARD-FORM
CATEGORICAL SYLLOGISMS

Now that we have identified and discussed standard-form categorical propositions, it is time to put them together to form arguments. Specifically, we are going to examine deductive, standard-form categorical syllogisms.

5.1 DEFINITION OF CATEGORICAL SYLLOGISMS

Let's start by reminding ourselves that, as Monty Python explained, an *argument* is "a connected series of statements intended to establish a proposition." Furthermore, a *deductive argument* is one which claims that the conclusion follows with necessity from the premise(s). So, the following is a deductive argument:

> If Socrates was a famous philosopher, then he would be in lots of books
> If Socrates was in lots of books, then many people would have heard of him
> Socrates *was* a famous philosopher
> _____
> Many people have heard of him[1]

While this *is* a deductive argument (and a valid one at that), it is not a syllogism. *A syllogism is a deductive argument that has exactly two premises.* So the following argument is a syllogism:

> If Socrates was a famous philosopher, then he would be in lots of books
> Socrates *was* a famous philosopher
> _____
> Socrates is in lots of books .

---

[1]From this point on we will drop the "P_1," "P_2," "C Therefore," and just list the premises. We will use a line to indicate that what follows is the conclusion.

This is a syllogism because it is a deductive argument with two premises. However, it is not a *categorical* syllogism. *A categorical syllogism is an argument with the following characteristics*:

1. The premises and conclusion are all categorical propositions.

2. There are exactly three terms.

3. Each term appears in two of the propositions that make up the argument.

Neither of the arguments given above meet even the first of these three criteria. But consider this argument:

Dogs are mammals
Mammals are animals
_____
Dogs are animals

This argument is a categorical syllogism. First, each of the three propositions making it up are categorical propositions—that is, they affirm class inclusion. Second, there are exactly three terms: "dogs," "mammals," and "animals." Third, each of these three terms appears in two of the propositions that together make up the argument: "dogs" is in the first premise and the conclusion; "mammals" is in both premises; and "animals" is in the second premise and the conclusion.

Assignment 5.1. Tell which of the following are categorical syllogisms. If it *is* a categorical syllogism, give the three terms.

Example: Socrates was an Athenian
                 Athenians were people who loved to debate ideas
                 _____
                 Socrates was a person who loved to debate ideas

Solution: Yes; terms: "Socrates," "Athenian," "people who loved to
                 debate ideas"

1. If I eat too much, I will get a stomachache.
   I eat too much
   _____
   I get a stomachache

2. Wooden desks are ugly things
   This desk is a wooden desk
   _____
   This desk is a beautiful thing

*3. If we have lunch at Subway, we will get a good deal
If we get a good deal, I will be happy

_____

If we have lunch at Subway, I will be happy

4. Some table lamps are broken things
This lamp is a table lamp

_____

This lamp is a broken thing

5. DVD-RWs are things that are no longer used much
Things that are no longer used much are valuable

_____

DVD-RWs are valuable

*6. Computer speakers are inexpensive items
Pens are inexpensive items

_____

Pens are computer speakers

7. Some of the clocks in our house are inaccurate things
This clock is a clock in our house

_____

This clock is an inaccurate thing

8. All storage containers are useful things
All filing cabinets are storage containers

_____

All filing cabinets are useful things

*9. Some children's books are boring things
No books by C. S. Lewis are boring things

_____

No books by C. S. Lewis are children's books

10. My printer is something that doesn't work
Things that don't work should be thrown away

_____

My printer should be thrown away

11. If I watered the lawn, then the grass is now wet
The grass is now wet

_____

I watered the grass

*12. No one sends greeting cards anymore
 Only old people send greeting cards
 _____
 Greeting cards are not a good investment

13. Shredders are things that are useful to have in an office with
  important papers
 Staples are things that do not work well in shredders
 _____
 Staples are things should not be used in an office with important papers

14. All printed encyclopedias are things nobody uses
 All things nobody uses are pointless to own
 Some printed encyclopedias are expensive items
 _____
 Some expensive items are pointless to own

*15. Some software are not useful things
 All expensive items are useful things
 _____
 All software are expensive items

5.2 DEFINITION OF STANDARD-FORM CATEGORICAL SYLLOGISMS

In this chapter, we want to consider a very specific type of categorical syllogism—namely, a "*standard-form* categorical syllogism." A *standard-form categorical syllogism is an argument with the following characteristics*:

1. It is a categorical syllogism.

2. The premises and conclusion are all standard-form categorical propositions.

3. It has the following order: the major premise comes first, then the minor premise, then the conclusion.

We defined categorical syllogisms in the previous section, and we have talked about standard-form categorical *propositions* in the previous chapter. But what about the terms *major premise* and *minor premise*? Well, the major premise is the premise that contains the major term while the minor premise contains the minor term. So what makes something a major or a minor term?

The *major term* is the predicate of the conclusion.

The *minor term* is the subject of the conclusion.

The *middle term* is the term in both premises, but not in the conclusion.

Consider the following standard-form categorical syllogism:

No dogs are cats

Some cats are pets

Some pets are not dogs

In this argument the major term (the predicate of the conclusion) is "dogs." This term appears in the major premise, "No dogs are cats." The minor term, "pets" (the subject of the conclusion), appears in the minor premise, "Some cats are pets." The middle term, "cats," is in both premises and not in the conclusion. Notice that the major term, "dogs," is the subject of the first premise, but it could just as easily have been the predicate. What makes it the major term is its position as the predicate in the conclusion.

In order to see the structure more clearly, let's use the place markers P, S, and M to stand for the major, minor, and middle terms. The argument above would then be,

No P are M

Some M are S

Some S are not P

Now this particular argument form is valid—and any argument with this structure will also be valid. That is, no matter what we substitute for P, S, and M, the resulting argument will be valid. That means this argument,

No remote controls are things that get lost

Some things that get lost are valuable things

Some valuable things are not remote controls

is valid (though it is clearly not sound as the first premise is false).

Assignment 5.2. Put the following categorical syllogisms into standard form and tell what is the major, minor, and middle term. (Remember to first find the conclusion. It may be helpful to consult the list of premise and conclusion indicators from chapter 1.)

Example: Some rare and costly substances are objects that are likely to be stolen, because some diamonds are rare and costly substances and some diamonds are objects that are likely to be stolen.

Solution: All <u>diamonds</u> are objects that are likely to be stolen
                 Some diamonds are rare and costly substances
                 _____
                 Some rare and costly substances are objects that are likely to be stolen

                 Major term: "objects that are likely to be stolen"
                 Minor term: "rare and costly substances"
                 Middle term: "diamonds"

1. No bulky coffee-table books are easily carried items, and all travel guidebooks are easily carried items, so no travel guidebooks are bulky coffee-table books.

2. Some useful things are not expensive computer accessories, because some high-capacity thumb drives are not expensive computer accessories and all high-capacity thumb drives are useful things.

*3. No dorm residents are students living off-campus, but some football players are students living off-campus; it follows that some dorm residents are not football players.

4. Some useful items for class are costly purchases, because some textbooks are costly purchases, and all textbooks are useful items for class.

5. Some plastic bags are not suitable toys for children, and some plastic bags are grocery bags, so some grocery bags are not suitable toys for children.

*6. Some conservatives are not advocates of high tariff rates, because all advocates of high tariff rates are Republicans, and some Republicans are not conservatives.

7. No laws are eternal laws, because all laws are things imposed on someone and no eternal laws are things imposed on someone.

8. All canines are dogs and some canines are not beagles, so some dogs are not beagles.

*9. Some cups are plastic, because some toys are plastic and some cups are toys.

10. All books are useful objects and all dictionaries are books, therefore all dictionaries are useful objects.

11. No HDMI cables are items supplied by the cable company and some connections between the cable box and the TV are items supplied by the cable company, so some connections between the cable box and the TV are not HDMI cables.

*12. No bank-giveaway pens are valuable items and no carnival prizes are valuable items, consequently no bank-giveaway pens are carnival prizes.

13. All diamonds are costly rocks and some wedding-ring stones are diamonds, so some wedding-ring stones are costly rocks.

14. No letter openers are deadly weapons since all letter openers are things sold at stationery stores and no deadly weapons are things sold at stationery stores.

*15. All good logic students are students who will know that this syllogism is invalid, and all students who do their homework carefully are good logic students. Therefore all students who will know that this syllogism is invalid are students who do their homework carefully.

5.3 MOOD AND FIGURE

To help identify standard-form categorical syllogisms, we use the letter names of the standard-form categorical propositions out of which they are formed. This is called the "mood" of the argument. Put more formally: *the "mood" of a standard-form categorical syllogism is the series of letters that are the names for the standard-form categorical propositions that make up the argument.*

So, for example, the following standard-form categorical syllogism,

All <u>minerals</u> are things that are mined

All <u>diamonds</u> are minerals

All <u>diamonds</u> are things that are mined

is made up of three universal affirmative standard-form categorical propositions, and so its mood is AAA. However,

All <u>things that are mined</u> are minerals

All <u>diamonds</u> are minerals

All <u>diamonds</u> are things that are mined

is also an AAA argument, yet unlike the first, this second one is invalid. Knowing the mood of an argument is not sufficient to identify the structure of the argument. We also need to know the position of the terms as they appear in the premises.

Now we know that, by definition, the major term will appear in the major premise, which comes first. But is the major term the subject or the predicate of the major premise? Similarly, we know the minor term will appear in the minor premise—but we don't know where. There are four possible combinations of positions for the major and minor terms, and this makes up the "figure" of the argument. Put more formally, *the "figure" of a standard-form categorical syllogism is a number that corresponds to the position of the middle term in the premises of the argument.*

Focusing just on the middle term (which is in both premises, but not in the conclusion), it could be the subject in the major premise and the predicate in the minor premise. That is called figure one. The middle term could be the predicate in both premises which is called figure two. The middle term could be the subject in both premises: figure three. Or the middle term could be the predicate in the major premise and the subject in the minor premise: figure four. For the moment, let's leave out the quantifier and the copula and again use S, P, M to stand for the minor term, the major term, and the middle term.

In that case we can schematize the four figures as follows:

Figure 1	Figure 2	Figure 3	Figure 4
M—P	P—M	M—P	P—M
S—M	S—M	M—S	M—S
S—P	S—P	S—P	S—P

The first argument above uses the middle term as the subject in the major premise and as the predicate in the minor premise, making it figure one. So combining the mood and figure, we say this is an AAA-1 argument. Now this argument happens to be valid—and any other argument that has the same mood and figure will also be valid. The second argument above has the middle term as the predicate in both premises (figure two), making it an AAA-2 argument. This mood and figure is invalid—and every instance of it will be invalid.

Several years ago, a student came up with a visual way of remembering the four figures. Put a line connecting the middle term in the premises in each of the figures and you get something like this:

Figure 1	Figure 2	Figure 3	Figure 4
M—P	P—M	M—P	P—M
S—M	S—M	M—S	M—S
S—P	S—P	S—P	S—P

Now remove the table, move the lines a bit closer and you get this:

If this is helpful, great. But one way or another, it is necessary to memorize the four figures and be able to pick them out quickly and easily.

Assignment 5.3a. Give the mood and figure of the categorical syllogisms from assignment 5.2 after you have put them into standard form.

Example: All <u>diamonds</u> are objects that are likely to be stolen
Some diamonds are rare and costly substances
_____
Some rare and costly substances are objects that are likely to be stolen

Solution: AII-3

Assignment 5.3b. For the mood and figure, give the standard-form categorical syllogism.

Example: OAO-4

Solution: Some P is not <u>M</u>
All <u>M</u> is S
_____
Some S is not <u>P</u>

1. AEE-2

2. AOO-3

*3. EIO-2

4. IAI-2

5. OAA-1

*6. EAE-1

7. EIO-4

8. OAO-3

*9. EEE-2

10. AEE-4

11. IAI-4

*12. IOI-2

13. OOI-4

14. AII-1

*15. AAA-1

5.4 VENN DIAGRAMS

Now that we have defined and named standard-form categorical syllogisms we can move on to the most important task: determining whether they are valid or invalid. In this section we will learn how to use Venn diagrams to determine validity.

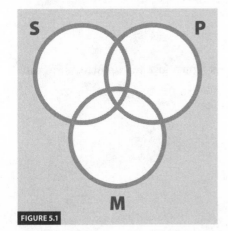

FIGURE 5.1

In the previous chapter, we learned how to diagram standard-form categorical propositions using two overlapping circles. To diagram a standard-form categorical *syllogism*, we will use three overlapping circles, as shown in figure 5.1.

We will agree to always label the upper left-hand circle as the minor term, the upper right-hand circle as the major term, and the bottom circle as the middle term. Now consider a basic AAA-1 syllogism:

All M̲ is P

All S̲ is M

All S̲ is P

To diagram the first (major) premise we would draw figure 5.2.
Now let's just rotate this drawing a bit (see fig. 5.3).

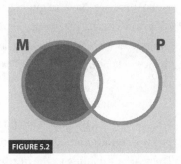

FIGURE 5.2

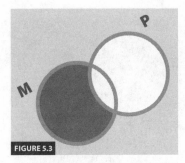

FIGURE 5.3

If we ignore the S circle in the generic three-overlapping-circle drawing, this
drawing shows the same thing (see fig. 5.4).

In the same way, if we diagram the second (minor) premise, we would draw
figure 5.5.

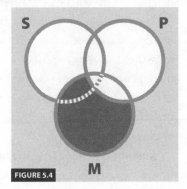

FIGURE 5.4

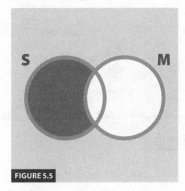

FIGURE 5.5

Rotating this drawing just a bit, we get figure 5.6.
If we ignore the P circle in the generic three overlapping circle drawing, figure
5.7 shows the same thing.

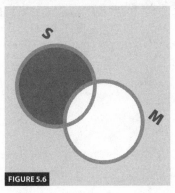

FIGURE 5.6

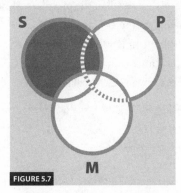

FIGURE 5.7

Now, if we put these two together—that is if we diagram both of the premises on the same generic three circle Venn diagram—we get figure 5.8.

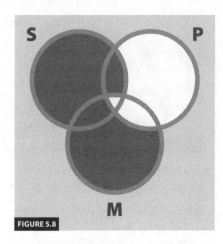

FIGURE 5.8

So here we have in one Venn diagram both premises represented. If we wanted to diagram the conclusion, "All S is P" we would do it like figure 5.9.

But to make this last diagram, we would not have to add *anything* to the diagram immediately above. The work of shading in the portion of S that is not in P has already been done. Yes, there is a little bit of the P circle that is shaded out that did not need to be to represent "All S is P." That is, there is a bit *more* that has been done in the drawing than is required—but there is not less. There is nothing that needs to be *added* to the drawing to get an adequate picture of the conclusion.

FIGURE 5.9

Since the conclusion has already been diagrammed once the premises are drawn, we can with confidence say that the AAA-1 syllogism is valid. Here is the general process for using the Venn-diagram method for determining the validity or invalidity of standard-form categorical syllogisms: Using the three-overlapping-circles Venn diagram, draw each of the premises. When you are done, if you have an adequate drawing of the conclusion—that is, there is nothing you need to *add*—then the syllogism is valid. If you need to add *anything* to get an adequate drawing of the conclusion, the syllogism is invalid.

Let's try an AAA-3 argument:

All M is P

All M is S
_____

All S is P

We would diagram the premises as shown in figure 5.10.

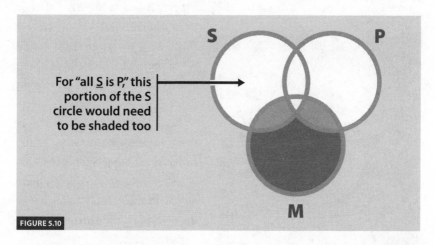

For "all S̲ is P," this portion of the S circle would need to be shaded too

FIGURE 5.10

Notice that part of the M circle gets shaded twice. And do we have an adequate drawing of the conclusion, "All S̲ is P"? Not at all. A portion of the S circle outside the P circle is unshaded, meaning there could be some member(s) of the class of S that is/are *not* P. We would have to shade out all the S outside of the P circle to get an adequate diagram of the conclusion. Now maybe there aren't any members of S outside of P—that is certainly a possibility. But "valid" means that if the premises are true the conclusion *must* be true—not just that it is possibly true.

Diagramming standard-form categorical syllogisms that have particular premises raises a challenge: where do we put the "X" that indicates that at least one member of the class is or is not a member of the other class? Consider the following EIO-2 syllogism:

No P̲ is M̲

Some S is M

Some S is not P̲

The first (major) premise is easy to diagram (see fig. 5.11).

When we go to diagram the second (minor) premise, we have to put an "X" in the part that S and

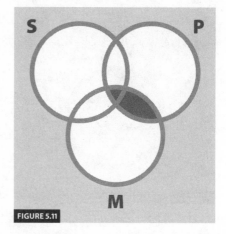

FIGURE 5.11

M share. But should it also be *inside* the P circle or *outside*? Well, actually, the decision has been made for us. The part that S, P, and M share has already

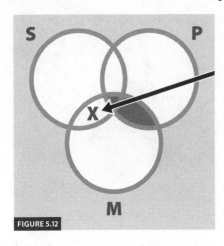

FIGURE 5.12

been shaded out—it no longer exists. So if we are going to put an "X" in the part that S and M share, it will have to go as shown in figure 5.12.

Now look at the drawing: Is there an adequate drawing of the conclusion, "Some S is not *P*"? That is, without adding anything is there an "X" in the S circle that is not in the P circle? Yes. The EIO-2 syllogism is valid.

What about an IAI-4 argument?

Some P is M

All <u>M</u> is S

———————

Some S is P

The first (major) premise will leave us with a quandary: Should we put the "X" that P and M share inside the S circle our outside of it? If we put the "X" inside the S circle as shown in figure 5.13.

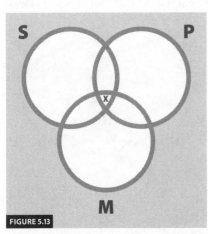

FIGURE 5.13

We would be saying "Some P is M—oh, and it is also an S." But that is more information than the first (major) premise expresses. Of course, if we put the "X" in the part that the P and M circles do not share with S (see fig. 5.14), it would not be any better. We would be saying "Some P is M—but it is not an S." Again, we would be asserting something the first (major) premise did not say.

There is a general rule here that will often (but not always) help with this problem: *always diagram any universal premise first*. If we diagram the second (minor) premise first, we get figure 5.15.

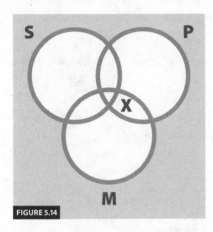

FIGURE 5.14

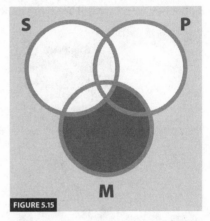

FIGURE 5.15

Now it is clear where the "X" goes that is shared by both M and P. There is only one part of the overlap between the two circles that remains, and so the "X" would have to go as shown in figure 5.16.

We now have an adequate drawing of the conclusion, "Some S is P," so we know the IAI-4 argument form is valid.

Sometimes, however, even if we diagram the universal premise first it is still not clear where to put the "X." Consider an AII-2 syllogism:

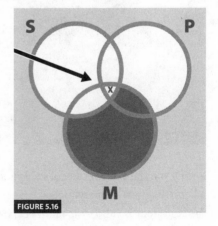

FIGURE 5.16

All P̲ is M

Some S is M

_____

Some S is P

If we diagram the universal premise first (which also happens to be the first premise here), we get figure 5.17.

But now when we go to diagram the second premise by putting an "X" in the part that S and M share, we are stuck. Should the "X" also go in the P circle or not? Either way we go, we will be saying something that is not warranted (see fig. 5.18).

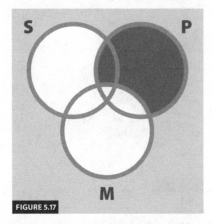

FIGURE 5.17

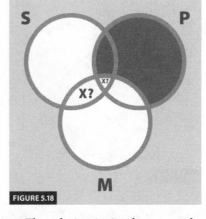

FIGURE 5.18

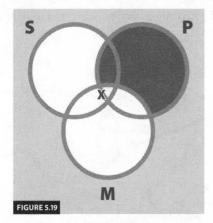

FIGURE 5.19

The solution is simple: we put the "X" on the line indicating that we do not know to which side it belongs (see fig. 5.19).

Do we now have an adequate drawing of the conclusion, "Some S is P"? Maybe. If the "X" is also in the P circle we would have a diagram of the conclusion. So is this syllogism 50 percent valid? No. Remember, "valid" means if the premises are true, then the conclusion *must be true*.

Assignment 5.4a. For the following standard-form categorical syllogisms, give the mood and figure, draw a Venn diagram of the syllogism, and on the basis of that diagram tell whether the argument is valid or invalid. Feel free to abbreviate all terms.

Example: Some eyeglasses are not <u>things made of glass</u>
              All <u>things made of glass</u> are optical devices
              _____
              Some optical devices are not <u>eyeglasses</u>

Solution: OAO-4; invalid, as there needs to be an X in the optical-devices (O. D.) circle that is not in the eyeglasses (E.) circle. We are not even close to that.

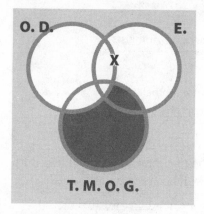

1. Some smartphones are useful devices
   All <u>TV remotes</u> are useful devices

   Some TV remotes are smartphones

2. All <u>bulky mail items</u> are things that are expensive to send
   No <u>postcards</u> are <u>bulky mail items</u>

   No <u>postcards</u> are <u>things that are expensive to send</u>

*3. All <u>sociopaths</u> are criminals
   Some criminals are not <u>neurotics</u>

   Some neurotics are not <u>sociopaths</u>

4. No <u>unicorns</u> are <u>creatures visible to the impure</u>
   All <u>unicorns</u> are animals with a horn

   Some animals with a horn are not <u>creatures visible to the impure</u>

5. All <u>Presbyterians</u> are Protestants
   Some Christians are not <u>Protestants</u>

   Some Christians are not <u>Presbyterians</u>

*6. No <u>logic students</u> are <u>idiots</u>
   Some logic students are gamers

   Some gamers are not <u>idiots</u>

7. No <u>bacon</u> is <u>kosher</u>
   No <u>ham</u> is <u>kosher</u>
   _____
   No <u>ham</u> is <u>bacon</u>

8. All <u>dogs</u> are mammals
   Some animals are not <u>mammals</u>
   _____
   All <u>animals</u> are dogs

*9. All <u>philosophers</u> are football fans
    No <u>musicians</u> are <u>football fans</u>
    _____
    Some musicians are not <u>philosophers</u>

10. Some difficult accomplishments are not <u>things worth doing</u>
    All <u>marathons</u> are difficult accomplishments
    _____
    Some marathons are not <u>things worth doing</u>

11. All <u>animal furs</u> are things obtained through cruelty
    Some things obtained through cruelty are expensive things
    _____
    Some expensive things are animal furs

*12. Some dreams are nightmares
     No <u>nightmares</u> are <u>experiences we actively seek</u>
     _____
     Some experiences we actively seek are not <u>dreams</u>

13. No <u>red staplers</u> are <u>things that should be taken from Milton</u>
    All <u>things that should be taken from Milton</u> are things that
       Lumbergh takes
    _____
    All <u>things that Lumbergh takes</u> are red staplers

14. All <u>French outlets</u> are fixtures with two holes
    Some electrical outlets are fixtures with two holes
    _____
    Some electrical outlets are not <u>French outlets</u>

*15. Some trees are evergreens
     Some plants are trees
     _____
     Some plants are evergreens

Assignment 5.4b. For the following standard-form categorical syllogism forms, write out the syllogism using S, P, and M. Then draw a Venn diagram of the syllogism, and on the basis of that diagram tell whether the argument is valid or invalid.

Example: OAO-3

Solution: Some M is not P̲
                 All M̲ is S
                 ─────────────
                 Some S is not P̲

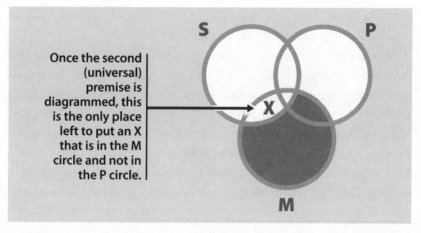

Once the second (universal) premise is diagrammed, this is the only place left to put an X that is in the M circle and not in the P circle.

Valid (there is an "X" in the S circle that is not in the P circle without having to add anything to the diagram).

1. AAA-1

2. AII-1

*3. OOI-4

4. IOI-2

5. AEE-4

*6. IAI-4

7. EEE-2

8. OAO-3

*9. EIO-4

10. EAE-1

11. OAO-1

*12. IAI-2

13. EIO-2

14. AOO-3

*15. AEE-2

5.5 THE RULES

Another way to test for the validity or invalidity of standard-form categorical syllogisms is to use the rules. *If a standard-form categorical syllogism does not violate any of the following five rules, it is valid.*[2]

Before we examine the five rules, it is important to first emphasize that these rules *only* apply to standard-form categorical syllogisms. Some logic books add a sixth rule stating that there can only be three terms each appearing in two of the premises. To violate this is called the fallacy of four terms. However, if there are four terms, there is not a violation of any syllogistic rules—it is not even a syllogism, so it cannot violate rules relating to standard-form categorical syllogisms. Still, students should be on their guard for equivocations that might lead to having four terms when it looks like there are only three. For example, consider this *apparent* standard-form categorical syllogism that was circulating in the 1930s:

All attempts to end hostilities are efforts which should be approved by all nations

All Japan's present activities in China are attempts to end hostilities

All Japan's present activities in China are efforts which should be approved by
   all nations[3]

Now at first glance, this appears to be an AAA-1 syllogism—which is valid. However, the term "attempts to end hostilities" is being used equivocally. In the first premise it refers to negotiating peace treaties, proposing an armistice, and so on. This premise is probably true. However, although the same words are used in the second premise, they mean something entirely different. Here "attempts to end hostilities" means the attempt to beat the

---

[2]It is certainly possible that a given syllogism could violate more than one of the five rules. It is only necessary to show one rule that is violated to show it is invalid.

[3]Irving M. Copi, *Introduction to Logic,* 6th edition (New York: Macmillan, 1982), 170-71.

Chinese into submission. While the same words are being used, we actually have four different classes that are being referenced here, and so this is not really a syllogism at all. With this caveat in mind, let us turn to the five rules.

Rule 1: No valid standard-form categorical syllogism has two negative premises. Think about it this way. In a syllogism, the major term is said to have some kind of relationship to the middle term. The minor term is also said to have some kind of relationship to the middle term. And on the basis of those two relationships, we conclude that the major and minor terms have some kind of relationship. This is shown diagrammatically in figure 5.20.

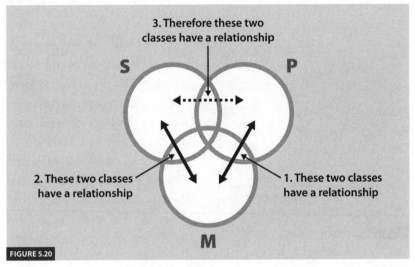

FIGURE 5.20

But if we begin by saying "the middle term is *not* related to the major term in this way . . . and the middle term is *not* related to the minor term in this way . . ." then how can we conclude anything about how the minor and major terms are related? In at least one of the premises we must assert some affirmation of relationship if we want to conclude with a relationship. Of course, this rule means that entire groups of standard-form categorical syllogisms will be invalid. Any syllogism whose mood starts with EE, EO, OE, or OO will necessarily be invalid because it has two negative premises.

Rule 2: If either premise of a valid standard-form categorical syllogism is negative, the conclusion must also be negative. If a conclusion affirms (either particularly or universally) class inclusion, it does so on the basis of the premises affirming class inclusion. But if one of the premises is denying class inclusion, how can we conclude anything about class *inclusion*?

Arguments that break this rule are so implausible that it is usually obvious that they are invalid.[4]

Rule 3: No valid standard-form categorical syllogism has two universal premises and a particular conclusion. With the Venn diagrams we can see this clearly. If both premises are universal, there will be no "X" in the diagram, yet the particular conclusion requires an "X" somewhere.

This rule brings up an interesting concept: the idea of *existential import*. This is a fairly recent development in logic. Aristotle assumed that whenever he was talking about a class, it had at least one member. So if he had known about Venn diagrams, he would have diagrammed an A proposition, "All S is P," like figure 5.21.

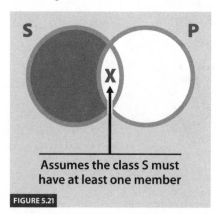

Assumes the class S must have at least one member

FIGURE 5.21

However, in contemporary logic, when we assert an A or an E proposition, we are not actually saying that the subject or predicate classes have any members. So we can say, "All *living things on Mars* are organisms capable of surviving without oxygen," whether or not there is life on Mars. This can be useful, as we may want to see what follows logically from our premises without making any claim about whether the classes being discussed have any members. But using Aristotle's traditional logic and moving from universal premises (without existential import) to a particular conclusion (with existential import) we might end up with something like this AEO-2 syllogism:

All <u>organisms on Mars</u> are organisms capable of surviving without oxygen

No <u>mammals</u> are <u>organisms capable of surviving without oxygen</u>

Some organisms on Mars are not <u>mammals</u>

---

[4]Now some logicians would add another rule as the converse of rule two: "If the conclusion of a valid standard-form categorical syllogism is negative, there must be a negative premise." It probably doesn't take too much figuring to realize that this purported rule is true. But there is no need for it as such an argument will of necessity break one of the other rules. Our goal is to come up with as small a set as possible for the rules—and five is the minimum that will get the job done. Could we add more? Of course—we could have a rule for each of the 256 possible argument forms declaring it either valid or invalid. But these five will form a sufficient set.

The problem here is that given our definition of "some," the conclusion is saying "*there is at least one* organism on Mars that is not a mammal." This is a claim that the class "organisms on Mars" has at least one member.

Rule 4: In a valid standard-form categorical syllogism, the middle term must be distributed (which we show by <u>underlining</u>) in at least one premise. Finally we come to see the value of the distribution rules. Remember that a term is distributed if we are saying anything about *every member of that class*. If the middle term is the "bridge" that connects the minor and major terms, at some point in the argument we must be talking about every member of that class. Imagine if the major premise talked about the relationship of the major term to the middle term—but what was asserted only applied to some members of the middle-term class. Then imagine that the minor premise talked about the relationship of the minor term to the middle term, but was talking about only some members of that middle-term class. The second group of members of the middle-term class might be entirely different from the first—so how could we conclude anything that connects the minor and major terms? We could not; at least not with the necessity that is required for an argument to be valid. For example, consider this argument:

Some campsites are places safe from bears

All <u>clearings in the high country of Yosemite</u> are campsites

---

All <u>clearings in the high country of Yosemite</u> are places safe from bears

The members of the class campsites referred to in the major premise are not necessarily the same members mentioned in the minor premise. Neither premise says anything about *all* the members of the class of campsites, and so the middle term is not distributed at least once. The premises here could be true without the conclusion necessarily being true.[5]

Now an astute student will soon figure out that, in fact, the middle term in a valid argument must also be distributed *at most* once. That is, if the middle term is underlined in both premises, the syllogism will be invalid. But, again, this will occur for other reasons, and we do not need this as one of our five rules. For our purposes we simply say the middle term must be distributed *at least* once.

Rule 5: In a valid standard-form categorical syllogism, if either term is distributed in the conclusion (which we show by <u>underlining</u>), then it must

---

[5] And a wise camper would know this argument was invalid and would take all necessary precautions when backpacking in the mountains of Yosemite.

be distributed in the premise in which it appears. This rule is somewhat intuitive: How can we conclude something about every member of a class (distribution) unless we have been talking about every member of the class in the premise? Consider the following invalid AAA-3 argument:

All <u>horses</u> are animals that can be domesticated

All <u>horses</u> are mammals

All <u>mammals</u> are animals that can be domesticated

The problem here is that the term "mammals" is distributed in the conclusion, but not in the second (minor) premise. The conclusion is saying something about *every member* of the class of "mammals" while the second premise was only discussing some of them (namely, those that are horses). By breaking rule five we end up concluding way more about "mammals" than the first premise supported.

Summary of the Rules for Testing Validity of Standard-Form Categorical Syllogisms

Rule 1: Can't have two negative premises.

Rule 2: If either premise is negative, the conclusion must also be negative.

Rule 3: Can't have two universal premises and a particular conclusion.

Rule 4: The middle term must be distributed in at least one premise.

Rule 5: If either term is distributed in the conclusion, then it must be distributed in the premise in which it appears.

Assignment 5.5a. For the following standard-form categorical syllogisms, give the mood and figure and determine whether they are valid by applying the five rules. If it is invalid, tell which rule it breaks.

Example: Some pens are good writing utensils
                Some items given away by banks are not <u>pens</u>
                _____
                Some items given away by banks are not <u>good</u>
                    <u>writing utensils</u>

Solution: IOO-1; invalid; breaks rule five: the major term is distributed (underlined) in the conclusion, but not in the major premise.

1. All <u>videotapes</u> are means of recording video
   Some videotapes are VHS-format tapes
   _____
   Some VHS-format tapes are means of recording video

2. Some members of Congress are efficient and capable represetatives
   All <u>efficient and capable representatives</u> are people likely to get reelected

   All <u>people who are likely to get reelected</u> are members of Congress

*3. No <u>athletes who have won national championships</u> are <u>marginal players</u>
   Some subs are athletes who have won national championships

   Some subs are not <u>marginal players</u>

4. Some members of the Sanhedrin were not <u>people who persecuted Jesus</u>
   No <u>Romans</u> were <u>members of the Sanhedrin</u>

   Some Romans were not <u>people who persecuted Jesus</u>

5. Some brilliant students are frosh
   All <u>State University students</u> are brilliant students

   Some State University students are frosh

*6. Some personal digital assistants are electronic gadgets
   All <u>personal digital assistants</u> are things that are outdated

   Some things that are outdated are electronic gadgets

7. Some thumb drives are not <u>expensive items</u>
   All <u>thumb drives</u> are small items

   No <u>small items</u> are <u>expensive items</u>

8. No <u>desks</u> are <u>pieces of furniture</u>
   All <u>credenzas</u> are pieces of furniture

   No <u>credenzas</u> are <u>desks</u>

*9. Some electrical wirings are cables
   All <u>cables</u> are wires

   Some wires are electrical wirings

10. No <u>logic books</u> are <u>valuable items</u>
    No <u>logic books</u> are <u>books that are fun to read</u>

    Some books that are fun to read are not <u>valuable items</u>

11. Some elementary school buildings are not <u>buildings that are
    certified fire-safe</u>
    Some wooden structures are not <u>buildings that are certified fire-safe</u>

    Some wooden structures are not <u>elementary school buildings</u>

*12. No <u>wind-up clocks</u> are <u>accurate timekeepers</u>
     Some accurate timekeepers are not <u>quartz watches</u>

     Some quartz watches are not <u>wind-up clocks</u>

13. Some prescription pills are habit-forming narcotics
     No <u>heart medicines</u> are <u>habit-forming narcotics</u>

     No <u>heart medicines</u> are <u>prescription pills</u>

14. No <u>purses</u> are <u>impulse purchases</u>
     Some online sale items are purses

     Some online sale items are impulse purchases

*15. All <u>students who finish this assignment</u> are happy students
     All <u>students who do their best</u> are happy students

     All <u>students who do their best</u> are students who finish this assignment

Assignment 5.5b. For the following standard-form categorical-syllogism forms, write out the syllogism using S, P, and M. Then give a Venn diagram. If it is invalid, tell which rule it breaks.

Example: EAO-1

Solution: No <u>M</u> is <u>P</u>
            All <u>S</u> is M

            Some S is not <u>P</u>

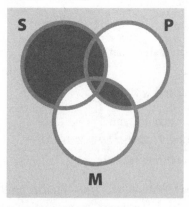

            Invalid; breaks rule three with two universal premises and a particular conclusion.

1. AEE-2

2. AOO-3

*3. EIO-2

4. IAI-2

5. OAA-1

*6. EAE-1

7. EIO-4

8. OAO-3

*9. EEE-2

10. AEE-4

11. IOI-2

*12. IAI-4

13. OOI-4

14. AII-3

*15. AAI-1

Assignment 5.5c. Using the rules, tell which of the 256 possible standard-form categorical-syllogism forms are valid. (Yes, this sounds hard, but once you start applying the rules you will see whole groups of arguments disappearing. For example, we know that any argument that begins EE, EO, OE, or OO violates rule one. That alone eliminates 64 of the possible 256.)

6

SYLLOGISMS IN
ORDINARY LANGUAGE

In ordinary language, people rarely use the highly structured syllogisms we examined in the previous chapter. Standard-form categorical syllogisms are virtually nonexistent in the real world. But while these highly stylized syllogisms are rare, it is not uncommon to find arguments than can be reformulated into standard-form categorical syllogisms without changing the propositions they assert. In this chapter we will look at such arguments as they naturally occur in ordinary language. We will then develop techniques for translating these arguments into standard-form categorical syllogisms. One warning: while the arguments in the previous chapter were artificial and stilted, they were also very clear and easy to test for validity once we learned the Venn diagrams and the rules for standard-form categorical syllogisms. The arguments in this chapter will be much harder to decipher. In fact, a general rule of thumb in logic applies here: the clearer and more precise an argument, the less real-life value it probably has. And vice-versa, the more natural an argument is, the muddier and less precise it is likely to be.

Take this argument from Boethius in *The Consolation of Philosophy*:

> "There is free will," Philosophy answered, "and no rational nature can exist which does not have it. For any being, which by its nature has the use of reason, must also have the power of judgment by which it can make decisions and, by its own resources, distinguish between things which should be desired and things which should be avoided."[1]

---

[1]Boethius, *The Consolation of Philosophy*, trans. Richard Green, Library of the Liberal Arts (New York: Macmillan, 1962), book 5, prose 2.

In this passage, Lady Philosophy is giving a syllogism with the conclusion, "No rational creatures can exist [without free will]." But this quotation does not fit the form of a standard-form categorical syllogism. So how do we get from this original argument to something like this?

All <u>creatures with judgment</u> are creatures with free will

All <u>rational creatures</u> are creatures with judgment

All <u>rational creatures</u> are creatures with free will

That is the subject of this chapter—how to translate categorical syllogisms in ordinary language into standard form.

6.1 SYNONYMS

Sometimes a syllogism seems to contain more than three terms, but two or more of these terms may be synonyms for each other. In this case, though two different words or phrases are being used, they actually name the same class. We can simply eliminate the synonymous terms to clarify the argument. In some cases, that will be sufficient to allow us to put a categorical syllogism into standard form. For example, consider this argument:

All <u>lawyers</u> are well-educated persons

All <u>doctors</u> are well-educated persons

All <u>physicians</u> are attorneys

Now this syllogism has five terms. But "lawyers" and "attorneys" both refer to the same class. "Doctors" and "physicians" do as well. By replacing the synonymous terms, we would get the following AAA-2 standard-form categorical syllogism:

All <u>lawyers</u> are well-educated persons

All <u>doctors</u> are well-educated persons

All <u>doctors</u> are lawyers

Assignment 6.1. Put the following syllogisms into standard form using synonyms as needed, give the mood and figure, then check for validity using the rules. If it is invalid, give the rule it violates.

Example: All <u>TVs</u> are electrical appliances with circuit boards
              Some idiot boxes are Sonys
              _____
              Some Sonys are electronic devices

Solution: AII-3; valid
              All <u>TVs</u> are electronic devices
              Some TVs are Sonys
              _____
              Some Sonys are electronic devices

1. Some enjoyable places to live are places patrolled by cops
   No <u>prisons</u> are <u>fun places to live</u>
   _____
   Some jails are not <u>places patrolled by cops</u>

2. All <u>maps</u> are articles designed to help you find your way
   All <u>GPS devices</u> are things to keep you from getting lost
   _____
   All <u>satellite-based navigation systems</u> are maps

*3. All <u>pieces of plumbing equipment</u> are things that are difficult to install
    All <u>toilets</u> are pieces of plumbing equipment
    _____
    All <u>porcelain thrones</u> are things that are a pain to put in

4. Some snowboarders are not <u>thoughtful people</u>
   No <u>skiers</u> are <u>boarders</u>
   _____
   No <u>skiers</u> are <u>polite people</u>

5. No <u>conformists</u> are <u>people who are appointed to office</u>
   All <u>public servants</u> are rule-followers
   _____
   Some bureaucrats are not <u>unelected people</u>

*6. Some antiques are not <u>things for sale</u>
    All <u>old collectibles</u> are valuable things
    _____
    Some expensive items are not <u>purchasable things</u>

7. Some veggies are delicious things
   All <u>broccoli</u> are greens
   _____
   Some broccoli is not <u>yummy things</u>

8. No <u>action features</u> are <u>movies without Morgan Freeman or Samuel L. Jackson</u>
   All <u>Marvel Comics film adaptations</u> are boom-boom movies

   No <u>Marvel movies</u> are <u>Morgan Freeman or Samuel L. Jackson–free</u>

*9. Some cars are very fast machines
   All <u>racers</u> are dangerous contraptions

   Some hazardous vehicles are automobiles

10. All <u>small children</u> are exhausting
    Some houseguests are not <u>people who wear you out</u>

    Some company are not <u>kids</u>

6.2 IMMEDIATE INFERENCES: CONVERSION, OBVERSION, AND CONTRAPOSITION

Let's return to our standard-form categorical propositions from chapter four and see what we can immediately infer from them. We will find that using these immediate inferences will be very helpful in translating syllogisms into standard form.

Conversion. In an E proposition, the claim is made that not a single member of the subject class belong to the predicate class: "No S is P." But if this is the case, it would follow that no member of the predicate class would belong to the subject class either. That is, we could switch the subject and predicate terms—"No P is S"—and it would be logically equivalent. So "No dogs are cats" and "No cats are dogs" are logically equivalent. Literally, they are both expressing the same proposition. We can substitute one for the other without any change in the truth value of the proposition. The Venn diagram for the E proposition shows this clearly. The Venn diagram for "No S is P" is shown in figure 6.1.

If we just rotate this drawing 180 degrees we get figure 6.2.

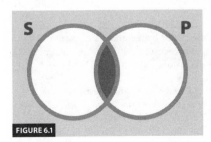

FIGURE 6.1

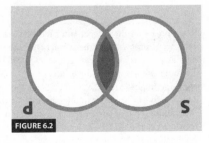

FIGURE 6.2

Now the letters may be upside down, but this is the Venn diagram for "No P is S."[2]

In the same way, consider the I proposition "Some S is P." If there is at least one S that is a P, then there is at least one P that is an S. So if "Some dogs are animals,"[3] then "Some animals are dogs." Once again the Venn diagram for this standard-form proposition (see fig. 6.3) is exactly the same as the Venn diagram for "Some P is S" (see fig. 6.4).

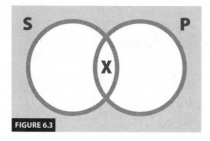

FIGURE 6.3

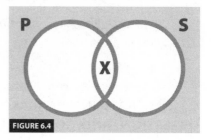

FIGURE 6.4

So the subject and predicate can be flipped in an E or an I proposition and the result is logically equivalent to the original. In other words, both an E or I proposition and its converse express the same proposition.

In the case of the O proposition "Some S is not P," it is clear that switching the subject and the predicate would yield a converse that was *not* logically equivalent to the original proposition. If we say "Some dogs are not beagles," that is not saying the same thing as "Some beagles are not dogs." An O proposition simply cannot be converted.

The A proposition is an unusual case. We cannot switch the subject and predicate of an A proposition and expect to get something logically equivalent. To say that "All dogs are animals" is clearly not saying the same thing as "All animals are dogs." However, in traditional—that is, Aristotelian—logic, it is claimed that there *is* a kind of conversion that can be done. This is called

---

[2]Remember that the subject and predicate are determined by the order of the standard-form categorical proposition. The subject is whatever comes between the quantifier and the copula, and the predicate is whatever comes after the copula. It does not matter what letters—S, P, M, or anything else—stand for the terms.

[3]Now one might object, "But *all* dogs are animals!" Remember, "some" means "at least one"—and at least one dog is an animal. In ordinary language when we say "some . . . are . . . ," we are often implying that some are *not*. But in logic all we are asserting with a particular standard-form proposition is that at least one member of the subject class is or is not a member of the predicate class.

"conversion by limitation (in traditional logic)," and it involves switching the subject and the predicate *and changing it to an I proposition*. So if "All <u>dogs</u> are animals," then "*Some* animals are dogs." The second proposition here is *not* logically equivalent to the first proposition—but in traditional logic, it follows from the first.

The problem here is that this assumes existential import. Consider the A proposition "All <u>living things on Mars</u> are organisms capable of surviving with virtually no oxygen." The converse of this by traditional logic would be "Some organisms capable of surviving with virtually no oxygen are living things on Mars." But remember, "some" means "at least one," so this latter proposition is claiming that the class of living things on Mars has at least one member— that is, there *are* Martians. The conversion of an A proposition by limitation in traditional logic is included here only because it occasionally arises in some older arguments.

So, in summary, here are the rules for conversion.

CONVERSION			
Original Proposition		**Converse**	
A	All <u>S</u> is P	I	*Some P is S—by limitation*
E	No <u>S</u> is <u>P</u>	E	No <u>P</u> is <u>S</u>
I	Some S is P	I	Some P is S
O	Some S is not <u>P</u>		(not valid)

Obversion. While conversion only really applies to two of our standard-form categorical propositions, obversion can be used in all four. To explain the inference of obversion, we must first return to the concept of a "class" we discussed at the beginning of chapter five. We defined a class as "any group that has a common characteristic." To understand obversion, we must introduce a new concept. *The "complement of a class" is the class of everything that is not a member of the original class.* We usually express this by using the prefix *non-*. So the complement of the class of "athletes" would be "non-athletes." Now the class of "non-athletes" includes *everything* that is not in the class of athletes. This would include not only folks who spend all day lying on a couch eating pizza but also the couch and the pizza—anything that is not an athlete.

Using our Venn diagrams, we can say that for the class P (see fig. 6.5), the

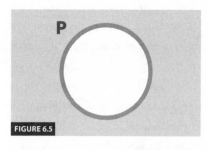

FIGURE 6.5

class of non-P is everything outside that circle on this sheet of paper if the paper were extended out to infinity. (One side note: the complement of non-P would be P—not "non-non-P." Everything that is not in the class of non-P is P. A sort of "double negative" is at work here.)

Strictly speaking, the complement of a class is *everything* outside that class. Yet there is often an implied "universe of discourse" that limits the complementary class. For example, when we speak of the class of non-athletes, we usually are assuming that the "universe of discourse" is "people." So while a couch and a pizza are outside the class of athletes, when we said "non-athletes" we were probably not intending to include them. Using a slightly modified

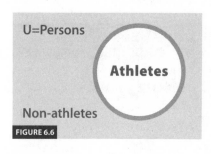

FIGURE 6.6

Venn diagram, we can indicate the universe of discourse within which we were discussing the class of athletes (see fig. 6.6).

In the given context, the universe of discourse here is diagrammed with the large rectangle, and the "U" tells us that this discourse is limited to persons. So, in this context when we talk about the complement of the class of "athletes," we are limiting ourselves to persons who are non-athletes. That is, pizzas and couches are no longer part of what we mean here by "non-athletes." In ordinary language, it is often understood that we are limited by a universe of discourse. So the complement of the class of "Ford sedans" would probably be any car that is not a Ford—that is, we are assuming a universe of discourse of automobiles.

With this concept of complementary classes in mind, we are now ready to define obversion. *In obversion, the subject term and the quantity remain the same, but we change the* quality *of the proposition and take the complement of the predicate.* So,

To obvert a standard-form categorical proposition:

1. Leave the subject term and the quantity (universal or particular) alone

2. Change the quality (from affirmative to negative or vice versa)

3. Replace the predicate term with the complement of the predicate

With the A and the E propositions, this is clear. To say

All <u>dogs</u> are animals

is logically equivalent to stating the obverse:

No <u>dogs</u> are <u>non-animals.</u>

When we look at the Venn diagram for this A proposition (see fig. 6.7) it is clear that there is nothing outside the animals circle ("non-animals") that is left in the dogs circle—it is all shaded out. So "No <u>dogs</u> are <u>non-animals.</u>"

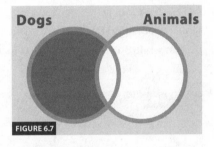

FIGURE 6.7

For the E proposition, "No <u>dogs</u> are <u>cats</u>" we have the Venn diagram, figure 6.8.

If we look at this diagram, we can see that anything remaining in the dogs circle is outside the cats circle— namely, non-cats. So the obverse of the original E proposition would be "All <u>dogs</u> are non-cats."

When we come to the I and the O propositions, it gets a little bit trickier. Remember that for both of these

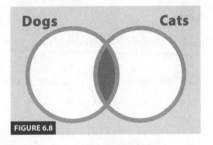

FIGURE 6.8

propositions, the quality is indicated by the *copula*, not by the quantifier. So to change the quality of the proposition, we must change from "Some . . . is . . ." to "Some . . . is not. . . ." This makes for some rather awkward sentences. The I proposition

Some dogs are beagles

is obverted to the O proposition

Some dogs are not <u>non-beagles.</u>

Now we immediately want to say, "But 'not non-' is just a double negative that can be eliminated!" Well, yes, if we drop both the "not" and the "non-" we do have a logically equivalent proposition—the one with which we began. But the "not" is part of the copula and the "non-" is part of the predicate term so there *is* a structural difference. This distinction will become important later as we try to translate ordinary language into standard-form categorical propositions.

In the case of the O proposition

Some students are not <u>conformists</u>

is obverted to the I proposition

Some students are nonconformists.

Again, these two sentences look very similar—and they clearly express the same proposition. But they are structurally different: one is denying class inclusion while one is affirming class inclusion.

Here are all the valid obversions:

OBVERSION			
Original Proposition		**Obverse**	
A	All <u>S</u> is P	E	No <u>S</u> is <u>non-P</u>
E	No <u>S</u> is <u>P</u>	A	All <u>S</u> is non-P
I	Some S is P	O	Some S is not <u>non-P</u>
O	Some S is not <u>P</u>	I	Some S is not non-P

Contraposition. The third immediate inference is known as contraposition. To form the contrapositive of a proposition, one uses the preceding two inferences as follows:

1. Obvert

2. Convert

3. Obvert

For example, beginning with the A proposition,

All <u>dogs</u> are animals

we obvert it to

No <u>dogs</u> are <u>non-animals</u>

then convert that to

No <u>non-animals</u> are <u>dogs</u>

and finally obvert *that* to get the contrapositive,

All <u>non-animals</u> are <u>non-dogs.</u>

Looking at the final result after obverting, converting, and obverting again, and comparing it to the original A proposition, we can see that *the contrapositive switches the subject and predicate terms and takes the complement of each.*

Turning to the case of the O proposition,

Some students are not <u>conformists</u>

we obvert it to

Some students are nonconformists

then we convert that to

Some nonconformists are students

and finally obvert *that* to get the contrapositive,

Some nonconformists are not <u>non-students</u>.

It ends up being quite a mouthful. But once again we can see that we have simply switched the subject and predicate terms of the O proposition and taken the complement of each.

The middle step of the contrapositive inference leads to a bit of a problem. We saw above that an O proposition cannot be converted at all and the A proposition can be converted only under certain conditions—and the result is not logically equivalent. Considering the first of these issues, if we try to give the contrapositive of an I proposition like

Some dogs are beagles

we can begin by obverting it to

Some dogs are not <u>non-beagles</u>.

But this is now an O proposition—and we cannot perform the conversion step: O propositions are "unconvertible." It turns out that we just cannot do contraposition on an I proposition for this reason.

For the E proposition,

No <u>dogs</u> are <u>cats</u>

we find a different problem. We can easily obvert this to the A proposition,

All <u>dogs</u> are non-cats

but as we attempt the next step, we encounter the problem with converting an A proposition. We can only convert by limitation in traditional logic to

Some non-cats are dogs

but this is not logically equivalent at all. From here we can obvert this I proposition, and we get

Some non-cats are not <u>non-dogs</u>.

So once again, this follows in traditional—that is, Aristotelian—logic, but it is not logically equivalent. Here are the rules for contraposition:

CONTRAPOSITION		
Original Proposition		**Contrapositive**
A	All <u>S</u> is P	A	All <u>non-P</u> is non-S
E	No <u>S</u> is <u>P</u>	O	*Some non-P is not <u>non-S</u>—by limitation*
I	Some S is P		
O	Some S is not <u>P</u>	O	Some non-P is not <u>non-S</u>

Here are all the immediate inferences summarized:

	Original	Converse	Obverse	Contrapositive
A	All <u>S</u> is P	*(Some P is S)**	No <u>S</u> is <u>non-P</u>	All <u>non-P</u> is non-S
E	No <u>S</u> is <u>P</u>	No <u>P</u> is <u>S</u>	All <u>S</u> is non-P	*(Some non-P is not <u>non-S</u>)**
I	Some S is P	Some P is S	Some S is not <u>non-P</u>	
O	Some S is not <u>P</u>		Some S is non-P	Some non-P is not <u>non-S</u>

*By limitation in traditional logic.

Assignment 6.2. For the following standard-form categorical propositions give the converse, the obverse, or the contrapositive for the following.

Convert the following (if possible):

Example: All <u>State University students</u> are smart people.

Solution: Some smart people are State University students. (By limitation—not logically equivalent.)

1. No <u>US Marines</u> are <u>cowards</u>.

2. Some Christians are fundamentalists.

*3. All <u>McDonald's restaurants</u> are moneymakers.

4. No <u>school playgrounds</u> are <u>quiet places</u>.

5. Some bridges are not <u>well-maintained structures</u>.

Obvert the following:

Example: All <u>State University students</u> are smart people.

Solution: No <u>State University students</u> are <u>non-smart people</u>.

*6. No <u>boat anchors</u> are <u>things that weigh less than ten pounds</u>.

7. All <u>Pixar movies</u> are delightful films.

8. Some Nicolas Cage films are not <u>moneymaking movies</u>.

*9. Some prescription pills are habit-forming drugs.

10. Some runners are not <u>athletes</u>.

Contrapose (i.e., give the contrapositive of) the following (if possible):

Example: All <u>State University students</u> are smart people.

Solution: All <u>non-smart people</u> are non–State University students.

11. Some prescription glasses are not <u>well-fitted items</u>.

*12. No <u>iPhones</u> are <u>cheap items</u>.

13. All <u>mousepads</u> are nonessential things.

14. Some posters are not <u>beautiful things</u>.

*15. Some Coke cans are specially themed items.

6.3 USING IMMEDIATE INFERENCES TO TRANSLATE CATEGORICAL SYLLOGISMS

An argument consisting of categorical propositions with more than three terms is not a syllogism. However, if one or more of the terms is the complement of another, we can use the immediate inferences described above to reduce the number of terms. In this way we may be able to "translate" the argument into a standard-form categorical syllogism. Consider the following argument:

Some rocks are valuable things
No <u>minerals</u> are <u>non-rocks</u>

Some minerals are valuable things

This argument is not a syllogism (yet) as it has four terms: "minerals," "valuable things," "rocks," and "non-rocks." However, these last two are complements of each other. If we obvert the second premise we get the following IAI-1 standard-form categorical syllogism:

Some rocks are valuable things
All <u>minerals</u> are rocks

Some minerals are valuable things

Of course, it is invalid because the middle term ("rocks") was never distributed. But now it is a standard-form categorical syllogism.

Sometimes we must make more than one immediate inference to get the argument into standard form. For instance, if the term we want to change to its complement is the subject of an E or an I proposition, we will need to first convert and then obvert the proposition. In the first premise of this argument,

Some worthless things are rocks
All <u>rocks</u> are minerals

Some minerals are not <u>valuable things</u>

if we replace "worthless things" with "non-valuable things," convert, and then obvert, we will get

Some rocks are not <u>valuable things</u>
All <u>rocks</u> are minerals

Some minerals are not <u>valuable things</u>.

This is now the valid OAO-3 standard-form categorical syllogism.

Notice that if we convert or do contraposition (which includes a conversion step) on the *conclusion* of an argument, we will change the subject and predicate and, hence, the major and minor terms. This means we will need to change the order of the premises so the major premise (which contains the major term) will still come first. For example, in the following argument,

All <u>Green Berets</u> are soldiers
All <u>soldiers</u> are brave people

All <u>cowards</u> are non–Green Berets

if we substitute the synonym "non-brave people" for "cowards" and do contraposition, the conclusion becomes

All <u>Green Berets</u> are brave people.

But by switching the original subject and predicate of the conclusion, we also switched what was apparently the major premise and the minor premise. So we will need to swap the two premises, and we will end up with the following valid AAA-1 standard-form categorical syllogism:

> All <u>soldiers</u> are brave people
> All <u>Green Berets</u> are soldiers
>
> ---
>
> All <u>Green Berets</u> are brave people.

In using the immediate inferences, there are often multiple ways to translate the same argument into standard form while preserving the logical equivalence of the argument. So the argument,

> No <u>writing tools</u> are <u>non-office supplies</u>
> No <u>pens</u> are <u>non-writing tools</u>
>
> ---
>
> No <u>pens</u> are <u>non-office supplies</u>

can be translated as

> No <u>writing tools</u> are <u>non-office supplies</u>
> All <u>pens</u> are writing tools
>
> ---
>
> No <u>pens</u> are <u>non-office supplies</u>

or as

> All <u>writing tools</u> are office supplies
> All <u>pens</u> are writing tools
>
> ---
>
> All <u>pens</u> are office supplies.

This brings up an interesting point. If this argument can be turned into an EAE-1 *or* an AAA-1, does that mean that any EAE-1 can be turned into an AAA-1? Yes. This means that we really don't even need the EAE-1: we could just translate it into an AAA-1:

> No <u>M</u> is <u>P</u>   obvert to ⟶   All <u>M</u> is non-P
> <u>All S is M</u>   <u>All S is M</u>
> No <u>S</u> is <u>P</u>   obvert to ⟶   All <u>S</u> is non-P

Of course, we could easily make the EAE-1 into an EAE-2 by converting the major premise. So AAA-1, EAE-1, and EAE-2 are all logically equivalent.

Is it possible to use these immediate inferences to translate this AAA-1 argument into even more standard-form categorical syllogisms? If we translated them, how far could we reduce the number of valid standard-form categorical syllogisms? In the last chapter we found that there are fifteen valid forms. What is the minimum number to which we can translate all the others? That is an extra-credit problem for your homework assignment.

Assignment 6.3. For the following arguments, using synonyms and the immediate inferences, translate them into standard-form categorical syllogisms, give the mood and figure, tell whether they are valid, and if invalid, tell what rule they violate.

Example: Some household decorations are real plants, but no artificial plants are things that need watering; therefore some things that need watering are not household decorations.

Solution: Some household decorations are not <u>artificial plants</u>
(by obversion)
No <u>artificial plants</u> are <u>things that need watering</u>
_____
Some things that need watering are not <u>household decorations</u>

OEO-4 invalid; breaks rules one (has two negative premises) and five (the major term, "household decorations," is distributed in the conclusion, but not in the major premise). Note that this argument could have been translated into standard form without making both premises negative, but it would still break at least one of the rules.

1. Some elected officials are Democrats. No elected officials are non-conformists. Therefore some conformists are Democrats.

2. All fireworks are hazardous materials, so all safe things are non-explosives, since all fireworks are things that blow up.

*3. No church organs are portable instruments, so, since no contemporary instruments are permanently installed in churches, all church organs are outdated instruments.

4. All times he goes out are times he is with others, and all times he is by himself are times he has fun, so it follows that all times he is bored are times he stays home.

5. All academic successes are things that are hard to achieve, for no goals worth having are easily attained ends, and no academic successes are worthless pursuits.

*6. No State University students are dumb, since all State students are folks who got admitted, and all people who got accepted are smart.

7. No scientific instruments are things you can't find for sale on the internet, and some scientific instruments are things besides microscopes, so it follows that some possible online purchases are microscopes.

8. All objects easily seen are material things; therefore no immaterial substances are non-molecules, because all molecules are things that cannot be seen by the naked eye.

*9. Some untamed creatures are not carnivores, since no carnivores are vegetarians, and some wild animals are plant eaters.

10. Some programs purchased for smartphones are rubbish, because some valuable apps are freebies, and all worthwhile applications are things worth downloading.

11. All professors are smart, but all ignorant people are vain people, so no professors are conceited.

*12. No valid syllogisms are syllogisms with two negative premises, and no EEA arguments are arguments without two negative premises, so all EEA arguments are invalid.

13. All valid syllogisms are arguments with three terms, so no arguments in this exercise are invalid, because all syllogisms in this homework assignment are arguments with three classes.

14. No poor people are bankers, and some shady operators are bankers, so it follows that some wealthy individuals aren't honest.

*15. Some NBA players are six feet tall or less, since no top-level American professional basketball players are lacking in skills, and some talented athletes are not over six feet tall.

Extra credit: Translate the valid standard-form categorical syllogisms into each other until you have the fewest number possible. What is the fewest number necessary? Show your work.

6.4 TRANSLATING CATEGORICAL PROPOSITIONS

Unfortunately, syllogisms we encounter in ordinary language are typically not made up of standard-form categorical propositions. This means using synonyms and immediate inferences will not be sufficient. We must think hard about what proposition a given sentence is trying to express. While there really are no hard-and-fast rules that tell us what to do in these cases, there are some general guidelines that we can use to help us translate ordinary sentences into standard form.

1. Propositions that have adjectives instead of **terms.** In a sentence like "Some drinks are refreshing," there really is no predicate *term*. That is, we do not have a substantive class of things that all share the property of being refreshing. We have only the property "refreshing." This can easily be turned into a term by adding the word "things," thus forming the I standard-form categorical proposition "Some drinks are refreshing things." The sentence "No people were waiting for the bus" can be translated to "No <u>people</u> were <u>people waiting for the bus</u>" or "No <u>people</u> were <u>bus-waiters</u>." The grammar may prove awkward, but both these E standard-form categorical propositions are logically equivalent to the ordinary-language sentence.

2. Singular propositions. Singular propositions in ordinary language pose a bit of a problem. Consider the following sentence:

Beyoncé Giselle Knowles-Carter is a famous singer.

The subject of this categorical proposition is not really a class, but an individual who is being claimed to belong to a class. We could translate this as a particular standard-form categorical proposition (albeit with some awkward grammar):

Some Beyoncé Giselle Knowles-Carter are famous singers.

This tells us that "there was at least one" Beyoncé Giselle Knowles-Carter who belongs to the class of famous singers. But this leaves open the possibility that there are other members of the class of Beyoncé Giselle Knowles-Carter who are not famous singers. If we choose the universal standard-form categorical proposition

All <u>Beyoncé Giselle Knowles-Carter</u> are famous singers, we have a different problem. Since this is a universal proposition, it does not have existential import—that is, it does not say that there actually *is* a Beyoncé. So what should we do?

The answer is that, in essence, a singular proposition is asserting *both* the universal and the particular. Using our Venn diagrams, we can show the affirmative singular proposition is asserting the diagram shown in figure 6.9, while the negative singular proposition is asserting the diagram shown in figure 6.10.

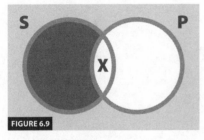

FIGURE 6.9

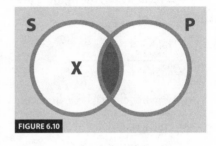

FIGURE 6.10

So, for example, the classic syllogism

All <u>persons</u> are mortal

Socrates is a person

Socrates is mortal

can be translated

All <u>persons</u> are mortal

All <u>Socrates</u> are persons

All <u>Socrates</u> are mortal.

This is a valid AAA-1 syllogism—though the grammar is awkward at best.

Similarly, the syllogism

All <u>Sophists</u> were paid teachers

Socrates wasn't a paid teacher

Socrates wasn't a Sophist

can be translated

All <u>Sophists</u> were paid teachers

No <u>Socrates</u> was <u>paid teachers</u>

No <u>Socrates</u> was <u>Sophists</u>.

In each of these cases we have taken the singular proposition and translated it as a universal.

Since a singular proposition is asserting more than a single standard-form categorical proposition can express, when translating we must consider both propositions. If the translation of the singular as a universal leads us to an invalid argument, we must try translating it as a particular to see whether that makes for a valid argument.[4] So if we translate the singular propositions as universals in the following valid argument,

> Socrates is mortal
>
> Socrates is a person
> _____
>
> Some persons are mortal

we get the invalid AAI-3 syllogism

> All <u>Socrates</u> is mortal
>
> All <u>Socrates</u> is persons
> _____
>
> Some persons are mortal

which violates rule three. But since the singular proposition is expressing *both* the particular and the universal, the following valid AII-3 syllogism is a proper translation of the original argument:

> All <u>Socrates</u> is mortal
>
> Some Socrates is persons
> _____
>
> Some persons are mortal.

3. *Categorical propositions without a copula.* In ordinary language we rarely use a copula (some form of the verb "to be") to connect two classes. So we say things like

> Some people cheat.

Now there is no copula here, but we can easily turn the verb "cheat" into a class and translate this as

> Some people are cheaters.

---

[4]An astute student might object, "But I thought to be valid the conclusion *had* to be true if the premises were true. So what is this giving-the-syllogism-a-second-chance nonsense?" The problem is that a singular proposition is communicating more than can fit into one standard-form categorical proposition. We are not "cheating," but rather acknowledging that a singular proposition is making both a universal and a particular claim.

4. Categorical propositions with a different quantifier. Frequently, categorical syllogisms will have quantifiers other than the standard-form *all*, *no*, or *some*. Words like *every*, *many*, and *most* are often used. In any case where the quantifier being used indicates less than every member of the class, we use the quantifier *some*. It is true that translating *many* into *some* loses some of the intended meaning, but given the limitations of standard-form categorical propositions, that will suffice.[5] So a categorical proposition like

Every rose has its thorn

translates into the A standard-form categorical proposition

All <u>roses</u> are things with thorns.

Sentences that begin with either *every* or *any* usually translate with the universal quantifier *all*. However, sentences that begin by denying these two are translated in very different ways. To say "not every" indicates the particular negative "some . . . are not. . . ." On the other hand, "not any" means the universal negative, "no."

So, in summary,

"every" or "any"	=	All . . .
"not any" or "none"	=	No . . .
"many" or "most"	=	Some . . .
"not all" or "not every"	=	Some . . . are not . . .

5. Categorical propositions without a quantifier. In some categorical propositions, no quantifier is given. Then one has to think about what the sentence probably means before translating it as a particular or a universal. For example,

Dogs are animals

clearly indicates the universal affirmative

All <u>dogs</u> are animals.

On the other hand,

Dogs are barking

is *not* making a universal claim at all and should be translated

Some dogs are barking (things).

While it is obvious in this case, there are often times when it is not clear whether the speaker is intending to refer to every member of a class or only some.

---

[5]Even in a case where a number is given, such as "two of the flowers," we still need to translate the sentence as "some flowers."

6. "Exceptive" propositions. One type of categorical proposition is the type that uses words like *only* or *none but* to indicate that the predicate applies exclusively to the subject. In such a case, we need to switch the *apparent* subject and predicate and translate the sentence as a universal. For example, to translate

Only seniors were present

we switch the apparent subject, "seniors," and the apparent predicate, "persons who were present," and we get

All <u>persons who were present</u> were seniors.

7. Categorical propositions in some other order. There are a myriad of other ways a proposition may indicate that one class does or does not belong to another—in whole or in part. There really are no "rules" that can tell us what to do. We simply need to read the sentence and do our best to figure out what proposition, exactly, is being asserted. Sometimes it is helpful to use a Venn diagram to guide our thinking. But in the final analysis, we just have to ask ourselves, What is the author/speaker saying?

Assignment 6.4. Translate the following into standard-form categorical propositions.

Example: A mind is a terrible thing to waste.

Solution: All <u>minds</u> are terrible things to waste.

  1. Bicycles are common.

  2. Seek and you will find.

*3. Many football games are fun to watch.

  4. If it isn't indexed on Google, it doesn't exist.

  5. Children are playing in the park.

*6. Only *you* can prevent forest fires.

  7. Everyone who saw the latest *Star Wars* film was blown away!

  8. Not everyone appreciated his pranks.

*9. The unexamined life is not worth living.

  10. Nothing is both true and false.

  11. A person who never made a mistake never tried anything new.

*12. What happens in Vegas stays in Vegas.

13. "Girls just wanna have fun" (Cyndi Lauper).

14. Only Costco card holders are permitted in the warehouse.

*15. Non-prescription glasses do not work for correcting astigmatism.

6.5 USING PARAMETERS

Sometimes a categorical proposition cannot be translated into standard form without specifying time or place. In such cases we add a *parameter: an auxiliary word or phrase that helps with translation by giving temporal or spatial limitations.* For example, consider the following statement:

He is always at the Mariners home baseball games.

This is not saying that he lives at the Mariners ballpark and never leaves. Nor is it saying that the Mariners play baseball twenty-four hours a day. Instead if we focus on the word "always," we can see that the statement is claiming that *when* there are Mariners games at home, he is there. So we can add the parameter "times when" and we translate the passage into standard form as

All times when the Mariners are playing a home baseball game are times he will be there.

Whenever we encounter words like *always, never, whenever*, and so on, it is likely that we will need to include a time parameter to translate the sentence into a standard-form categorical proposition.

In a similar way, we may need to use a parameter that indicates space rather than time. The proverb that claims

Where there is no vision, the people perish (Prov 29:18 KJV).

can be translated into

All places where there is no vision are places where the people perish.

So we can use the parameters "times when" and "places where" to help translate individual sentences into standard form. These standard-form categorical propositions can then be combined to form standard-form categorical syllogisms—as long as we translate in a uniform manner. Consider the following argument:

Whenever I'm in trouble, I pray. And since I'm in trouble all the time, [there is not a day when I don't pray].[6]

---

[6]Isaac Bashevis Singer, "A Night with Isaac B. Singer and His Demons," *The New York Times* (June 15, 1982).

We can start by finding the conclusion and putting the argument into a rough form like this,

Whenever I'm in trouble, I pray

I'm always in trouble

There is not a day when I don't pray.

Using the temporal parameter "times" and taking "there is not a day" to mean "all times," we can translate this into the valid AAA-1 standard-form categorical syllogism,

All <u>times I am in trouble</u> are times I pray

All <u>times</u> are times I am in trouble

All <u>times</u> are times I pray.

Assignment 6.5a. Translate the following sentences into standard-form categorical propositions using parameters.

Example: He gets sunburned every time he goes to the beach.

Solution: All <u>times he goes to the beach</u> are times he gets sunburned.

  1. It's never not a good time for a Mike's.

  2. He can turn into a werewolf whenever he feels like it.

 *3. She doesn't find people she knows everywhere she goes.

  4. No justice, no peace.

  5. She always corrected his grammar.

 *6. Whenever he goes to the store, he buys things he doesn't need.

  7. She talks about movies everywhere she goes.

  8. If he knows what she wants, he always makes it happen.

 *9. If you see something, say something.

 10. She drives where she wants.

 11. Everywhere that Mary went, the lamb was sure to go.

*12. When the boogeyman goes to sleep every night, he checks his closet for Chuck Norris.

 13. She never talks about music without mentioning Schubert.

14. "Somewhere out there beneath the pale moonlight, someone's thinking of me and loving me tonight" (Fievel Mousekewitz, *An American Tail*).

*15. Visa: It's everywhere you want to be.

Assignment 6.5b. Translate the following into standard-form categorical syllogisms. Using the rules, check for validity. If it is invalid, tell which rule it breaks. Note that many of these will *not* require parameters.

Example: "It would seem that it is always sinful to wage war. Because punishment is not inflicted except for sin. Now those who wage war are threatened by Our Lord with punishment, according to Matth. xxvi. 52: *All that take the sword shall perish with the sword.* Therefore all wars are unlawful" (Thomas Aquinas, *Summa theologiae*).[7]

Solution: All <u>times we are punished by Our Lord</u> are times we sin
All <u>times we wage war</u> are times we are punished by Our Lord

All <u>times we wage war</u> are times we sin

AAA-1; valid.

1. Tomorrow's game won't be boring, because it is against State, and games against State are never boring.

2. He never expected it to happen, and when it happened he was not prepared, so when he was prepared, he was not expecting it.

*3. Not everyone loves jazz, but everyone loves some kind of music, so some people love something other than jazz.

4. Yes, "with great power comes great responsibility," but I don't have any power, so I don't have any responsibility!

5. "My cousins are none of them judges, because all my cousins are unjust and all judges are just" (Lewis Carroll, *Symbolic Logic*).

*6. Larry: If it doesn't have a tail, it's not a monkey . . .
Bob: But, Larry, a kite has a tail.
Larry: Then it's a monkey! (VeggieTales, "Silly Song: Monkey")

---

[7]This is an argument with which Thomas Aquinas disagrees.

7. "Some animals are white and No stone is an animal, so Not everything white is a stone" (Ibn al-Salah, *On the Fourth Figure of the Categorical Syllogism*).

8. "Soldiers have the power to hold fast continually to the right and lawful. Anyone who has such power exhibits courage. Therefore soldiers are courageous" (Plato, *Republic* [paraphrased]).

*9. "Cool people work at Krispy Kreme, and me and Katie are cool, therefore me and Katie work at Krispy Kreme" (YouTube video).

10. "When a man irritates you, you must know that it is your own opinion which has irritated you. When your own opinion irritates you, you are being carried away by the appearance. Therefore when a man irritates you, you are being carried away by the appearance" (Epictetus, *Handbook* [paraphrased]).

11. "A law implies order to an end. But nothing ordered to an end is eternal, for the last end alone is eternal. Therefore no law is eternal" (Thomas Aquinas, *Summa theologiae*).[8]

*12. Flavius: Have you forgot me, sir?
    Timon: Why dost ask that? I have forgot all men;
        Then, if thou grant'st thou'rt a man, I have forgot thee.
        (William Shakespeare, *Timon of Athens*)

13. "Intense heat is nothing else but a particular kind of painful sensation; and pain cannot exist but in a perceiving being; it follows that no intense heat can really exist in an unperceiving corporeal substance" (George Berkeley, *Three Dialogues Between Hylas and Philomous*).

14. "All love is wonder; if we justly do
    Account her wonderful, why not lovely too?" (John Donne, "Elegy II: The Anagram").

*15. "Of the supernatural [talents man] has been wholly deprived. [Supernatural talents are necessary] for the attainment of a heavenly life and eternal happiness. Therefore, . . . he is exiled from the kingdom of God" (John Calvin, *Institutes of the Christian Religion*).

---

[8]Again, this is an argument Thomas Aquinas rejects.

6.6 ENTHYMEMES

Many times a syllogistic argument is given where one of the premises or the conclusion is "assumed" and not explicitly stated. The listener or reader is expected to supply the missing piece to complete the syllogism. For example, if I argue

Mary was there, so the lamb was sure to be there too

you can supply the missing premise,

Everywhere that Mary went, the lamb was sure to go

and complete the syllogism as follows:

Everywhere Mary goes, the lamb goes
Mary was there

The lamb was there

or in standard form (but horrid grammar),

All <u>places Mary goes</u> are places the lamb goes
All <u>there</u> were places Mary goes

All <u>there</u> were places the lamb goes.

In this particular case, the major premise was assumed. That is, a premise had to be supplied by the reader. To identify which part of the argument is missing, we class enthymemes as follows:

1. First-order enthymeme: major premise is missing.[9]

2. Second-order enthymeme: minor premise is missing.

3. Third-order enthymeme: conclusion is missing.

Now, are enthymemes useful or not? Some argue that enthymemes make an argument more powerful. By forcing the listeners or readers to supply part of the argument, you get them to "buy in," which may lead to acceptance. As Aristotle said in *Rhetoric*, "An enthymeme is, in general, the most effective of the modes of persuasion." Others have argued that enthymemes actually weaken an argument. By allowing the listener or reader to supply the missing

---

[9]Note that if one does conversion or contraposition on the conclusion while getting the syllogism into standard form, the enthymeme will change from first to second order or vice versa.

proposition, the arguer is giving up some control of the argument. What is to prevent the listener from supplying a proposition that makes the entire argument invalid?

In order to translate an enthymeme into a standard-form categorical syllogism, it is best to first ask what is missing and state the missing premise or conclusion in ordinary language. Like all the other kinds of arguments, we begin by asking, What is the speaker trying to convince me of? In the case of a third-order enthymeme, that will not be given, but only implied. We then ask what is given in support of the conclusion. In a first- or second-order enthymeme, part of the support for the conclusion will only be implied. In all cases, we should first get clear on the missing piece of the syllogism as it fits the ordinary language of argument.

We also have an epistemic responsibility to attempt to supply a missing proposition that will make the argument valid. We could always supply a missing proposition that would be absurd and make the argument totally fallacious. For example, the enthymeme

Dark chocolate is delicious and people like delicious things

is clearly missing the conclusion,

So people like dark chocolate.

If instead I added the following as the missing conclusion,

So dark chocolate likes people,

the result would be invalid. However, I would have "violated" my responsibility to at least try to fill in the syllogism in such a way as to make it valid. Of course, sometimes it is just not possible to make the enthymeme valid no matter what proposition we might add. For example, no matter what missing premise you supply for the enthymeme,

All dogs are mammals because all mammals are animals,

you cannot make it valid.

Assignment 6.6. Translate the following enthymemes into standard-form categorical-syllogism forms and tell which order enthymeme it is. If it is invalid, tell which rule it breaks.

Example: "Sense perception is common to all, and therefore easy and no mark of Wisdom" (Aristotle, *Metaphysics*).

Solution: First order

Put into rough order:
Things that are common to all are easy and no mark
    of Wisdom (assumed)
Sense perception is common to all

Sense perception is easy and no mark of Wisdom

In standard form; AAA-1, Valid:
All <u>things that are common to all</u> are things that are easy
    and no mark of Wisdom
All <u>sense perceptions</u> are things that are common to all

All <u>sense perceptions</u> are things that are easy and no mark
of Wisdom

1. Apple computers are different, and different is good.

2. The jury should not believe his testimony, because he has perjured himself in the past.

*3. You always grab your purse and shopping list when you go to the store, but you left them on the kitchen counter.

4. You never study, so there is no way you are going to pass this next logic test.

5. You must surely understand what enthymemes are because this book explained it with lots of examples.

*6. Where there is smoke, there is fire, but there is no smoke in the basement.

7. Nobody buys VHS tapes anymore and no hipsters buy VHS tapes.

8. "The social contract is not binding on the sovereign, so there is no legal limitation on the sovereign's power" (Thomas Hobbes, *Leviathan*).

*9. "Lend them [the soldiers] a hand. Buy war bonds" (British WWI poster).

10. "All segregation statutes are unjust because segregation distorts the soul and damages the personality" (Martin Luther King Jr., "Letter from a Birmingham Jail").

11. "Yond Cassius has a lean and hungry look. He thinks too much. Such men are dangerous" (William Shakespeare, *Julius Caesar*).

*12. "There is no law against composing music when one has no ideas whatsoever. The music of Wagner, therefore, is perfectly legal" (Mark Twain).

13. "If [the glove] doesn't fit, you must acquit" (Attorney Johnny Cochran in the O. J. Simpson murder trial, 1995).

14. "Throughout history [women] have always been subordinated to men, and hence their dependency is not the result of a historical event" (Simone de Beauvoir, *The Second Sex*).

*15. "Our ideas reach no farther than our experience: We have no experience of divine attributes and operations: I need not conclude my syllogism: You can draw the inference yourself" (David Hume, *Dialogues Concerning Natural Religion*).

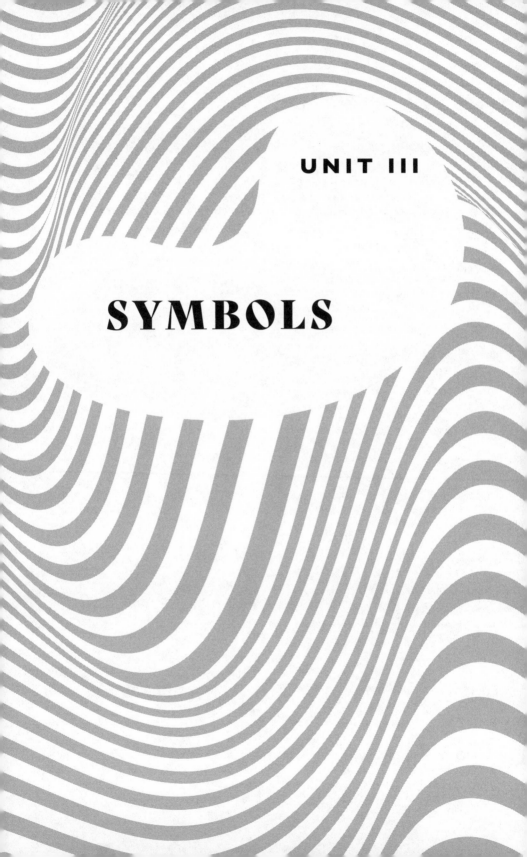

UNIT III

SYMBOLS

7

SYMBOLS AND STATEMENTS

Now that we have looked at ordinary language and a very stylized kind of argumentation, it is time to examine the underlying structure of arguments. In order to understand how a body bends and moves, it is useful to understand the bones and muscles without getting distracted by the skin. In the same way, in logic it is essential to examine the basic logical structure of arguments. To do this, we will need a set of symbols. These symbols will allow us to present, in a formal way, the underlying structure of everyday arguments. In this chapter we will be exploring *sentential* logic. That is, we will be dealing with arguments made up of whole sentences that express statements.[1]

In order to proceed, we need to agree on certain conventions. First, we must distinguish between simple and compound statements. A simple statement is something like "Jim is kind," while a compound statement is something like "Jim is kind and Jim is handsome." Simple statements do not have any other statements as components, while compound statements do.

Second, we will use capital letters to represent complete simple statements. For example, we might use the capital letter "K" to stand for the simple statement, "Jim is kind." Using "H" to stand for "Jim is handsome," if we wanted to say "Jim is kind and handsome," we could symbolize it as "K and H."

Third, sometimes we will want to refer to statements in general. To do this we will need "statement variables" and will use lowercase letters beginning in the middle of the alphabet with p, q, r, and so on. *These statement variables will be used to indicate any statement whatsoever—whether simple or compound.* It might be helpful to think of them like the "X" and "Y," which are used in math to stand for any number whatsoever.

---

[1]For our purposes in this chapter, we will equate "propositions" with the particular "statements" that express them and just use the word *statements*.

7.1 THE SYMBOLS FOR CONJUNCTION, NEGATION, AND DISJUNCTION

Conjunction. When we consider the example above, "K and H," we notice that we have formed a compound statement by connecting two simple statements with the word *and*. However, this word *and* has uses beyond being a connector. For example, the statement "Frankie and Johnny were lovers" is describing the relationship between Frankie and Johnny. The word *and* is not giving us a compound of the statements "Frankie was a lover" and "Johnny was a lover," but stating that Frankie and Johnny loved each other.

Given the ambiguity of the word *and*, we will use the symbol · to indicate conjunction.[2] So to symbolize "Jim is kind and Jim is handsome," we would write "K · H"—though we would read it out loud as "K and H."

Now since every statement is (by definition) true or false, we say it has a "truth value." In the case of a compound statement made up of the conjunction of two simple statements, the truth value will depend on the statements being conjoined (the "conjuncts"). So "K · H" will be true if Jim is kind *and* Jim is handsome. If Jim is kind, but homely, then the compound "K · H" would be false. If Jim is handsome, but mean, the compound would still be false. And, of course, if Jim is cruel and ugly the compound "K · H" is false. Now these conditions would be the same regardless of what statements we were joining with the · connector. That is, with any two statements the conjunction of them

would only be true if both of the statements were true. In any other case the conjunction would be false. If we show the truth values "true" and "false" with the letters "T" and "F," and use statement variables p and q to stand for any statement what-soever, we can define the dot symbol (·) as shown.

p	q	$p \cdot q$
T	T	T
T	F	F
F	T	F
F	F	F

This is called a "truth table," and it shows us all the possible truth-functional combinations that we can have in a conjunction. With any two statements, there are four possible truth values: (1) they are both true; (2) the first is true and the second is false; (3) the first is false and the second is true; or (4) they are both false. In all but the first of these possibilities, the conjunction of the two statements is false. Only if both statements are true is the conjunction true.

---

[2]Some logicians use the symbol ∧ or &.

We should note that in English there are many words that denote a conjunction. For example, when someone says "I don't mean to be critical, but . . ." we know that the next thing they are going to say will add a criticism. The word *but* is usually used to mean simply "and." Yet, *also, still, moreover,* and many, many more words have the logical function of conjunction. The compound statements they form will be true only if the individual statements of which they are made are true.

Negation. The sentence "It is not the case that Jim is kind" is also a compound statement. That is, it has as a component the simple statement "Jim is kind." The sentence "It is not the case that Jim is kind" is the negation of the statement "Jim is kind." In English we often simply put the word *not* in front of a statement to indicate the negation of the original statement. In symbolic logic we will use the symbol ~ and say "not" or "it is not the case that. . . ."[3] Since negation applies to only one statement, there are only two possible truth values: the negation will be false if the original statement is true, or true if the original statement is false. Using the statement variable *p* to stand for any statement whatsoever, the truth table that defines *not* is shown on the right.

p	~p
T	F
F	T

Disjunction. A third logical connection is *or*. Now in English we can use the word *or* in an exclusive or inclusive way. In the exclusive *or* we assert that one or the other is the case, *but not both*. So if I tell my granddaughters they can have cookies or ice cream, the unspoken assumption is "but not both." In logic, however, we will use *or* in the inclusive way to mean "at least one, possibly both." We will use the ∨ symbol for *or*, and we can define it with this truth table on the right.

p	q	p∨q
T	T	T
T	F	T
F	T	T
F	F	F

So the disjunction of two statements will be true in every case except if both of the statements are false.

But what if I want to tell my granddaughters "You can have cookies or ice cream, but not both"? Well, let's turn that sentence into symbols using "C" for "You have cookies" and "I" for "You have ice cream." In that case my instructions can be symbolized as follows:

(C ∨ I)	•	~	(C • I)
cookies or ice cream	but	not	both cookies and ice cream

---

[3]Some logicians use the symbol ¬.

Logical punctuation. This compound statement brings up an important point. In order to understand the proposition that a compound statement is asserting, it is necessary to use parentheses to make sense of the statement. For example, the compound statement

A ∨ B · C

is completely ambiguous. Is it claiming "(A or B) and C" or "A or (B and C)"? This compound statement has very different truth values depending on where we place the parentheses. For example, if I tell my granddaughters, "You can have cookies or ice cream and go to bed," what am I saying? If they stay up late eating cookies, have they done what I asked? Or should they have either cookies or ice cream for desert and then promptly go to bed?

This is especially true when we use negation. If we negate A and B, we get a very different truth value than when we negate A and negate B. For example, let "A" stand for "Alice was there" and "B" stand for "Bob was there." The statement, "Alice and Bob were not both there" would be written

~ (A · B)

while the statement "Alice was not there and Bob was not there" would be written

~ A · ~ B

The first of these two statements would still be true if one of them showed up—but not the second. So these are two very different claims and have different truth values. That is, it would take different circumstances to make them true.

One problem we sometimes have is that we think of the negation as being like the minus sign in math. In math, the sum of -(6 + 4) is the same as the sum of -6 + -4; in both cases the total is -10, so we can say that mathematically they mean the same thing. While the two compound statements above look like these two sets of numbers, the meanings are *not* the same. The truth tables for these two compound statements will be very different.

Assignment 7.1. Which of the following compound statements are true?

Example: ~ (Fire is hot · Water is wet)

Solution: False (Fire is hot and water is wet, so the conjunction in the parentheses is true, so the overall negation of it is false.)[4]

1. ~ Fire is cold · ~ Water is wet

2. ~ Fire is cold ∨ ~ Water is wet

*3. (Fire is hot · Water is dry) ∨ (Fire is hot · ~ Water is dry)

4. Water is wet · ~ (Fire is hot ∨ Water is dry)

5. ~ [~ (~ Fire is hot ∨ Water is wet) ∨ ~ (Sugar is sweet ∨ ~ Water is dry)]

*6. ~ [(~ Diamonds are hard · Sugar is sweet) ∨ ~ (~ Sugar is sweet · Fire is cold)]

7. [Diamonds are hard · (Water is wet ∨ Ice is cold)] · ~ [(Diamonds are hard · Water is wet) ∨ (Diamonds are hard · Ice is cold)]

For the following compound statements, assume that A, B, and C are true and X, Y, and Z are false.

Example: ~ [A · (X ∨ Y)]

Solution: True (Since X and Y are false, the part inside the parentheses is false. If either half of a conjunction is false, then the conjunction is false, so the part inside the brackets must be false—so the negation of the part inside the brackets must be true.)

8. ~ Y ∨ B

*9. (A · B) ∨ (X · Y)

10. (A ∨ B) · (X ∨ Y)

11. (A ∨ Z) · (X ∨ C)

*12. (X ∨ Y) · (X ∨ Z)

13. [Y ∨ (Z · X)] ∨ ~ [(Y ∨ Z) · (Y ∨ X)]

14. [B · (C ∨ A)] · ~ [(B · A) ∨ (B · C)]

*15. ~ { ~ [(A · ~ B) ∨ (Z · ~ Y)] · [(~ A ∨ X) ∨ (A ∨ ~ Z)]}

---

[4]Students have pointed out to me that there is an interesting debate about whether water itself is wet. You can Google "Is water wet?" to read more. For the purpose of this assignment, we will assume this proposition to be true.

7.2 CONDITIONALS OR HYPOTHETICALS (IMPLICATION)

In everyday language we use hypothetical or conditional ("if . . . then . . .")
statements in many different ways:

1. If Francis is the pope, then he is Catholic.

2. If you drop a ball, then it will fall.

3. If all dogs are mammals and all mammals are animals, then all dogs
   are animals.

The first of these uses is a definition, the second is a scientific claim, and the
third is a deductive argument. But there is one common characteristic to each
of these statements: the second part (called the "consequent") is claimed to
follow from the first part (the "antecedent"). For these three statements to be
true, it cannot be the case that the antecedent is true and the consequent false.
For example, if you drop a ball and it flies up in the air, then the compound
statement "If you drop a ball, then it will fall" is false. Similarly, since the pope
is the head of the Roman Catholic Church, if Francis is the pope, then by
definition he is Catholic. So it is not possible for the first half of this hypothetical to be true without the second half also being true.

In these "if . . . then . . ." compound statements, we say the
consequent is implied by the antecedent, so there is an essential relation of implication between the two. The
statement is not saying that the antecedent *is* true—only that
if it is true, the consequent will also be true. We will use the
symbol, → for the "if . . . then . . ." compound statement[5] and
the truth table looks here.

Notice that the compound hypothetical statement is true in every case
except where the antecedent is true and the consequent false. This means in
those cases where the antecedent is *false* the overall compound statement is
always true. Now this seems odd. Why would the entire statement always be
true when the first half is false? Take a silly example like "If we lose the conference finals tomorrow, then I will eat my hat!" The reason someone makes a
statement like this is because they are so sure the antecedent will be false, they
can promise *anything* as a consequent without making a false statement. Their
original claim would only be false if they did lose and then did not eat their hat.

---

[5]Some logicians use the symbol ⊃.

Assignment 7.2. Which of the following compound statements is true?

Example: ~ (Fire is cold → Water is dry)

Solution: False (The part inside the parentheses begins "if [false]. . . ." A hypothetical that begins with a false statement is always true. But then the entire thing is negated making the entire compound statement false.)

1. Fire is cold → Ice is warm

2. Fire is cold → Ice is cold

*3. Water is wet → ~ Diamonds are hard

4. (Water is dry → Diamonds are soft) → Sugar is sour

5. [The pope is Catholic → (Fire is cold · Water is dry)] → [(The pope is Catholic → Fire is cold) ∨ (The pope is Catholic → Diamonds are soft)]

*6. [(Sugar is sweet · Diamonds are soft) ∨ (~ Sugar is sweet · ~ Diamonds are soft)] → [(Sugar is sweet → Diamonds are soft) · (Diamonds are soft → Sugar is sweet)]

7. [(The pope is Catholic → ~ Fire is hot) → Ice is cold] → Diamonds are soft

For the following compound statements, assume that A, B, and C are true and X, Y, and Z are false.

Example: ~ [A · (X ∨ Y)] → Z

Solution: False (Since X and Y are false, the part inside the parentheses is false. If either half of a conjunction is false, then the conjunction is false, so the part inside the brackets must be false. So the negation of the part inside the brackets must be true. This means that overall we end up with "if true then false," which is false.)

8. Z → X

*9. (X → Y) → Z

10. [A → (A · Z)] ∨ (~ A · ~ Z)

11. [(B · X) ∨ (~ B · ~ X)] → [(B → X) · (X → B)]

*12. B → ~ C

13. $[A \rightarrow (X \cdot Z)] \rightarrow [(A \rightarrow X) \vee (A \rightarrow Y)]$

14. $[(B \cdot Y) \vee (\sim B \cdot \sim Y)] \rightarrow [(B \rightarrow Y) \cdot (Y \rightarrow B)]$

*15. $[(A \rightarrow \sim B) \rightarrow A] \rightarrow Y$

7.3 BICONDITIONALS

p	q	p ↔ q
T	T	T
T	F	F
F	T	F
F	F	T

There is one more truth-functional symbol we must discuss. We can say that *two statements are materially biconditional if they have the same truth value*—that is, they are both true or they are both false. We express this notion by using the symbol ↔, which we read as "if and only if."[6] Here is the truth table that defines this.

For example:

$p \leftrightarrow \sim \sim p$

is asserting that in every case where p is true, $\sim \sim p$ will also be true and every case where p is false, $\sim \sim p$ will be false.

SUMMARY OF TRUTH TABLES						
p	q	p · q	p ∨ q	~p	p → q	p ↔ q
T	T	T	T	F	T	T
T	F	F	T		F	F
F	T	F	T	T	T	F
F	F	F	F		T	T

Assignment 7.3. Which of the following compound statements are true?

Example: Water is wet ↔ ~ Water is dry

Solution: True

1. ~ (The pope is Catholic · Fire is hot) ↔ (~ The pope is Catholic ∨ ~ Fire is hot)

2. ~ (The pope is Catholic ∨ Fire is hot) ↔ (~ The pope is Catholic · ~ Fire is hot)

---

[6]Some logicians use the symbol ≡. Also, the English phrase "if and only if" is sometimes abbreviated "iff."

*3. [Water is wet ∨ (Diamonds are hard · Ice is cold)] ↔ [(Water is wet ∨ Diamonds are hard) · (Water is wet ∨ Ice is cold)]

4. (Fire is cold → Water is wet) → (Diamonds are hard ↔ ~ Water is wet)

5. [(The pope is Catholic ↔ Fire is cold) ∨ Sugar is sweet] → (Ice is cold · ~ Fire is hot)

*6. ~ [The pope is Catholic → (Fire is cold · Water is dry)] ↔ [(The pope is Catholic → Fire is cold) ∨ (The pope is Catholic → ~ Diamonds are soft)]

7. [Honey is sticky ↔ (Diamonds are hard · Water is dry)] · Ice cream is yummy

For the following compound statements, assume that A, B, and C are true and X, Y, and Z are false.

Example: ~ [A · (X ↔ B)] → Z

Solution: False (Since X and B have different truth values, the part inside the parentheses is false. If either half of a conjunction is false, then the conjunction is false, so the part inside the brackets must be false. So the negation of the part inside the brackets must be true. This means that overall we end up with "if true then false," which is false.)

8. (A → Z) ↔ A

*9. Z ↔ (~ B → ~ Z)

10. (A · Z) ↔ (~ A · ~ Z)

11. (B ↔ X) ↔ [(B → X) · (X → B)]

*12. Z ↔ ~ C

13. (A → B) ↔ (~ A ∨ B)

14. [(B · Z) ∨ (~ A · ~ X)] ↔ [(B → Y) · (Y → B)]

*15. ~ (A ∨ Z) ↔ (~ A · ~ Z)

7.4 UNPACKING COMPOUND STATEMENTS

To this point we have been using simple statements whose truth or falsehood was either given or obvious. But what are we to do if we are given a compound statement and we don't know the truth value of the simple statements that make it up? In that case we can use a truth table to "unpack" the compound statement. We begin by writing out the statement on the right-hand side of the paper and then drawing a line under it and to the left of it, like this:

	~(A ∨ B) ↔ (~A · ~B)

Now, we ask ourselves, What would I need to know in order to know whether this entire compound statement is true or false? To answer that question, we must determine which symbol applies to the *entire* compound statement. In this example, the first ~ applies only to what is inside the first set of parentheses (i.e., "A ∨ B"). The second and third ~ apply only to the individual letters, while the · connects them. The one symbol that applies to the entire compound statement is the ↔. To know whether the complete compound statement is true or false, we would need to know each half of the material biconditional—that is, what is on each side of the ↔ sign. If the parts on each side have the same truth value, then the overall compound statement will be true—otherwise it will be false. In essence, we are treating "~ (A ∨ B)" as if it were *p* (remember, *p* can stand for *any* proposition whatsoever), and "~ A · ~ B" as if it were *q*. So to the left of the compound statement above we would write each of these separated by another line as follows:

(acting as "p")	(acting as "q")	(acting as "p ↔ q")
~(A ∨ B)	~A · ~B	~(A ∨ B) ↔ (~A · ~B)

We now know that the truth value of the entire compound statement " ~ (A ∨ B) ↔ (~ A · ~ B)" depends on whether the two component statements have the same truth value.

So now let us move to "~ A · ~ B"—what would we need to know in order to know whether *that* is true? Let's write that to the left of what we have separated by a line:

(acting as "p")	(acting as "q")		(acting as "p · q")	
~A	~B	~(A ∨ B)	~A · ~B	~(A ∨ B) ↔ (~A · ~B)

We now know if "~ A · ~ B" is true—it is true if both ~ A and ~ B are true. What about ~ (A ∨ B)? Well, to know whether that statement is true or false we would need to know the truth value of "A ∨ B," which we write to the left:

(acting as "p")			(acting as "~p")		
A ∨ B	~A	~B	~(A ∨ B)	~A · ~B	~(A ∨ B) ↔ (~A · ~B)

To know what "A ∨ B" or "~ A" or " ~ B" are, we need to know the truth values of the simple statements A and B. As a convention, we will always put them in alphabetical order and write them on the far left side:

A B	A ∨ B	~A	~B	~(A ∨ B)	~A · ~B	~(A ∨ B) ↔ (~A · ~B)

There are four possible truth values for these simple statements, so we write them under the simple statements to the left of the other elements as follows:

A B	A ∨ B	~A	~B	~(A ∨ B)	~A · ~B	~(A ∨ B) ↔ (~A · ~B)
T T						
T F						
F T						
F F						

Now that we have completely "unpacked" the compound statement from right to left, we can move from left to right filling in the truth table. This will give us:

A B	A ∨ B	~A	~B	~(A ∨ B)	~A · ~B	~(A ∨ B) ↔ (~A · ~B)
T T	T	F	F	F	F	T
T F	T	F	T	F	F	T
F T	T	T	F	F	F	T
F F	F	T	T	T	T	T

So this truth table shows us that regardless of the truth or falsity of A and B, "~ (A ∨ B)" and "~ A · ~ B" are materially biconditional.

Notice that to do a truth table we start on the right and ask ourselves, What do I need to know in order to know whether this proposition is true or false?

and we write what is needed to the left (separated by a line). We continue to do this until we are down to the "simples"—the simple statements or statement variables. Then we fill in all the possible combinations of true and false. (If there are two simples, that will be four possibilities.) Finally we go from left to right using our truth tables to determine the truth value of each column until we finally arrive at the far right-hand column—the compound statement we were analyzing.

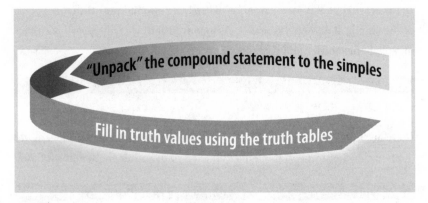

If a compound statement includes three simple statements, we will need to double the truth table shown above. That is, we will need to examine all the cases listed for two statements where the third is true and all the cases for the two statements where the third is false. Such a truth table will look like this: (Again, always put the "simples" in alphabetical order, left to right.)

For 3 statements	For 2 statements	For 1 statement				
A	B	C	A ∨ B	~(A ∨ B)	~C	~(A ∨ B) • ~C
T	T	T	T	F	F	F
T	T	F	T	F	T	F
T	F	T	T	F	F	F
T	F	F	T	F	T	F
F	T	T	T	F	F	F
F	T	F	T	F	T	F
F	F	T	F	T	F	F
F	F	F	F	T	T	T

If there were four different statements, it would require sixteen rows; if five, thirty-two rows; and so on.

Assignment 7.4. Use a truth table to "unpack" the following compound statements.

Example: $(C \lor I) \cdot \sim (C \cdot I)$

Solution:

C	I	C·I	C∨I	~(C·I)	(C∨I)·~(C·I)
T	T	T	T	F	F
T	F	F	T	T	T
F	T	F	T	T	T
F	F	F	F	T	F

  1. $\sim (A \lor \sim A)$

  2. $(A \lor B) \rightarrow \sim (A \cdot B)$

*3. $(A \lor B) \rightarrow (C \cdot B)$

  4. $\sim (C \lor I) \cdot \sim (C \cdot I)$

  5. $(L \rightarrow M) \leftrightarrow (\sim L \lor M)$

*6. $[D \rightarrow (D \rightarrow E)] \rightarrow E$

  7. $F \rightarrow [(F \rightarrow G) \rightarrow G]$

  8. $(H \cdot I) \cdot (H \rightarrow \sim I)$

*9. $J \rightarrow [\sim J \rightarrow (K \lor \sim K)]$

10. $(L \rightarrow L) \rightarrow M$

11. $[N \cdot (O \lor P)] \leftrightarrow [(N \cdot O) \lor (N \cdot P)]$

*12. $[\sim Q \rightarrow (R \lor \sim Q)] \rightarrow (R \lor Q)$

13. $S \rightarrow [S \rightarrow (T \cdot \sim T)]$

14. $U \leftrightarrow [U \lor (U \rightarrow V)]$

*15. $W \leftrightarrow [W \cdot (W \rightarrow X)]$

7.5 STATEMENTS AND STATEMENT FORMS

In order to clearly see how statements are used to make up arguments, we must first make a distinction between statements and statement forms. A *statement form is a combination of logical symbols and statement variables.* When the statement variables (which we identify by using lowercase letters beginning with *p*) are replaced with statements (for which we use capital letters), the result will be a compound statement. So "*p* $\lor$ *q*" is a statement form because if we substitute statements for p and q, the result will be a compound statement. Now the statements we use to substitute for p and q need not be simple statements. Both of the following are *substitution instances* of the statement form, "$p \vee q$":

1. Susan is hungry or Susan is thirsty

2. If Susan has any more soup, then Susan will be sick or Susan will take a drink if and only if the drink is Coke.

So, in symbols,

H $\vee$ T

and

$(S \rightarrow B) \vee (D \leftrightarrow C)$

are both substitution instances of $p \vee q$. But while these are both *substitution instances* of the statement form, "$p \vee q$," this statement form is the *specific form* of the compound statement "H $\vee$ T."

So, as long as the logical connectors are kept the same and the same statement is used for each statement variable, any replacement of statement variables by statements will be a *substitution instance* of the statement form. The statement form that matches up exactly to the original compound statement with each statement replaced by a statement variable will be the *specific form* of the compound statement. So,

A $\cdot$ B

$(C \rightarrow D) \cdot \sim [E \leftrightarrow \sim (F \vee G)]$ are all substitution $p \cdot q$
                                          instances of

(H $\vee$ I) $\cdot$ ~J

but

$p \cdot q$ is the specific form of   A $\cdot$ B

As we examine statement forms, we find three kinds: tautologies, contradictions, and contingencies. A statement form that has only true substitution instances is a tautology. Consider the statement form "$p \vee \sim p$." If we do a truth table on this and "unpack" it we will find this:

p	~p	$p \vee$ ~p
T	F	T
F	T	T

The final column is all true—and no matter what statement we "plug in" for the p, the same result will happen. In other words, no matter what statement we make—simple or compound—to assert it or its negation will always be true.[7] On the other hand, the statement form, "$p \cdot \sim p$" will have only false substitution instances. The truth table following makes it clear that this statement form is a contradiction:

p	$\sim p$	$p \cdot \sim p$
T	F	F
F	T	F

Of course, in most statement forms the truth value depends on the individual statement variables that make it up. That is, it is contingent—maybe true, maybe false. So the truth of the statement form "$p \cdot q$" depends on what p and q are as we can see in the last column on the right below.

p	q	$p \cdot q$
T	T	T
T	F	F
F	T	F
F	F	F

---

[7]Aristotle called this the "law of excluded middle": for any statement whatsoever, it is either true or false.

Assignment 7.5. For each statement in the left-hand column, indicate which of the statement forms in the right-hand column have that statement as a substitution instance. What is the specific form of the given statements?

Example: (C ∨ P) · ~ (C · P)

Solution: It is a substitution instance of a, e, f, and m (but not j; j does not have a ~). The specific form of this statement is m.

1. A · ~B

2. B · A

*3. (A · B) ∨ A

4. (A → B) → C

5. [(A → B) → C] → D

*6. (A ∨ B) · (A · B)

7. (A ∨ B) · ~ (B · B)

8. (A → B) · (B → A)

*9. [(A → A) → A] → A

10. (A ∨ B) · (C · ~D)

11. [(C ∨ ~D) → ~ (A · B)] ∨ ~ (~A → B)

*12. (A → B) · [(B → (A ↔ B)]

13. (A ∨ B) → ~ [C ∨ (A ↔ B)]

14. [~A → ~ (B · C)] · ~ [A → (D → ~E)]

*15. ~ [A → (B · C)] ∨ (C ↔ A)

a. p · q

b. p → q

c. p ∨ q

d. p ↔ q

e. p · ~q

f. (p ∨ q) · r

g. (p · q) ∨ p

h. (p → q) · (q → p)

i. (p → p) → p

j. (p ∨ q) · (p · q)

k. [(p → q) → r] → s

l. [(p → q) → p] → r

m. (p ∨ q) · ~ (p · q)

n. (p → q) ∨ r

o. (p · q) → r

8

SYMBOLS AND ARGUMENTS

8.1 ARGUMENTS AND ARGUMENT FORMS

We are now ready to examine arguments and argument forms. *An argument form is a series of statement forms such that when statements are substituted for the statement variables, the result will be an argument.*

For example,

$p \rightarrow q$

p

$\therefore q^1$

is an argument form because if we substitute statements for p and q, the result will be an argument. Now the statements we use to substitute for p and q need not be simple statements. Both of the following are *substitution instances* of the argument form above:

If I water my lawn, then the lawn is wet

I water my lawn

$\therefore$ The lawn is wet

If I water my lawn and don't fertilize it, then it won't turn green and I will
   be disappointed

I water my lawn and don't fertilize it

$\therefore$ [My lawn] won't turn green and I will be disappointed

---

[1]The symbol $\therefore$ means "therefore"—just as we sometimes use a line to mean "therefore."

So, in symbols,

$$L \rightarrow W$$
$$L$$
$$\therefore W$$

and

$$(W \cdot \sim F) \rightarrow (\sim G \cdot D)$$
$$W \cdot \sim F$$
$$\therefore \sim G \cdot D$$

are both substitution instances of the argument form above. But while these are both *substitution instances* of the argument form above, that argument form is the *specific form* of the argument.

$$L \rightarrow W$$
$$L$$
$$\therefore W$$

So, as long as the logical connectors are kept the same and the same statement is used for each statement variable, any replacement of statement variables by statements will be a *substitution instance* of the argument form. The argument form that matches up exactly to the original argument with each statement replaced by a statement variable will be the *specific form* of the argument. So,

$$L \rightarrow W$$
$$L$$
$$\therefore W$$

		$p \rightarrow q$
$(W \cdot \sim F) \rightarrow (\sim G \cdot D)$	are all substitution instances of	p
$W \cdot \sim F$		$\therefore q$
$\therefore \sim G \cdot D$		
but		
$p \rightarrow q$	is the specific form of	$L \rightarrow W$
p		L
$\therefore q$		$\therefore W$

This leads us to a very important point. *Any substitution instance of a valid argument form is valid*. The argument form above is valid. (It even has a name, *modus ponens.*) Thus, both of the substitution instances are also valid. It does not matter what "L," "W," "F," "G," and "D" are—these arguments are valid.[2] If the premises are true in either of these arguments, the conclusion *must be* true.

On the other hand, *a substitution instance of an invalid argument form may or may not be invalid.* Consider the following, obviously invalid, argument form:

p

q

$\therefore r$

If we replace each statement variable here with a simple statement, we would get something like

A

B

$\therefore$ C

or in ordinary language,

Alligators are dangerous

Birds have feathers

$\therefore$ Cats never purr

which is clearly invalid. (The premises here are true and the conclusion false.) But remember that "p," "q," and "r" can stand for *any statement whatsoever.* So substituting "D ∨ E" for p, "~ D" for q, and "E" for r, this valid argument would be a substitution instance of the same argument form:

D ∨ E

~ D

$\therefore$ E

or

He is on a diet or he will eat anything

He is not on a diet

$\therefore$ He will eat anything

---

[2]Of course whether these arguments are *sound* or *persuasive* does depend on what statements these capital letters represent.

So a substitution instance of a valid argument form must be valid. But a substitution instance of an invalid argument form could be valid or invalid, depending on what statements are substituted for the variables.

Assignment 8.1. For each argument in the left-hand column indicate which of the argument forms in the right-hand column have that argument as a substitution instance. What is the specific form of the given argument?

Example: $(C \cdot P) \to (U \cdot S)$

$C \cdot P$

$\therefore (U \cdot S)$

Solution: It is a substitution instance of a. The specific form of this argument is not given.

1. $A \to \sim B$
   $\sim B$
   $\therefore A$

2. $(C \lor D) \to \sim (A \cdot C)$
   $\sim \sim (A \cdot C)$
   $\therefore \sim (C \lor \sim D)$

3. $\sim [A \lor (B \leftrightarrow C)] \lor [(A \lor B) \to \sim (C \cdot D)]$
   $\sim \sim [A \lor (B \leftrightarrow C)]$
   $\therefore (A \lor B) \to \sim (C \cdot D)$

4. $(A \lor B) \to (B \cdot A)$
   $\therefore [(A \lor B) \to (B \cdot A)] \lor (C \leftrightarrow D)$

5. $(A \lor B) \to (C \cdot D)$
   $\therefore (A \lor B) \to [(A \lor B) \cdot (C \cdot D)]$

6. $[M \to (\sim N \cdot O)] \to (O \lor M)$
   $[M \to (\sim N \cdot O)]$
   $\therefore O \lor M$

7. $A \lor B$
   $\sim A$
   $\therefore B$

8. $(\sim A \to B) \cdot [(C \lor \sim D) \to (E \cdot C)]$
   $\sim A \lor (C \lor \sim D)$
   $\therefore B \lor (E \cdot C)$

*9. $(\sim A \to B) \cdot [(C \cdot \sim D) \to \sim (E \cdot F)]$
   $\therefore \sim A \to B$

10. $(\sim H \to I) \cdot [(J \lor \sim K) \lor \sim (L \cdot C)]$
   $\therefore \{(\sim H \to I) \cdot [(J \lor \sim K) \lor \sim (L \cdot C)]\} \lor (U \cdot S)$

a. $p \to q$
   p
   $\therefore q$

b. $p \to q$
   $q \to r$
   $\therefore p \to r$

c. $(p \to q) \cdot (r \to s)$
   $p \lor r$
   $\therefore q \lor s$

d. $p \cdot q$
   $\therefore p$

e. p
   $\therefore p \lor q$

f. $p \to q$
   q
   $\therefore p$

g. $p \to q$
   $\sim q$
   $\therefore \sim p$

h. $p \lor q$
   $\sim p$
   $\therefore q$

i. $p \to q$
   $\therefore p \to (p \cdot q)$

j. $p \to q$
   $\therefore p$

8.2 USING TRUTH TABLES TO TEST ARGUMENTS FOR VALIDITY

A valid argument is one where if the premises are true, the conclusion *must* be true. So if we could examine every possible case where the premises are true and we find that the conclusion is also true, then the argument would be valid. Using truth tables we can determine if this is the case. Take an argument like this:

> My granddaughters may have cookies or ice cream, but not both
> They each have cookies
> _____
> They may not have ice cream

We could symbolize this as

$(C \lor I) \cdot \sim (C \cdot I)$
C
$\therefore \sim I$

So how can we tell whether this argument is valid? Well, let's try a truth table. First we write down the premises and the conclusion separated by lines as follows:

We have now written out the argument with the premises and the conclusion, so we mark it off with a double line.[3]

Now we ask ourselves what we would need to know in order to know whether each of these columns was true or false. We continue to ask this and write the answer to the left until we get to the "simples"—the individual statement forms without any logical connecters. That is, we unpack the argument to the left just as we did when "unpacking" statements and statement forms.[4] In each

---

[3] We do this to remind ourselves that the part on the right-hand side of the double line is the argument and the part on the left hand side is the "unpacking" we have done to determine the truth value of the premise(s) and conclusion.

[4] Again, always put the "simples" at the far left side in alphabetical order from left to right.

column we ask, What do I need to know to determine the truth value here?
and we write it to the left. We continue doing this until we get to the simples.
So it would look like this:

C I	C • I	C ∨ I	~(C • I)	(C ∨ I) • ~(C • I)	C	∴ ~I

Then we fill in the truth table as we did in the previous chapter:

C I	C • I	C ∨ I	~(C • I)	(C ∨ I) • ~(C • I)	C	∴ ~I
T T	T	T	F	F	T	F
T F	F	T	T	T	T	T
F T	F	T	T	T	F	F
F F	F	F	T	F	F	T

We have now considered every possible combination there is. There are no
other truth-functional possibilities for this argument. So we look and see, *Is
there any case where the premises are true and the conclusion false?* If so, the
argument is invalid; if not, the argument is valid. That is, if the premises are
true, the conclusion *must* be true. We look at the truth table and we see that
only in line two are the premises both true, so we circle them and draw a line
pointing to the truth value of the conclusion, as follows:

C I	C • I	C ∨ I	~(C • I)	(C ∨ I) • ~(C • I)	C	∴ ~I
T T	T	T	F	F	T	F
T F	F	T	T	ⓣ──────────────────ⓣ──────▶		T
F T	F	T	T	T	F	F
F F	F	F	T	F	F	T

We have now considered all the possible combinations, and there is only one
case where the premises are true—line two—and in that case the conclusion
is also true. This argument is valid.

Let's try another example. Consider this argument:

If it rained last night, my lawn will be wet

My lawn is wet
_____

It rained last night

We could symbolize this as

R → W

W

∴ R

This truth table will be very simple:

R	W	R → W	W	∴ R
T	T	T	T	T
T	F	F	F	T
F	T	T	T	F
F	F	T	F	F

Now we don't really have to write R and W twice here. But let's agree to always write the complete argument to the right of the double line and then "unpack" it to the left until we get down to the simples.

In this truth table we see that in lines one and three the premises are true, so we circle the truth values of the premises here and look to see whether the conclusion is also true:

R	W	R → W	W	∴ R	
T	T	(T)	(T) → T		
T	F	F	F	T	
F	T	(T)	(T) → F		x—invalid
F	F	T	F	F	

Since line three shows that it is possible for the premises to be true and the conclusion to be false, we put an "x" next to it and write "invalid." (After all, my lawn could be wet from the sprinklers, even if it did not rain.)

Let's try one final example:

> If Susan continues her hitting slump, then if Nancy hits leadoff then Julie will have to hit cleanup. Nancy does hit leadoff. So if Julie hits cleanup, then Susan will continue her hitting slump.

In symbols this becomes

S → (N → J)

N

∴ J → S

Since there are three statements here, our truth table will have eight lines. Line five of the truth table shows this argument to be invalid.

J N S	N → J	S → (N → J)	N	∴ J → S
T T T	T	T	T	T
T T F	T	T	T	F	x—invalid
T F T	T	T	F	T
T F F	T	T	F	F
F T T	F	F	T	T
F T F	F	T	T	T
F F T	T	T	F	T
F F F	T	T	F	T

Assignment 8.2a. Use a truth table to determine the validity or invalidity of the following arguments.

Example: (A ∨ B) → (B · A)
                ∴ (A → B) · (B → A)

Solution: Valid: There are two possibilities where the premise is true and in both cases the conclusion is also true.

A B	A ∨ B	B · A	A → B	B → A	(A ∨ B) → (B · A)	∴ (A → B) · (B → A)
T T	T	T	T	T	T	T
T F	T	F	F	T	F	F
F T	T	F	T	F	F	F
F F	F	F	T	T	T	T

1. (E ∨ F) → (E · F)
   E · F
   ∴ E ∨ F

2. C → D
   ~ D
   ∴ ~ C ∨ D

*3. A ∨ B
   A
   ∴ ~ B

4. (G ∨ H) → I
    I → (G · H)
    ∴ (G ∨ H) → (G · H)

5. J
    ∴ J → K

*6. L → (M · N)
    ~ N ∨ ~ M
    ∴ ~ L

7. O → P
    P → O
    ∴ P ∨ ~ P

8. Q ∨ (R · ~ R)
    Q
    ∴ ~ (R · ~ Q)

*9. S ∨ T
    (S · T) → T
    ~ S
    ∴ T

10. (W ∨ X) → (W · X)
    ~ (W ∨ X)
    ∴ ~ (W · X)

Assignment 8.2b. Put the following argument into symbols and then use a truth table to determine their validity or invalidity.

Example: If a student passes logic, then that student will be better prepared to take the LSAT. If a student is better prepared to take
the LSAT, that student will be more likely to get into a good
law school. So if a student passes logic, that student will be
more likely to get into a good law school.

Solution: S → B
                 B → L
                 ∴ S → L

Valid: There are four possibilities where the premises are true and in all four cases the conclusion is also true:

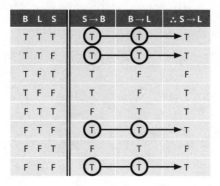

B	L	S	S→B	B→L	∴ S→L
T	T	T	T	T	T
T	T	F	T	T	T
T	F	T	T	F	F
T	F	F	T	F	T
F	T	T	F	T	T
F	T	F	T	T	T
F	F	T	F	T	F
F	F	F	T	T	T

1. If he eats a chocolate bar or a donut, then he will eat both a chocolate bar and a donut. So if he eats a chocolate bar then he will eat a donut and if he eats a donut, he will eat a chocolate bar.

2. If it is sunny, then he will put on sunblock, but he doesn't put on sunblock, so it must not be sunny.

*3. If I buy a lamp and a desk, then I will buy a lamp and not a desk. I buy a lamp. So I buy a desk.

4. It is hot or it is the case that it is cold or it is not cold. It *is* hot. So it is not the case that it is cold and not cold.

5. If Superman is strong and brave, then either Superman is strong or he is not brave. But Superman is brave, so he must be strong.

*6. If Batman is either crazy or good, then he is crazy *and* good. So if Batman is crazy then he is good and if he is good then he is crazy.

7. If I eat a big meal, then I get heartburn. Therefore if I eat a big meal, then I eat a big meal and get heartburn.

8. If this assignment is easy or fun, then it will be easy and fun. This assignment is easy and fun, therefore it is easy or fun.

*9. If you do well at logic, then you will enjoy this class. If you enjoy this class, then you do well in logic. So you will enjoy this class.

10. If you either win or die trying, then you win and die trying. It is not the case that you either win or die trying. Therefore it is not the case that you win and die trying.

8.3 PROVING VALIDITY

While the truth-table method is effective at testing for validity, it can get un-wieldy. Consider the following argument:

If Alice goes to work, then Betty gets the day off
If Betty gets the day off, then Charlie will spend the day with Betty
If Charlie will spend the day with Betty, then Charlie will go with Betty to
     visit Donna
If Charlie will go with Betty to visit Donna, then Edward will be upset
Alice goes to work
Therefore, Edward will be upset

In symbols this is

$A \rightarrow B$
$B \rightarrow C$
$C \rightarrow D$
$D \rightarrow E$
A
$\therefore E$

To prove this is valid, we would need a truth table with thirty-two rows. This means lots of chances to misread a line or get a truth value wrong. But what if we find a simpler way of proving validity? To do this, we divide this argument into a series of smaller arguments. Consider the argument form called *hypothetical syllogism*:

$p \rightarrow q$
$q \rightarrow r$
$\therefore p \rightarrow r$

We could do a truth table of eight lines and easily prove this valid. This means every substitution instance of this argument form is also valid. So we know that if the first two lines of this argument,

$A \rightarrow B$
$B \rightarrow C$

are true, then

$A \rightarrow C$

must also be true. Using this substitution and combining it with the third premise of the original argument, we can create an argument as follows:

A → C (which we got from using *hypothetical syllogism* on the first and
   second premises)

C → D

∴ A → D

We can take the conclusion from *this* little argument and combine it with the
fourth premise of the original argument and create this argument:

A → D (which we got from using *hypothetical syllogism* above)

D → E

∴ A → E

We can now combine the conclusion from this argument with the original
fifth premise. Thus, we make an argument using the argument form known
as *modus ponens* to create a final "mini-argument":

A → E (which we got from using *hypothetical syllogism* above)

A

∴ E

So, if the original premises are true, and all the intermediate argument forms
are valid, the final conclusion must also be true. We will consider which argument forms are valid in a moment. But first, let's organize our argument by
numbering it:

   1. A → B
   2. B → C
   3. C → D
   4. D → E
   5. A /∴ E

We will always put the conclusion on the final line after a forward slash (/) and
the symbol for "therefore" (∴). We do this so we never get confused and treat
the conclusion as one of the premises.

   Now we can begin to give a formal proof of validity for this argument.
When we write out a formal logical proof, we begin by adding a line six. This
is a line that comes from two of the previous lines. We cite the lines we used
to conclude line six and the rule of inference that justifies that conclusion:

   6. A → C 1, 2, Hypothetical Syllogism (or "H. S." for short)

Now we know that if lines one and two are true, then line six must be true.

Then we add line seven using lines six and three and the same rule of inference as follows:

    7. A → D 6, 3, H. S.

Notice that we list the lines we used, "6, 3," in the order they were *used* to form a hypothetical syllogism that led to the statement on line seven.

    We do this same step one more time and get

    8. A → E 7, 4, H. S.

Finally, we use the *modus ponens* (M. P.) rule of inference to combine line eight with line five and conclude

    9. E 8, 5, M. P.

Which is what we were trying to prove. The completed formal proof of validity looks like this:

    1. A → B

    2. B → C

    3. C → D

    4. D → E

    5. A / ∴ E

    6. A → C   1, 2, H. S.

    7. A → D   6, 3, H. S.

    8. A → E   7, 4, H. S.

    9. E   8, 5, M. P.

In this formal proof of validity, lines one through five were the original premises (with the conclusion placed on the side of the last line) and everything that followed was justified by using a basic rule of inference and lines above it. So if lines one through five are true, then line six must be true; if lines six and three are true, then line seven must be true; if lines seven and four are true, then line eight must be true; if lines eight and five are true, then the conclusion, "E," must be true. So if the premises are true, the conclusion *must* be true. We can see this clearly, using these intermediate steps to get us there. Hence the argument is valid.

We will use nine basic argument forms as Rules of Inference in constructing formal proofs of validity, using the method outlined above. Each of these nine can be easily proved by using a truth table.

RULES OF INFERENCE

Modus Ponens (M. P.)

$p \rightarrow q$

p

$\therefore q$

Modus Tollens (M. T.)

$p \rightarrow q$

$\sim q$

$\therefore \sim p$

Hypothetical Syllogism (H. S.)

$p \rightarrow q$

$q \rightarrow r$

$\therefore p \rightarrow r$

Disjunctive Syllogism (D. S.)

$p \vee q$ or $p \vee q$

$\sim p$ $\sim q$

$\therefore q$ $\therefore p$

Constructive Dilemma (C. D.)

$(p \rightarrow q) \cdot (r \rightarrow s)$

$p \vee r$

$\therefore q \vee s$

Conjunction (Conj.)

p

q

$\therefore p \cdot q$

Simplification (Simp.)

$p \cdot q$ or $p \cdot q$

$\therefore p$ $\therefore q$

Addition (Add.)

p or p

$\therefore p \vee q$ $\therefore q \vee p$

Absorption (Abs.)

$p \rightarrow q$

$\therefore p \rightarrow (p \cdot q)$

Assignment 8.3a. For each of the valid arguments below, state the rule of inference that justifies the conclusion.

Example: $\sim (A \cdot B) \rightarrow (C \vee D)$

              $\sim (A \cdot B)$

              $\therefore (C \vee D)$

Solution: M. P. (though it looks complicated, if p is replaced by "$\sim (A \cdot B)$" and q is replaced by "$(C \vee D)$," this is the *modus ponens* argument form.

1. $(B \rightarrow C) \cdot \sim (A \vee B) / \therefore (B \rightarrow C)$

2. $(D \vee E) \rightarrow \sim [(F \vee G) \leftrightarrow (D \cdot C)]$
   $\sim C \rightarrow (D \vee E) / \therefore \sim C \rightarrow \sim [(F \vee G) \leftrightarrow (D \cdot C)]$

*3. $(\sim H \rightarrow I) \cdot [J \rightarrow (K \cdot L)]$

4. $\sim H \vee J / \therefore I \vee (K \cdot L)$
   $M \rightarrow (\sim N \cdot O)$

5. [M → (~ N · O)] → (O ∨ M) /∴ O ∨ M
   1. [(P ∨ Q) → ~ (P · Q)] · (P → R) /∴ (P → R)

*6. (S ∨ T) → ~ [U ∨ (S ↔ T)]
   /∴ {(S ∨ T) → ~ [U ∨ (S ↔ T)]} ∨ [(U ∨ S) → ~ (T · V)]

7. (W · X) → ~ (Y ∨ Z)
   ~ ~ (Y ∨ Z) /∴ ~ (W · X)

8. A ∨ (B ↔ C)
   ~ (B ↔ C) /∴ A

*9. (D ∨ ~ G) → ~ (H · I)
   ~ E → F /∴ (~ E → F) · [(D ∨ ~ G) → ~ (H · I)]

10. (K ∨ L) → [(J · K) ∨ ~ M]
    /∴ (K ∨ L) → {(K ∨ L) · [(J · K) ∨ ~ M]}

11. ~ N → (O · P) /∴ [~ N→ (O · P)] ∨ (O · P)

*12. U → {[~ R → [(S ∨ T) · ~ V]}
    {[~ R → [(S ∨ T) · ~ V]} → R /∴ U → R

13. ~ [(W ∨ X) · ~ Y]
    { ~ W → [(Z ∨ Y) · ~ X]}→ [(W ∨ X) · ~ Y] /∴ ~ { ~ W → [(Z ∨ Y) · ~ X]}

14. ~ ~ (~ A → B)
    ~ (~ A → B) ∨ [(C ∨ ~ D) → ~ (A · B)] /∴ [(C ∨ ~ D) → ~ (A · B)]

*15. (~ E → F) · [(G ∨ ~ H) → ~ (I · J)]
    ~ E ∨ (G ∨ ~ H) /∴ F ∨ ~ (I · J)

Assignment 8.3b. Construct a formal proof of validity for each of the following arguments. (Note: there may be multiple ways of proving these valid.)

Example: A · ~ B
             B ∨ C /∴ C

Solution: 1. A · ~ B
             2. B ∨ C /∴ C
             3. ~ B   1, Simp.
             4. C   2, 3, D. S.

1. A
   B /∴ (B ∨ C) · A

2. D → F
   D · E /∴ F

*3. G → H
   ~ H /∴ ~ G ∨ I

4. (J ∨ K) → L
   J /∴ L

5. M → N
   (M · N) → O /∴ M → O

*6. P → Q
   R → P
   P ∨ R /∴ Q ∨ P

7. S → T
   ~ T · ~ U /∴ ~ S

8. V ∨ W
   ~ V /∴ W ∨ X

*9. Y · ~ Z
   ~ Z → (Y ↔ Z) /∴ (Y ↔ Z) ∨ (~ Y · ~ Z)

10. A → (B · C)
    C → (D · E)
    A /∴ E

11. (H → I) · (I → H)
    (K → J) · (J → K)
    H ∨ J /∴ I ∨ K

*12. (L → M) · (N → O)
    L /∴ M ∨ O

13. P → Q
    Q → S
    ~ S /∴ ~ P

14. $(T \rightarrow U) \cdot (V \rightarrow W)$

   $T \lor V$

   $\sim U / \therefore W$

*15. $(X \rightarrow Y) \rightarrow Z$

   $(X \rightarrow Y) \lor X$

   $\sim Z / \therefore X$

Assignment 8.3c. Construct a formal proof of validity for each of the following arguments.

Example: $A \cdot B$

         $B \rightarrow (C \lor D)$

         $\sim D \cdot \sim E / \therefore C$

Solution: 1. $A \cdot B$

         2. $B \rightarrow (C \lor D)$

         3. $\sim D \cdot \sim E / \therefore C$

         4. B 1, Simp.

         5. $C \lor D$ 2, 4, M. P.

         6. $\sim D$ 3, Simp.

         7. C 5, 6, D. S.

1. $A \rightarrow B$

   $B \rightarrow C$

   $\sim C / \therefore \sim A \cdot \sim B$

2. $(D \cdot E) \rightarrow \sim F$

   $F \lor G$

   D

   $E / \therefore G$

*3. $(K \lor J) \rightarrow H$

   $K / \therefore H \lor I$

4. $J \lor K$

   $J \rightarrow (K \lor L)$

   $\sim K / \therefore L$

5. $(M \rightarrow N) \cdot (O \rightarrow P)$
   $M \lor O$
   $\sim P / \therefore N$

*6. $[(Y \leftrightarrow Z) \rightarrow Z] \lor (Y \lor Z)$
   $\sim (Y \lor Z)$
   $Y \leftrightarrow Z / \therefore Z$

7. $[(A \cdot B) \rightarrow C] \rightarrow (D \lor E)$
   $\sim E \rightarrow [(A \cdot B) \rightarrow C]$
   $\sim E / \therefore D$

8. $(F \leftrightarrow G) \rightarrow [H \rightarrow (I \lor J)]$
   $\sim G \rightarrow I$
   $\sim I$
   $(F \leftrightarrow G) \lor \sim G / \therefore H \rightarrow (I \lor J)$

*9. $K \rightarrow L$
   $(K \cdot L) \rightarrow [M \rightarrow (O \lor P)]$
   K
   $\sim (O \lor P) / \therefore \sim M$

10. $(Q \lor R) \rightarrow [(R \cdot S) \lor T]$
   $\sim R \rightarrow Q$
   $\sim R$
   $\sim T / \therefore S$

11. $(U \cdot V) \rightarrow W$
   $\sim W \rightarrow [\sim (U \cdot V) \rightarrow Z]$
   $\sim W / \therefore Z$

*12. $[(\sim A \rightarrow B) \cdot C] \cdot (D \leftrightarrow E)$
   $(B \cdot C) \rightarrow E$
   $(D \leftrightarrow E) \rightarrow \sim E / \therefore \sim (B \cdot C)$

13. $F \rightarrow \{ \sim G \rightarrow [H \cdot (I \lor J)] \}$
   $G \rightarrow \sim F$
   $F \rightarrow \sim \sim F$
   $F / \therefore I \lor J$

14. $[(\sim K \rightarrow L) \rightarrow M] \cdot \{ [(N \cdot K) \rightarrow L] \rightarrow P \}$
   $(O \lor P) \rightarrow \{ (\sim K \rightarrow L) \lor [(N \cdot K) \rightarrow L] \}$
   $O / \therefore M \lor P$

*15. $(Q \cdot R) \rightarrow [\sim (R \leftrightarrow S) \vee T]$

    $\sim \sim (R \leftrightarrow S)$

    $[(T \cdot \sim S) \rightarrow R] \rightarrow Q$

    R

    $(T \cdot \sim S) \rightarrow R /\therefore T$

8.4 REPLACEMENT RULES

While the Rules of Inference allow us to prove many arguments, there are some obviously valid arguments that we cannot prove with just these rules. Consider, for example, the following argument:

$(A \vee B) \rightarrow C$

$B \vee A$

$\therefore C$

This argument is *almost* a substitution instance of the argument form *modus ponens*:

$p \rightarrow q$

p

$\therefore q$

But if we substitute "A ∨ B" for the p in the first line, then we cannot substitute "B ∨ A" for p in the second line. Still, it seems intuitively obvious that "A ∨ B" and "B ∨ A" have the same truth value and that they are asserting the same proposition.

We can say that two statements are *logically equivalent* if and only (iff) they have the same truth value regardless of the simple statements that make them up. Notice, this is more than just *material* equivalence. For example, these two compound statements are *materially* equivalent as they have the same truth value:

1. Diamonds are hard and diamonds are expensive

2. Fire is hot and fire can burn things.

But these two statements are not asserting the same proposition, and the fact that they have the same truth value is a contingent feature of the simple statements that make them up. If we found a way to make diamonds cheaply, the first statement would then be false while the second continued to be true.

On the other hand, the following two statements are *logically* equivalent:

   3. Diamonds are hard and diamonds are expensive

   4. Diamonds are expensive and diamonds are hard.

Regardless of what happens to the simple statements making up these compound statements, they will have the same truth value and are, in fact, expressing the same proposition. This means when we see statement three, we can properly substitute statement four—and vice versa. Now this would be true of any disjunctive ("or") compound statement. Using :: to indicate logical equivalence, we can say

$p \lor q :: q \lor p$.

This particular substitution is called "commutation (Com.)," so we can prove the argument above as follows:

   1. $(A \lor B) \rightarrow C$

   2. $B \lor A / \therefore C$

   3. $A \lor B$ 2, Com.

   4. C 1, 3, M. P.

The ten commonly used Rules of Replacement can be seen here:

RULES OF REPLACEMENT	
De MORGAN'S THEOREM (DeM.)	$\sim (p \cdot q) :: (\sim p \lor \sim q)$ $\sim (p \lor q) :: (\sim p \cdot \sim q)$
COMMUTATION (COM.)	$(p \lor q) :: (q \lor p)$ $(p \cdot q) :: (q \cdot p)$
ASSOCIATION (ASSOC.)	$[p \lor (q \lor r)] :: [(p \lor q) \lor r]$ $[p \cdot (q \cdot r)] :: [(p \cdot q) \cdot r]$
DISTRIBUTION (DIST.)	$[p \lor (q \cdot r)] :: [(p \lor q) \cdot (p \lor r)]$ $[p \cdot (q \lor r)] :: [(p \cdot q) \lor (p \cdot r)]$
DOUBLE NEGATION (D. N.)	$p :: \sim\sim p$
TRANSPOSITION (TRANS.)	$(p \rightarrow q) :: (\sim q \rightarrow \sim p)$
MATERIAL IMPLICATION (IMPL.)	$(p \rightarrow q) :: (\sim p \lor q)$
EXPORTATION (EXP.)	$[(p \cdot q) \rightarrow r] :: [p \rightarrow (q \rightarrow r)]$
TAUTOLOGY (TAUT.)	$p :: p \lor p$ $p :: p \cdot p$
MATERIAL EQUIVALENCE (EQUIV.)	$(p \leftrightarrow q) :: [(p \rightarrow q) \cdot (q \rightarrow p)]$ $(p \leftrightarrow q) :: [(p \cdot q) \lor (\sim p \cdot \sim q)]$

It is very important to recognize the difference between the Rules of Inference and the Rules of Replacement. *In the Rules of Inference, the conclusion follows from the premises, but not the other way around.* So from $p \cdot q$ the simplification rule allows us to conclude p. But from p we certainly cannot properly conclude $p \cdot q$. If we put the rule of simplification into ordinary English, we mean that if two statements are both true, then one of them is true. However, if one statement is true, that does not mean that statement *and any other statement* are *both* true. For example, if we know that "John is hungry and John is sleepy," we can conclude that "John is hungry." However, knowing that "John is hungry" does *not* also tell us that he is sleepy.

Furthermore, the *Rules of Inference must apply to an entire line.* So from

$(M \cdot F) \rightarrow B$

we cannot use the *simplification* rule to conclude,

$M \rightarrow B.$

For example, when we say,

If you have a match and firewood, then you can build a bonfire

we could not conclude from that

Therefore if you have a match, then you can build a bonfire.

In the Rules of Replacement, we can *change just part of a line.* So, for example,

$(M \cdot F) \rightarrow B$

is logically equivalent to

$(F \cdot M) \rightarrow B.$

So if we say,

If you have a match and firewood, then you can build a bonfire

that is logically equivalent to saying

If you have firewood and a match, then you can build a bonfire.

That is, we can do *commutation* on the antecedent part of this compound statement without changing the truth value.

Furthermore, *the Rules of Replacement can go "either direction."* That is, we can replace the statement form on the left side of the material-equivalence sign with the right side or vice versa. So if we have the statement, "$\sim \sim A$," we can replace it with "A"—and if we have the statement "A," we can replace it with "~ ~ A." For example, if it is not the case that it is not sunny, then it *is* sunny. If it *is* sunny, then it is not *not* sunny.

If we consider this ability to replace statements with other statements that have the same truth value, we find some interesting implications. In the first place, it means that some of the Rules of Inference and Rules of Replacement are redundant. For example, consider the following *modus ponens* argument:

A → B
A
∴ B

We could prove this argument valid *without using modus ponens*:

1. A → B
2. A / ∴ B
3. ~ A ∨ B   1, Impl.
4. ~ ~ A   2, D. N.
5. B   3, 4, D. S.

This means that every time we encounter a *modus ponens* argument form, we could use the Rules of Replacement and then prove it using a disjunctive syllogism. Of course, we could prove the *modus ponens* argument above without using *modus ponens* or disjunctive syllogism by doing transposition on the first premise and then setting up a *modus tollens*:

1. A → B
2. A / ∴ B
3. ~ B → ~ A   1, Trans.
4. ~ ~ A   2, D. N.
5. ~ ~ B   3, 4, M. T.
6. B   5, D. N.

So not all of the Rules of Inference or the Rules of Replacement are needed. But we will keep all nineteen of these rules for the sake of their "naturalness" and the way they fit our ordinary way of arguing. While not all of these rules are necessary, together they are sufficient to construct a formal proof of any valid truth-functional argument.[5]

---

[5]If you are interested in a proof that this set of rules is complete, see also John A. Winnie, "The Completeness of Copi's System of Natural Deduction," *Notre Dame Journal of Formal Logic* 11, no. 3 (July 1970): 379-82.

As you move on to construct proofs, you would be well advised to keep a copy of the rules handy. A one-page summary of all the rules can be found on the following page. (There is also a copy on the last page of this book.)

Assignment 8.4. For each of the valid arguments below, state the rule of replacement that justifies the conclusion.

Example: (A · B) ∨ (A · C) / ∴ A · (B ∨ C)

Solution: Dist. (remember that the Rules of Replacement can go from right to left as well as from left to right.)

1. ~ A ∨ (B · C) / ∴ A → (B · C)

2. (D ∨ E) → ~ [(F ∨ F) ↔ (D · C)] / ∴ (D ∨ E) → ~ [F ↔ (D · C)]

*3. [(~ H → I) · (J ∨ ~ K)] ∨ [(~ H → I) · ~ (L · G)]
    / ∴ (~ H → I) · [(J ∨ ~ K) ∨ ~ (L · G)]

4. [M → (~ ~ N · O)] → (O ∨ M) / ∴ [M → (N · O)] → (O ∨ M)

5. [(P ∨ Q) → ~ (P · Q)] · (P → R) / ∴ [~ (P ∨ Q) ∨ ~ (P · Q)] · (P → R)

*6. (S ∨ T) → ~ [U ∨ (S ↔ T)] / ∴ (T ∨ S) → ~ [U ∨ (S ↔ T)]

7. [(W · X) ∨ Z] → ~ (~ Y ∨ V) / ∴ [(W · X) ∨ Z] → ~ (Y → V)

8. 8~ [A ∨ (B · C)] ∨ [(C → A) · (A → C)] / ∴ ~ [A ∨ (B · C)] ∨ (C ↔ A)

*9. [(D ∨ ~ E) · F] → [~ G → (D ∨ F)] / ∴ (D ∨ ~ E) → {F → [~ G → (D ∨ F)]}

10. {~ H → [(K ∨ J) · ~ I]} → [(H ∨ I) ∨ ~ J]
    / ∴ { ~ H → [(K ∨ J) · ~ I]} → [H ∨ (I ∨ ~ J)]

11. (L ∨ ~ M) → ~ (N · O) / ∴ (L ∨ ~ M) → (~ N ∨ ~ O)

*12. ~ [P ∨ (Q · R)] ∨ [(R · P) ∨ (~ R · ~ P)] / ∴ ~ [P ∨ (Q · R)] ∨ (R ↔ P)

13. S → [~ T → ~ (U · V)] / ∴ (S · ~ T) → ~ (U · V)

14. (W ∨ ~ X) → ~ (Y · Z) / ∴ ~ ~ (Y · Z) → ~ (W ∨ ~ X)

*15. A → { ~ B → [~ A · (C ∨ D)]} / ∴ A → { ~ B → [(~ A · C) ∨ (~ A · D)]}

190 HOW DO WE REASON?

RULES OF INFERENCE (must apply to the *entire* line)

Modus Ponens (M. P.)

$p \rightarrow q$
p
$\therefore q$

Modus Tollens (M. T.)

$p \rightarrow q$
$\sim q$
$\therefore \sim p$

Hypothetical Syllogism (H. S.)

$p \rightarrow q$
$q \rightarrow r$
$\therefore p \rightarrow r$

Disjunctive Syllogism (D. S.)

$p \vee q$ or $p \vee q$
$\sim p$ $\sim q$
$\therefore q$ $\therefore p$

Constructive Dilemma (C. D.)

$(p \rightarrow q) \cdot (r \rightarrow s)$
$p \vee r$
$\therefore q \vee s$

Conjunction (Conj.)

p
q
$\therefore p \cdot q$

Simplification (Simp.)

$p \cdot q$ or $p \cdot q$
$\therefore p$ $\therefore q$

Addition (Add.)

p or p
$\therefore p \vee q$ $\therefore q \vee p$

Absorption (Abs.)

$p \rightarrow q$
$\therefore p \rightarrow (p \cdot q)$

RULES OF REPLACEMENT (can apply to any *part* of a line)	
De MORGAN'S THEOREM (DeM.)	$\sim (p \cdot q) :: (\sim p \vee \sim q)$ $\sim (p \vee q) :: (\sim p \cdot \sim q)$
COMMUTATION (COM.)	$(p \vee q) :: (q \vee p)$ $(p \cdot q) :: (q \cdot p)$
ASSOCIATION (ASSOC.)	$[p \vee (q \vee r)] :: [(p \vee q) \vee r]$ $[p \cdot (q \cdot r)] :: [(p \cdot q) \cdot r]$
DISTRIBUTION (DIST.)	$[p \vee (q \cdot r)] :: [(p \vee q) \cdot (p \vee r)]$ $[p \cdot (q \vee r)] :: [(p \cdot q) \vee (p \cdot r)]$
DOUBLE NEGATION (D. N.)	$p :: \sim\sim p$
TRANSPOSITION (TRANS.)	$(p \rightarrow q) :: (\sim q \rightarrow \sim p)$
MATERIAL IMPLICATION (IMPL.)	$(p \rightarrow q) :: (\sim p \vee q)$
EXPORTATION (EXP.)	$[(p \cdot q) \rightarrow r] :: [p \rightarrow (q \rightarrow r)]$
TAUTOLOGY (TAUT.)	$p :: p \vee p$ $p :: p \cdot p$
MATERIAL EQUIVALENCE (EQUIV.)	$(p \leftrightarrow q) :: [(p \rightarrow q) \cdot (q \rightarrow p)]$ $(p \leftrightarrow q) :: [(p \cdot q) \vee (\sim p \cdot \sim q)]$

8.5 CONSTRUCTING PROOFS

With nineteen possible rules to use, it is often hard to know where to begin in constructing a proof. What follows are some general guidelines that may help us proceed.

1. Look at the conclusion and get some idea of what might be the step right before it. Looking at the conclusion will often help make clear what some of the steps in the proof are likely to be. For example, if there is a statement in the conclusion that is not in any of the premises, you can be sure that addition happened at some point in the proof. If the conclusion is an "if . . . then . . . ," it is likely that a hypothetical syllogism was used somewhere along the way.

2. Create a "got" and "want" list. On more complex proofs, it is helpful to make a "got" list and add all the statements you can properly infer from the premises—even if you don't yet see where they are leading. Then make a "want" list and work backward from the conclusion saying, "Well, if I had *this* I could get the conclusion by using rule . . ." and proceed to list the statements that could lead to the conclusion. At some point these two lists should match up. From there, you can "glue" the "got" and "want" lists together into a proof.

3. Does any line have an "and" in the middle? The nice part about any line with an "and" (·) as the primary logical connecter is that you can use simplification to get either side by itself.

4. Look to do a modus ponens *or a* modus tollens. Is the primary logical connecter for any premise an "if . . . then . . ." (→) statement? If so, is it possible to find the antecedent (the "if . . ." part) in one of the other premises? If so, do a *modus ponens*. Even if you cannot find the antecedent by itself, it may be possible to infer it by using simplification on some line or one of the other rules. If you cannot isolate the antecedent to the "if . . . then . . ." premise, is it possible to find the negation of the consequent (the ". . . , then . . ." part)? If so, do a *modus tollens*. Again, it may be necessary to use double negation or simplification or some other rule(s) to set this up.

5. See if a hypothetical syllogism is possible. If there are two premises that have an "if . . . then . . ." as the primary logical connecter, see if you can get the antecedent on one line to "match up" with the consequent on another line. Remember, this may require doing transposition or applying some other rule to get the two lines into the proper form for the hypothetical syllogism.

6. If you are not sure what else to do with an "if . . . then . . . ," consider doing material implication and changing it to an "or" (∨). This is especially true when there is only one premise. If there is only one premise, it is not possible to do a *modus ponens*, a *modus tollens*, a hypothetical syllogism, or a constructive dilemma. All of those Rules of Inference require two premises.

7. Remember that any "or" (∨) statement can be changed into an "if . . . then . . . (→). It may be necessary to create a "not" (~) in front of the first half of the disjunction. This can be done by doing double negation (D. N.) and then removing *one* of the "nots" when doing material implication (Impl.).

8. If you have a ~ outside of parentheses with an "and" or an "or" inside the parentheses, try doing De Morgan's theorem. In the case of an "or" inside the parentheses, it will become an "and," which may allow you to do simplification. In the case of an "and" inside the parentheses, it will become an "or," which may allow for a material implication.

9. If you find a line with both an "and" and an "or," do distribution on it. Often when you distribute a line, you end up with an "and" in the middle and then you can simplify either side as described in guideline two.

10. When you must use addition, remember that it may be necessary to add "not something" ("~ p"). Remember that p and q stand for any statement whatsoever. So the addition rule of inference allows you to add anything you want. In some situations, it will be necessary to add the negation of a statement rather than just the statement.

11. Once you create a formal proof of validity, remember the steps as you may need to use them again in another proof. In constructing a formal proof of validity, there may be steps that can be used later in a longer proof. These recurring patterns help break down a longer proof into smaller parts that are more easily solved. It is a good idea to keep a list of these recurring patterns. Assignment 8.5b especially uses patterns that are often parts of more complex proofs.

Assignment 8.5a. Construct a formal proof of validity for each of the following simple arguments.

Example: ~ A → A / ∴ A

Solution: 1. ~ A → A / ∴ A

                2. ~ ~ A ∨ A   1, Impl. (see guideline no. 6)

                3. A ∨ A   2, D. N.

                4. A   3, Taut.

1. A · (B ∨ C)
   ~ C /∴ B

2. ~ D · ~ E
   F → D /∴ ~ F

*3. G /∴ H → G

4. J → K
   I → J
   ~ K /∴ ~ I

5. L ∨ (M · N) /∴ N ∨ L

*6. (O ∨ P) → Q
   P /∴ Q

7. ~ R ∨ (S · T) /∴ R → S

8. U → V
   ~ T → U
   ~ (T ∨ W) /∴ V

*9. X → Y
   Y → Z
   X ∨ Y /∴ Y ∨ Z

10. (A · B) ∨ (~ A · ~ B) /∴ (A → B) · (B → A)

11. C ∨ D
    C ∨ E /∴ C ∨ (D · E)

*12. F → (G · H)
    ~ G ∨ ~ H /∴ ~ F

13. ~ (I ∨ J)
    K → I /∴ ~ K

14. ~ (L → M) /∴ ~ M

*15. ~ (N → O) /∴ N

Assignment 8.5b. Construct a formal proof of validity for the following arguments. This set of proofs includes frequently recurring patterns that may be useful in constructing more complex proofs.

Example: A /∴ B → A

Solution: 1. A /∴ B → A

                    2. A ∨ ~ B   1, Add.

                    3. ~ B ∨ A   2, Comm.

                    4. B → A   3, Impl.

1. ~ A /∴ A → B

2. C → (D → E) /∴ D → (C → E)

*3. F → G /∴ (F · H) → G

4. I → (J · K) /∴ I → J

5. L → M /∴ L → (M ∨ N)

*6. (O ∨ P) → Q /∴ O → Q

7. S ∨ T /∴ ~ S → T

8. U → V
    U → W /∴ U → (V · W)

*9. X → Y
    Z → Y /∴ (X ∨ Z) → Y

10. A → B
     A → ~ B /∴ ~ A

Assignment 8.5c. Construct a formal proof of validity for the following arguments.

Example: A → (B · C)
              (B ∨ C) → D /∴ A → D

Solution: First look at the conclusion. If we could get A → *p* (some-
              thing) and if *p* (the same something) → D, we could do H. S.
              and get the conclusion. The key would be to get the con-
              sequent of the A → *p* to match the antecedent of *p* → D.
              Using what we learned from number four above (assignment
              8.5b), we know that from A → (B · C) we can get A → B.
              And using number three above, from (B ∨ C) → D we can
              get B → D.

1. A → (B · C)

2. (B ∨ C) → D / ∴ A → D

3. ~ A ∨ (B · C)	1, Impl.	
4. (~ A ∨ B) · (~ A ∨ C)	3, Dist.	The same steps used
5. ~ A ∨ B	4, Simp.	in assignment 8.5b
6. A → B	5. Impl.	no. 4
7. ~ (B ∨ C) ∨ D	2, Impl.	
8. (~ B · ~ C) ∨ D	7, DeM.	
9. D ∨ (~ B · ~ C)	8, Comm.	The same steps used
10. (D ∨ ~ B) · (D ∨ ~ C)	9, Dist.	in assignment 8.5b
11. D ∨ ~ B	10, Simp.	no. 6
12. ~ B ∨ D	11, Comm.	
13. B → D	12, Impl.	
14. A → D	6, 13, H. S.	Put them together

Now this is a perfectly good proof—however, it *is* possible to do this proof using fewer steps:

1. A → (B · C)

2. (B ∨ C) → D / ∴ A → D

3. ~ A ∨ (B · C)	1, Impl.	The first three steps
4. (~ A ∨ B) · (~ A ∨ C)	3, Dist.	used in assignment
5. ~ A ∨ B	4, Simp.	8.5b no. 4
6. ~ (A ∨ B) ∨ C	5, Add.	Using *Add.* to get a
7. ~ A ∨ (B ∨ C)	6, Assoc.	consequent that matches the
8. A → (B ∨ C)	7, Impl.	antecedent of line 2
9. A → D	8, 2, H. S.	Put them together

1. $A \rightarrow \sim B$
   $B \vee C /\therefore A \rightarrow C$

2. $(D \cdot E) \rightarrow F$
   $G \rightarrow D$
   $G \rightarrow E /\therefore G \rightarrow F$

*3. $H \rightarrow (I \rightarrow J)$
   $K \rightarrow I /\therefore K \rightarrow (H \rightarrow J)$

4. $L \rightarrow (M \cdot N)$
   $M \rightarrow O /\therefore L \rightarrow O$

5. $P \rightarrow Q$
   $R \rightarrow Q$
   $S \rightarrow (P \vee R) /\therefore S \rightarrow Q$

*6. $T \rightarrow U$
   $T \rightarrow \sim U$
   $V \rightarrow T /\therefore \sim V$

7. $W \rightarrow (X \cdot Y) /\therefore (\sim X \vee \sim Y) \rightarrow (\sim W \vee \sim Z)$

8. $A \rightarrow \sim A$
   $B \rightarrow A /\therefore \sim B$

*9. $(C \rightarrow D) \cdot (E \rightarrow F)$
   $(\sim C \vee D) \cdot E /\therefore (\sim C \vee D) \cdot F$

10. $H \rightarrow (\sim I \rightarrow J)$
   $I \rightarrow K /\therefore \sim K \rightarrow (H \rightarrow J)$

8.6 PROVING INVALIDITY

Consider the following argument:

> If Alex is a Democrat, then Alex would be in favor of raising the marginal tax rate.
> If Alex is a communist, then Alex would be in favor of raising the marginal tax rate.
> ∴ If Alex is a Democrat, then Alex is a communist.

We can symbolize this as

$D \rightarrow R$
$C \rightarrow R$
$\therefore D \rightarrow C$

If we try to construct a formal proof of validity, we will fail. No matter how many Rules of Inference and Rules of Replacement we use, we will never properly prove validity—because this argument is invalid.

So how do we prove it invalid? We will use a truth table in which we set up the truth table as we did in section 7.4 and "unpack" it as before:

But rather than look at all eight possible combinations of truth values for the simples, let's work backward to see if there is *any* combination that makes the premises true and the conclusion false. There is only one combination that will make the conclusion false: where "D" is true and "C" is false.

Since "D" is true and we want the premise "D → R" to also be true, then "R" must be true. The premise "C → R" will then be true as well. So the following modified truth table shows that there is a combination of truth values for the simples that makes the premises true and the conclusion false. Hence the argument must be invalid.

If we are not able to come up with a combination of truth values for the simples that makes the premises true and the conclusion false, does that prove the argument is valid? Unfortunately, no. While a complete truth table could be used to prove validity (as we did in section 8.2), there is always the possibility that we just made a mistake in the modified truth table. To prove validity we must use the rules and construct a formal proof as outlined in the preceding sections. So when we encounter an argument for the first time, we must do the following:

1. Do a modified truth table to see whether it is possible to assign truth values to the simples to make the premises true and the conclusion false. If so, then the argument is invalid and we can quit.

2. If we cannot come up with a combination of truth values that makes the premises true and the conclusion false, then we must move on to construct a formal proof of validity using the rules.

Assignment 8.6. Prove the following invalid by using a modified truth table. (The arguments in this assignment are all invalid.)

Example: 1. A → B

2. C → D

3. A ∨ D /∴ B ∨ C

Solution:

A	B	C	D	A → B	C → D	A ∨ D	∴ B ∨ C
F	F	F	T	T	T	T	F

1. A · B
~ (B · C) /∴ ~ A

2. ~ D ∨ E
E · [(D ∨ G) → F] /∴ ~ G → F

*3. H ∨ ~ I
~ H → J
(~ J ∨ H) → K /∴ I ∨ K

4. L → M
N → M /∴ L → N

5. (O → Q) → (P · R)
~ O · P
(~ Q ∨ R) · ~ O
[(O · P) · Q] → R /∴ O ↔ P

*6. (~ S → ~ T) · (U → V)
(~ U ∨ W) → S
(T · ~ U) ↔ [S → (V · W)] /∴ S → (V ∨ W)

7. (X ∨ Y) → (X ∨ ~ Z)
(~ X · Y) → (Y ↔ Z)
~ [(Z · X) ∨ (~ Z · ~ X)] → (Y ↔ X) /∴ [Y ∨ (X ↔ Z)] → (Y · ~ Z)

8. $\sim A \rightarrow (B \lor C)$
   $C \rightarrow (B \cdot E)$
   $(D \cdot E) \rightarrow (\sim A \cdot E)$
   $D \lor E /\therefore \sim (C \leftrightarrow D) \cdot \sim E$

*9. $F \rightarrow (G \cdot H)$
   $H \rightarrow (F \cdot G)$
   $I \rightarrow \sim (F \lor H)$
   $(F \cdot G) \rightarrow (H \cdot I)$
   $(G \lor \sim H) \rightarrow \sim (G \lor I) /\therefore I$

10. $(J \cdot K) \rightarrow [K \lor (L \cdot M)]$
   $(\sim N \rightarrow K) \rightarrow (L \lor O)$
   $M \cdot O /\therefore (J \lor L) \rightarrow (M \leftrightarrow N)$

8.7 INCONSISTENCY

There is one kind of argument that deserves special mention. Consider the following:

If the Los Angeles Lakers win the Western Conference, then the Cleveland Cavaliers win the NBA Championship

If the Los Angeles Lakers do not win the Western Conference, then the Oklahoma City Thunder win the NBA Championship

Neither the Cleveland Cavaliers nor the Oklahoma City Thunder win the NBA Championship

∴ The Saint Ignatius eighth-grade girls basketball team wins the NBA Championship

We can symbolize this as

$G \rightarrow C$
$\sim G \rightarrow O$
$\sim (C \lor O)$
$\therefore S$

Amazingly enough, this argument is valid, as we can prove:

1. $G \rightarrow C$
2. $\sim G \rightarrow O$

3. ~ (C ∨ O) /∴ S

4. ~ C · ~ O   3, DeM.

5. ~ C   4, Simp.

6. ~ G   1, 5, M. T.

7. O   2, 6, M. P.

8. ~ O   4, Simp.

9. O ∨ S   7, Add.

10. S   9, 8, D. S.

This argument is valid because there is an inconsistency hidden within it. By using the rules, we make clear this inconsistency: line seven and line eight are exact contradictions of each other. And what follows from a contradiction is not nothing, but *everything*!

Let's show this with a much simpler argument:

Albert is in the room

Albert is not in the room

∴ Betty is a unicorn

So

A

~ A

∴ B

The formal proof of validity is very simple:

1. A

2. ~ A ∴ B

3. A ∨ B   1, Add.

4. B   3, 2, D. S.

Any time we find two lines that are exact contradictions of each other, we need only add the conclusion (*any* conclusion) and do a disjunctive syllogism to prove validity.

Why is that? Recall that for a valid deductive argument, if the premises are true, then the conclusion must also true. But if the premises of an argument are contradictory, then there will be *no case* in which the premises are true. That is, if we construct a truth table for the argument, there will be no lines to circle where the premises are all true because one of them contradicts another.

So is it the case that "If the premises are true, then the conclusion must also true"? Yes. This sentence is a compound "if ... then ..." statement. When the antecedent of an "if ... then ..." statement is false, the entire statement is true. So in an argument with contradictory premises the antecedent "the premises are true" will always be false, making the entire statement true—and hence it will meet the definition for "valid."

This is why contradictions are so anathema to logicians. If you permit a contradiction in an argument, you can validly conclude anything.[6]

Now a further clarification about contradictions. Poets like Walt Whitman may say,

Do I contradict myself?

Very well then I contradict myself,

(I am large, I contain multitudes.)

But they are rarely talking about contradictions. What they usually mean is really a *paradox*, which we can define as an "apparent contradiction." For example, if you say, "I am here, but I am not here," we all know what you mean. You are actually equivocating on the word *I*: the first usage means "my body is here," while the second usage means "my attention or interest is not here." But if you said, "My physical body is present in this particular place at this particular time and my physical body is not present in this very same particular time and place," we would be worried about you.[7]

Assignment 8.7. For each of the following arguments, first try to prove it invalid by using a modified truth table. If that is not possible, construct a formal proof of validity.

---

[6]Of course, while an argument with contradictory premises is *valid*, it will never be *sound*.

[7]A note about contradictions and paradoxes. Sometimes people say that the basic belief of Christianity involves a contradiction: Jesus is both God and human. It is certainly a paradox, but is it a contradiction? If so, then to believe this claim one would either have to believe that anything and everything follows from it or admit that one is illogical. But for this basic Christian claim to be a contradiction, one would have to say that Jesus was both God and not God or human and not human—a belief that no orthodox Christian would hold. Now some would say, "The contradiction is not explicit, but implicit. To be God *means* to not be human—so if Jesus is God, he could not be human and yet you claim the contradiction that he *is* human." However, the claim "To be God *means* to not be human" is not a logical necessity. In fact, one need only have one example of a being that is both God and human to refute this claim. And Christians believe that Jesus fits the bill. To say that Jesus could not be both, one would have to come up with a complete definition of God that explicitly excludes being human. I, for one, do not have a complete definition of God of *any* sort— let alone one that excludes the possibility that God could become a human if God so chose. Now none of this has anything to do with the truth or falsehood of the claim that Jesus is God and human. The claim may very well be false. But note that this claim is *not* a contradiction. It is a contingent proposition whose truth value must be determined by other means than logical necessity.

Example: $A \rightarrow (B \cdot C)$

$B \rightarrow D$

$B \rightarrow E / \therefore A \rightarrow (D \cdot E)$

Solution:

A B C D E	B·C	D·E	A→(B·C)	B→D	B→E	∴ A→(D·E)
T T ? ? ?	T	F	T	?	?	F

It is not possible to find truth values to make the premise true and the conclusion false so we must construct a formal proof of validity.

1. $A \rightarrow (B \cdot C)$

2. $B \rightarrow D$

3. $B \rightarrow E / \therefore A \rightarrow (D \cdot E)$

4. $\sim A \vee (B \cdot C)$ 1, Impl.

5. $(\sim A \vee B) \cdot (\sim A \vee C)$ 4, Dist.   The same steps used in assignment 8.5b no. 4

6. $\sim A \vee B$ 5, Simp.

7. $A \rightarrow B$ 6, Impl.

8. $\sim B \vee D$ 2, Impl.

9. $\sim B \vee E$ 3, Impl.   The same steps used in assignment 8.5b no. 8

10. $\sim (B \vee D) \cdot (\sim B \vee E)$ 8, 9, Conj.

11. $\sim B \vee (D \cdot E)$ 10, Dist.

12. $B \rightarrow (D \cdot E)$ 11, Impl.

13. $A \rightarrow (D \cdot E)$ 7, 12, H. S.   Put them together

1. $A \rightarrow B$

$B \rightarrow C$

$B \rightarrow D / \therefore A \rightarrow (C \cdot D)$

2. $E \rightarrow F$

$E \rightarrow \sim F$

$(C \vee D) \rightarrow E / \therefore \sim D$

*3. $I \rightarrow (J \rightarrow K)$

$I \rightarrow J$

$I \cdot K / \therefore \sim J$

4. ~ L → ~ M
   N → L /∴ (M ∨ N) → L

5. (O ∨ P) → [~ Q → ~ (O · R)]
   Q · [P ↔ (R ∨ ~ Q)]
   ~ R /∴ ~ O

*6. S ∨ T
   U → ~ T /∴ (U · V) → S

7. (W → ~ Y) · (~ W → ~ Y)
   Y ∨ ~ (~ Y ∨ ~ Z)
   ~ W ∨ (~ Z ∨ Y) /∴ ~ Z

8. (~ A ∨ ~ B) → C
   C → (~ D ∨ ~ E)
   D → (~ B ∨ ~ C)
   E → (~ C ∨ ~ D) /∴ (A · B) ↔ E

*9. (F ∨ G) → (H → I)
   (~ J ∨ H) · (~ K ∨ F)
   (~ L ∨ G) · (K ∨ L) /∴ J → I

10. [M ∨ (N ∨ O)] → [M · (N ∨ O)] /∴ O → M

8.8 TRANSLATING STATEMENTS
INTO SYMBOLIC NOTATION

The real-life application of these lessons is, of course, to translate naturally occurring arguments into logical notations and test them for validity. Unfortunately, there are no hard-and-fast rules for this sort of translation work. One guideline, however, is to find the conclusion first. Then look for the reasons given as to why one should accept that conclusion. As much as possible, try to replace synonyms and, in general, use the same language throughout the argument. The goal is to be as generous as possible in the translation while still staying true to the meaning of the sentences that make up the argument.

Assignment 8.8a. For each of the following arguments, put them into symbolic notation using the suggested letters and then construct a formal proof of validity. (These arguments are all valid, so no need to make a modified truth table.)

Example: (Use letters LED)

If Genesis is literal history, then the earth existed three days before the sun was created and "day" is defined by reference to the sun. But if "day" is defined by reference to the sun, then it cannot be the case that the earth existed three days before the sun was created, so Genesis is not literal history.

Laid out: If Genesis is literal history, then the earth existed three days before the sun was created.

"Day" is defined by reference to the sun

If "day" is defined by reference to the sun, then it cannot be the case that the earth existed three days before the sun was created

Genesis is not literal history

Solution: 1. $L \rightarrow E$

2. D

3. $D \rightarrow \sim E / \therefore \sim L$

4. $\sim E$ 3, 2, M. P.

5. $\sim L$ 1, 4, M. T.

1. (Use letters AP)

   Army will beat Navy in football if and only if Army will learn how to pass, but Army will never learn how to pass, so Army will never beat Navy.

2. (Use letters AC)

   If you can always believe the TV, then Coke is better than Pepsi, but if you can always believe the TV, then Coke is not better than Pepsi! So you cannot always believe the TV.

*3. (Use letters WGAO)

   We must conclude that either God is not omnipotent or God is not all good. Because if God doesn't want to prevent evil, then God is not all good, and if God isn't able to prevent evil, then God is not omnipotent. It is clear that either God doesn't want to prevent evil or God is not able.

4. (Use letters TCDE)

If predestination is true, then God causes us to sin. And If God causes us to sin and still damns sinners to eternal punishment, then God is evil. So if God is not evil, then either predestination is not true or else God does not damn sinners to eternal punishment.

5. (Use letters BGO)

If our best arguments for "God exists" and for "I am not the only conscious being in the universe" fall apart at the same points, then belief in God is reasonable if—and only if—belief in other minds is reasonable. It seems clear that our best arguments for "God exists" and for "I am not the only conscious being in the universe" fall apart at the same points. So, since belief in other minds is reasonable, belief in God is reasonable.

*6. (Use letters FES)

If there is no first cause, then either there is an endless chain of causes and effects or else some being caused itself. But there is not endless chain of causes and effects. Furthermore, no being caused itself. So we have to conclude there is a first cause.

7. (Use letters GIA)

If God knows what I will do, then it would be impossible for me not to do it. And if it would be impossible for me not to do it, then my action is not free. But my actions are free, so God does not know what I will do.

8. (Use letters GPCNW)

If God exists, then God is perfect. And if God exists, then God is the creator of the universe. Furthermore, if God is perfect, God can have no needs or wants. But if God is the creator of the universe, God has needs or wants (e.g., needs or wants to create), so it is obvious that God does not exist.

*9. (Use letters KLBDUH)

If the Sacramento Kings make it to the NBA Finals, they will lose. If the Charlotte Hornets make it to the NBA Finals, they will be defeated. Both the Kings and the Hornets make it to the NBA Finals. Either the Kings will lose or the Hornets will be defeated, but not both. So the universe will explode in a fiery cataclysm and hell will freeze over.

10. (Use letters CWO)

If you can think clearly, then you would do well in logic. If you cannot think clearly, then you ought to study logic. And if you would do well in logic, then you ought to study logic. So no matter what, you ought to study logic.

Assignment 8.8b. For each of the following arguments, first translate them into symbolic notation. Second, try to prove them invalid by using a modified truth table. If that is not possible, construct a formal proof of validity.

| **Example:** | (Use letters RFO) |
| | In football, if you run and fumble, then the other team gets the ball. You run on the next play. You don't fumble. So the other team doesn't get the ball. |

Laid out:	If you run the football and fumble, then the other team gets the ball
	You run the football
	You do not fumble
	————————————————————
	The other team does not get the ball

Solution: 1. $(R \cdot F) \rightarrow O$

2. R

3. $\sim F \: / \therefore \: \sim O$

F	O	R	R•F	(R•F)→O	R	~F	∴ ~O
F	T	T	F	T	T	T	F

Invalid

1. (Use letters GMBS)

If God exists, then our lives have meaning and there is beauty in the world. If there is beauty in the world, then we can see it in the world around us. And we *can* see beauty in the world around us, so God exists.

2. (Use letters PGA)

If there is a perfectly loving God, then any given person who has not freely shut himself or herself off from God is capable of an explicit and positively meaningful relationship with God. And if any given person who has not freely shut himself or herself off from God is capable of an explicit and positively meaningful relationship with God, then all persons who have not freely shut themselves off from God believe God exists. But it is not the case that all persons who have not freely shut themselves off from God believe God exists. It follows that there is no perfectly loving God.

*3. (Use letters EFSH)

Either you enjoy doing these proofs or you find them frustrating. If you enjoy doing these proofs, then you are finding solutions for them. But if you find these proofs frustrating, then you are not happy right now, so either you are finding solutions for these proofs or you are not happy right now.

4. (Use letters WRQ)

If you live a wild life then you will have regrets. If you live a quiet life then you will have regrets. You must do one or the other. Therefore, you will have regrets.

5. (Use letters KDLVP)

SeaWorld is keeping orca whales in "constant involuntary physical confinement." If SeaWorld is keeping orca whales in "constant involuntary physical confinement," then SeaWorld is depriving the whales of "their ability to live in a manner of their choosing." And if SeaWorld is depriving the whales of "their ability to live in a manner of their choosing," then if whales have legal standing as persons, then SeaWorld is violating the 13th Amendment rights of the whales. Now if PETA's lawyers are correct, then whales have legal standing as persons. It follows that if PETA's lawyers are correct, then SeaWorld is violating the 13th Amendment rights of the whales.

*6. (Use letters PGBN)

Either Socrates's death will be perpetual sleep, or, if the gods are good, then Socrates's death will be an entry into a better life. If Socrates's death will be perpetual sleep, then Socrates has nothing to fear from death. Thankfully, the gods are good. Now if Socrates's death will be an entry into a better life, then Socrates has nothing to fear from death, so Socrates has nothing to fear from death.

7. (Use letters PWNV)

If a belief is proved, then it is worthy of acceptance. If a belief is not disproved but is of practical value to our lives, then it is worthy of acceptance. Of course, if a belief is proved, then it is not disproved. So if a belief is proved or is of practical value to our lives, then it is worthy of acceptance.

8. (Use letters FOBI)

If Socrates flees Athens to avoid death, then he will only obey the state when this pleases him. But if he will only obey the state when it please him, then he does not really believe what he says and he is inconsistent. So if Socrates really believes what he says, then he won't flee Athens to avoid death.

*9. (Use letters TWPEFL)

If I give a test in logic, then people either do well or poorly. If people do well, then I think that I made the test too easy and I am frustrated. If people do poorly, then I think that people didn't learn any logic and I am frustrated. Therefore, if I give a test in logic, then I am frustrated.

10. (Use letters GHFWCU)

The apostles' teaching is either from God or it is from humans. If it is from God and we fight it, we will be fighting God. If it is from humans, it will collapse of its own accord. If it will collapse of its own accord and we fight it, then our efforts will be unnecessary. So if we fight the apostles' teaching, either our efforts will be unnecessary or we will be fighting God.

ἀνάγκη δὴ στῆναι.

One must end somewhere.

ARISTOTLE, *METAPHYSICS* 10704

ANSWERS FOR SELECTED ASSIGNMENTS

3. Premise 1: Kids who go to preschool are more likely to go to college.
   Premise 2: We want more people to go to college.
   Conclusion: We should have public preschool for everyone.

6. Premise: From this equality of ability arises equality of hope in the attaining of our ends.
   Conclusion: If any two men desire the same thing, which nevertheless they cannot both enjoy, they become enemies. . . .

9. Premise: People sometimes are thirsty, and yet do not wish to drink.
   Conclusion: [Being thirsty and wishing to drink] are two principles [in the soul] distinct one from the other.

12. Premise: All the dignity of man consists in thought.
    Conclusion: Thought is by its nature a wonderful and incomparable thing.

15. Premise: If the presence were felt so clearly, the soul would find it impossible to be engaged in anything else or even to live among people.
    Conclusion: It should be understood that [God's] presence is not felt so fully, I mean so clearly, as when revealed the first time or at other times when God grants the soul this gift.

3. The conclusion is "All swans are white." Inductive.

6. The conclusion is "[Mars has] rock[s] that [were] formed in the presence of water." Inductive.

9. The conclusion is "[Jesus] was and is God." Probably inductive. If Lewis is saying there are only three possibilities and the second two are false, then it is deductive. But does "it seems obvious to me . . ." mean the second two options are false?

12. The conclusion is "We must have known equality previously to the time when we first saw the material equals." Deductive.

15. The conclusion here is both at the beginning and the end: "A pure democracy . . . can admit of no cure for the mischiefs of faction" and "such democracies have ever been spectacles of turbulence and contention." (In other words, "pure democracy is chaos!") Inductive.

1.3

3. Invalid (so also not sound or persuasive).
6. Valid, but not sound or persuasive. (At least I *hope* it is not sound.)
9. Valid, sound, and persuasive.
12. Valid—soundness and persuasiveness depend on what I did.
15. Valid, but the soundness and persuasiveness depends on your dating life.

UNIT I

2.1

3. Performative. (The words of the letter are *doing* the resigning.)
6. Expressive (though it does contain some information).
9. Ceremonial.
12. Given what is here, informative. However, he said this as advice to Henry Ford's attorney, Horace Rackham, telling him not to invest in the Ford Motor Company, so it was actually directive. By the way, Rackham ignored the advice and bought $5,000 worth of stock. He sold it several years later for $12.5 million.
15. Directive. (Say "thank you.")

2.2

3. Form: Declarative.
    Function: Directive. (If you think this is just informative, you are in trouble.)
    Reworded: Water the lawn.
6. Form: Declarative.
    Function: Assertion (informative).
    Reworded: At sea level water freezes at 32° F (0° C).
9. Form: Interrogative.
    Function: Assertion (informative).
    Reworded: Former vice president Al Gore and actor Tommy Lee Jones were freshman roommates at Harvard.
12. Form: Imperative.
    Function: Assertion (informative)—though if one already knows the number, it could be directive and telling how to use the number.
    Reworded: The PIN is 3356.
15. Form: Declarative and exclamatory.
    Function: Assertion (informative).
    Reworded: I'm the map.

2.3

3. Informative: Warriors should kill whatever stands in their way.
    Expressive: Expresses admiration for warriors.
    Directive: Suppress your emotions and compassions and kill whatever stands in your way.

6. Informative: Three classes of citizens, etc.
    Expressive: Disgust for the upper and lower classes.
    Directive: Let's help develop the middle class.

9. Informative: If anyone ever saved Gladstone from death, it would be a calamity. (It is a joke at Gladstone's expense. Got to love those clever Brits.)
    Expressive: Contempt for Gladstone.
    Directive: Think poorly of Gladstone.

12. Good grief. I have no idea what this is saying. Do you?

15. Informative: Christianity is false and does not do a good job of explaining the universe.
    Expressive: Expresses disgust at Christianity.
    Directive: Don't be a Christian.

2.5

3. **Agreement** *in belief about the facts*: as to the US Air Force's involvement in Cambodia.
    Disagreement *in attitude toward the facts*: in whether this is a good or bad thing.

6. **Disagreement** *in belief about the facts*: as to whether women need men.
    Disagreement *in attitude toward the facts*: about women's dependence on men.

9. **Disagreement** *in belief about the facts*: as to whether people congregate with those like them.
    (*An argument could be made either way about their respective attitudes toward the facts.*)

12. **Disagreement** *in belief about the facts*: as to whether religion is true.
    Disagreement *in attitude toward the facts*: about religion.

15. **Disagreement** *in belief about the facts*: as to the value of education.
    Disagreement *in attitude toward the facts*: about education.

3.1

Note: There are any number of analogies that could be used. Here are just some samples.

3. If you can't be seen, you can't be captured. Therefore, if you are seen you will be captured.

Put formally:

> If you can't be seen, you can't be captured
> ———————————————————
> If you are seen you will be captured

That's like saying,

> If you can't be available next Saturday night, you can't perform at Carnegie Hall
> ———————————————————
> If you can be available next Saturday night, you will perform at Carnegie Hall

6. If you have ADHD, then you will have trouble focusing on academic work. Therefore all gamers have ADHD since all gamers have trouble focusing on academic work.

Put formally:

> If you have ADHD, then you will have trouble focusing on academic work
> If you are a gamer, then you will have trouble focusing on academic work
> ———————————————————
> If you are a gamer, you have ADHD

That's like saying,

> If you are five years old, then you can't bench-press 150 pounds
> If you are an out-of-shape fifty-year-old, you can't bench-press 150 pounds
> ———————————————————
> If you are an out-of-shape fifty-year-old, you are a five year old

9. No people afraid of heights are mountain climbers, but all mountain climbers are fit, so no people afraid of heights are fit.

Put formally:

> All mountain climbers are fit
> No people afraid of heights are mountain climbers
> ———————————————————
> No people afraid of heights are fit

That's like saying,

> All paintings by Rafael are beautiful
> No paintings by Michelangelo are paintings by Rafael
> ———————————————————
> No paintings by Michelangelo are beautiful

3.2

3. Equivocation; on the word "run." The first use means "to move at a speed faster than a walk"; the second means "flows."

6. Division; the headline is talking about the lack of railroad track taken as a whole, but Leno is responding as if it meant this particular railroad line. There could also be an equivocation on "hurt," but that also involves a division ("hurt" in the headline means the entire system is lacking track, while Leno means they will be "hurt" by the lack of track on this particular train line.)

9. Hasty generalization; taking an unusual case (school-sponsored activity) and trying to make a general rule out of it.

12. Amphiboly; grammatically, the phrase "in Graves Gym tonight" modifies where the *jobs* are; the dean undoubtedly meant it to modify where the *talk* was going to be.

15. Hasty generalization; making a general rule from just two instances.

3.3

3. Straw man; a very simplistic argument that few, if any, feminists would make.

6. *Ad populum*; snob appeal.

9. Ignorance; no one has proved it true (that the secretary leaked the news), so it must be false.

12. *Ad hominem*; a version of circumstantial *ad hominem*.

15. False cause; a clear example of *post hoc, ergo propter hoc* reasoning—it is not clear what, if any, causal relationship there is here.

3.4

3. *Ad populum*?; seems to be appealing to emotions to excuse setting a devastating blaze. Perhaps this could be seen as a false cause if she is implying that her situation caused her to set the fire.

6. Begging the question; essentially this says, "I am attractive because I am attractive."

9. False cause; unless watching crime shows causes people to commit murder—in which case, why aren't there millions of murders?

12. Illegitimate authority; Cruise is an authority on acting, but psychiatry? Not so much.

15. Accent; quoting out of context to completely change the meaning.

3.5a

3. Looks like either appeal to pity or an odd *ad populum*. But do deer and elk have "feelings" that need to be regarded in the same way as those of humans? And is the answer to shoot them?

6. This looks like *ad populum*, but there is probably no fallacy here. Had he argued that there are eternal rewards and punishments because all nations think so, that would be a fallacy. But if, in fact, all nations believe there are eternal rewards and punishments, that would make it a "Common Notion."

9. Begging the question; it's not a *new* number, just changed—because it is a not different (i.e., "new") just changed.

12. Division; what is true of a group as a whole is not necessarily true of the parts (as Willis found out when his solo career bombed).

15. Equivocation; on the words "make sure." The 911 operator meant "check to see if" he is dead; the hunter took it to mean "do what is necessary to ensure that" he is dead.

3.   Force; clearly a threat.

6.   Equivocation on the words "a mighty nation." Croesus took it to mean his adversary's nation, the Oracle meant his own.

9.   Perhaps hasty generalization; there may be religions based on "voluntary slavery," but does that apply to all religions? Or it could be equivocation by implying that "obedience" and "corruption of the will" mean the same thing.

12.   Composition; seems to say that the attributes of the smallest class are true of the state taken as a whole.

15.   False cause; putting this disgusting stuff on her head is probably not what restored her hair after childbirth. Could also be considered a hasty generalization as she is taking two examples (hers and her grandmother's) and drawing a general rule from it.

UNIT II

4.1

3.   Quantifier: All
      Copula: are
      Subject: people who enjoy a great love story and quirky humor
      Predicate: people who should watch *Strictly Ballroom*

6.   Quantifier: Some
      Copula: are
      Subject: members of the clergy
      Predicate: disreputable people

9.   Quantifier: All
      Copula: will be
      Subject: usable pens
      Predicate: things we will need

12.   Quantifier: Some
      Copula: are
      Subject: drugs
      Predicate: habit-forming things

15.   Quantifier: Some
      Copula: are
      Subject: philosophical treatises
      Predicate: incredibly complicated and grammatically dense writings

4.2

3. Quality: Affirmative
    Quantity: Universal
    Name: A
    Distributed: "people who take a logic class" (subject)

6. Quality: Negative
    Quantity: Universal
    Name: E
    Distributed: "buildings in downtown Lisbon" (subject) and "buildings that survived the earthquake of 1755" (predicate)

9. Quality: Affirmative
    Quantity: Universal
    Name: A
    Distributed: "philosophy classes" (subject)

12. Quality: Affirmative
    Quantity: Particular
    Name: I
    Distributed: nothing

15. Quality: Affirmative
    Quantity: Particular
    Name: I
    Distributed: nothing

4.3

3. All picture frames are expensive items.

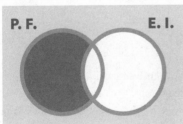

6. No skateboards are things allowed in this park.

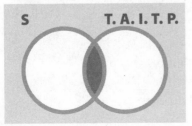

9.   All <u>pewter steins</u> are pencil holders.

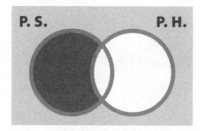

12. Some shampoo bottles are containers in the shape of cartoon characters.

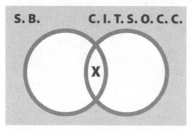

15. Some mechanical pencils are hard-to-find items.

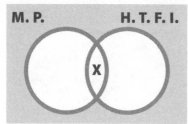

5.1

3.   No (this is a hypothetical syllogism)
6.   Yes; terms: "computer speakers," "inexpensive items," "pens"
9.   Yes; terms: "children's books," "boring things," "books by C. S. Lewis"
12. No (this has four terms: "[things] one sends," "greeting cards," "old people," "good investments")
15. Yes; terms: "software," "useful things," "expensive items"

5.2

3.   Some football players are students living off-campus
     No <u>dorm residents</u> are <u>students living off-campus</u>
     _____
     Some dorm residents are not <u>football players</u>

Major term: "football players"
Minor term: "dorm residents"
Middle term: "students living off-campus"

6. All <u>advocates of high tariff rates</u> are Republicans
    Some Republicans are not <u>conservatives</u>
    _____
    Some conservatives are not <u>advocates of high tariff rates</u>

Major term: "advocates of high tariff rates"
Minor term: "conservatives"
Middle term: "Republicans"

9. Some toys are plastic
    Some cups are toys
    _____
    Some cups are plastic

Major term: "plastic"
Minor term: "cups"
Middle term: "toys"

12. No <u>carnival prizes</u> are <u>valuable items</u>
    No <u>bank-giveaway pens</u> are <u>valuable items</u>
    _____
    No <u>bank giveaway pens</u> are <u>carnival prizes</u>

Major term: "carnival prizes"
Minor term: "bank-giveaway pens"
Middle term: "valuable items"

15. All <u>students who do their homework carefully</u> are good logic students
    All <u>good logic students</u> are students who will know that this syllogism is invalid
    _____
    All <u>students who will know that this syllogism is invalid</u> are students who do their
    homework carefully

Major term: "students who do their homework carefully"
Minor term: "students who will know that this syllogism is invalid"
Middle term: "good logic students"

5.3a

3. IEO-2
6. AOO-4
9. III-1
12. EEE-2
15. AAA-4

5.3b

3.   No <u>P</u> is <u>M</u>
        Some S is M
        _____

        Some S is not <u>P</u>

6.   No <u>M</u> is <u>P</u>
        All <u>S</u> is M
        _____

        No <u>S</u> is <u>P</u>

9.   No <u>P</u> is <u>M</u>
        No <u>S</u> is <u>M</u>
        _____

        No <u>S</u> is <u>P</u>

12.   Some P is M
        Some S is not <u>M</u>
        _____

        Some S is P

15.   All <u>M</u> is P
        All <u>S</u> is M
        _____

        All <u>S</u> is P

5.4a

3.   AOO-4; invalid, as it is not clear if the X is in the sociopath (S) circle or not.

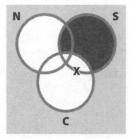

6.   EIO-3; valid

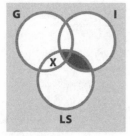

9. AEO-2; invalid, as there is no X at all.

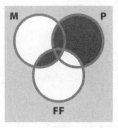

12. IEO-4; invalid, as there is no X in the experiences we actively seek (EWAS) circle that is outside the dreams (D) circle.

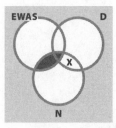

15. III-1; invalid, as it is not clear where either X is to go.

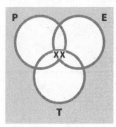

5.4b

3. OOI-4; invalid

Some P is not <u>M</u>

Some M is not <u>S</u>

Some S is P

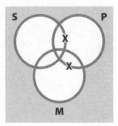

6. IAI-4; valid

> Some P is M
> All <u>M</u> is S
> _____
> Some S is P

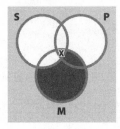

9. EIO-4; valid

> No <u>P</u> is <u>M</u>
> Some M is S
> _____
> Some S is not <u>P</u>

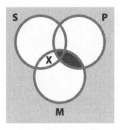

12. IAI-2; invalid

> Some P is M
> All <u>S</u> is M
> _____
> Some S is P

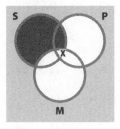

15.   AEE-2; valid

All <u>P</u> is M
No <u>S</u> is <u>M</u>

No <u>S</u> is <u>P</u>

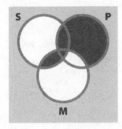

3.   EIO-1; valid
6.   IAI-3; valid
9.   IAI-4; valid
12.   EOO-4; invalid; rule one: Can't have two negative premises
15.   AAA-2; invalid; rule four: The middle term must be distributed in at least one premise

3.   EIO-2; valid

No <u>P</u> is <u>M</u>
Some S is M

Some S is not <u>P</u>

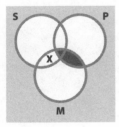

6.   EAE-1; valid

No <u>M</u> is <u>P</u>
All <u>S</u> is M

No <u>S</u> is <u>P</u>

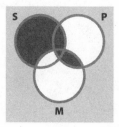

9. EEE-2; invalid; rule one: Can't have two negative premises

No P̲ is M̲
No S̲ is M̲
—————
No S̲ is P̲

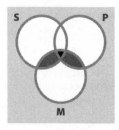

12. IAI-4; valid

Some P is M
All M̲ is S
—————
Some S is P

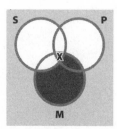

15. AAI-1; invalid; rule one: Can't have two universal premises and a particular conclusion

All M is P
All S is M
—————
Some S is P

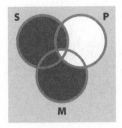

6.1

3. AAA-1; valid

> All <u>pieces of plumbing equipment</u> are things that are difficult to install
> All <u>toilets</u> are pieces of plumbing equipment
> ___
> All <u>toilets</u> are things that are difficult to install

6. OAO-3; valid

> Some antiques are not <u>things for sale</u>
> All <u>antiques</u> are expensive items
> ___
> Some expensive items are not <u>things for sale</u>

9. IAI-4; valid

> Some cars are racers
> All <u>racers</u> are hazardous vehicles
> ___
> Some hazardous vehicles are cars

6.2

3. Some money-makers are McDonald's restaurants. (By limitation; not logically equivalent.)
6. All <u>boat anchors</u> are non-things that weigh less than ten pounds. (Or All boat anchors are things that weigh ten pounds or more.)
9. Some prescription pills are not <u>non-habit-forming drugs</u>.
12. Some non-cheap items are not <u>non-iPhones</u>. (By limitation; not logically equivalent.)
15. —— (It is not possible to contrapose an I proposition.)

6.3
---

3.   AEE-2; valid

> All <u>contemporary instruments</u> are portable instruments (by obversion)
> No <u>church organs</u> are <u>portable instruments</u>
> _____
> No <u>church organs</u> are <u>contemporary instruments</u> (by obversion)

6.   EAE-1; valid

> No <u>people who got accepted</u> are <u>dumb people</u> (by obversion)
> All <u>State University students</u> are people who got accepted
> _____
> No <u>State University students</u> are <u>dumb people</u>

9.   EIO-2; valid

> No <u>carnivores</u> are <u>vegetarians</u>
> Some wild animals are vegetarians (by synonym)
> _____
> Some wild animals are not <u>carnivores</u> (by synonym)

12.   EAE-2; valid

> No <u>valid syllogisms</u> are <u>syllogisms with two negative premises</u>
> All <u>EEA arguments</u> are syllogisms with two negative premises (by obversion)
> _____
> No <u>EEA arguments</u> are <u>valid syllogisms</u> (by obversion)

15.   IAI-1; invalid; rule four: The middle term must be distributed in at least one premise

> Some talented athletes are six feet tall or less
> All <u>NBA players</u> are talented athletes (by obversion)
> _____
> Some NBA players are six feet tall or less

6.4
---

3.   Some football games are fun things to watch.
6.   All <u>forest fire preventers</u> are you. (This is an exceptive proposition.)
9.   No <u>unexamined lives</u> are <u>lives worth living</u>.
     (Or the converse and obverse: "All <u>lives worth living</u> are examined lives.")
12.   All <u>things that happen in Vegas</u> are things that stay in Vegas.
15.   No <u>non-prescription glasses</u> are <u>glasses that correct astigmatism</u>.
     (Or the converse and obverse: "All <u>glasses that correct astigmatism</u> are pre-scription glasses.")

6.5a

3. Some places she goes are not <u>places she finds people she knows</u>.

6. All <u>times he goes to the store</u> are times he buys things he doesn't need.

9. All <u>times you see something [suspicious]</u> are times you should say something [to an appropriate authority].

12. All <u>times the boogeyman goes to sleep</u> are times he checks his closet for Chuck Norris.

15. All <u>places you want to be</u> are places where Visa is found [or "is accepted as payment"].

6.5b

3. Roughly:

> Everybody loves some kind of music
> Not everyone loves jazz
> _____
> Some people love something other than jazz

Translated:

> Some people are not <u>jazz lovers</u>
> All <u>people</u> are music lovers
> _____
> Some music lovers are not <u>jazz lovers</u>

OAO-3; Valid

6. Roughly:

> All things without tails are non-monkeys
> Kites have tails
> _____
> Kites are monkeys

Translated:

> All <u>monkeys</u> are things with tails (by contraposition)
> All <u>kites</u> are things with tails
> _____
> All <u>kites</u> are monkeys

AAA-2; invalid; rule four: The middle term must be distributed in at least one premise. If we translate the singular propositions as I propositions, it won't help since the middle term will still not be distributed. (Bob seems to know there is a problem when he says, "Uh, I think there's something wrong with your logic, Larry.")

9.   Roughly:

> Cool people work at Krispy Kreme Doughnuts
> Me and Katie are cool
> _____
> Me and Katie work at Krispy Kreme

Translated:

> All <u>Krispy Kreme Doughnuts workers</u> are cool people*
> All <u>me and Katie</u> are cool people
> _____
> All <u>me and Katie</u> are Krispy Kreme Doughnuts workers

AAA-2; invalid; rule four: The middle term must be distributed in at least one premise. So we must try translating the singular propositions using the particular:

> All <u>Krispy Kreme Doughnuts workers</u> are cool people
> Some me and Katie are cool people
> _____
> Some me and Katie are Krispy Kreme Doughnuts workers

AII-2; but this is still invalid for the same reason.

12.   Roughly:

> I have forgot all men
> You are a man
> _____
> I have forgotten you

Translated:

> All <u>men</u> are persons I have forgotten
> All <u>you</u> are men
> _____
> All <u>you</u> are persons I have forgotten

AAA-1; valid; yes, the grammar is awkward, but it works.

15.   Roughly:

> Supernatural talents are necessary for attainment of a heavenly life and
>   eternal happiness
> Of the supernatural [talents man] has been wholly deprived
> _____
> Man is exiled from the kingdom of God

---

*If we translate this as "All <u>cool people</u> are Krispy Kreme Doughnuts workers," we would have a valid argument. But is the statement really making the claim that every cool person *in the world* works at Krispy Kreme Doughnuts?

Translated:

> All <u>persons who attain the kingdom of God</u> are persons with supernatural talents
> No <u>persons</u> are <u>persons with supernatural talents</u>
> ───
> No <u>persons</u> are <u>persons who attain the kingdom of God</u>

AEE-2; valid

6.6

3. Roughly:

> You always grab your purse and shopping list when you go to the store
> You did not grab your purse and shopping list
> ───
> You are not going to the store

Translated:

> All <u>times you are going to the store</u> are times you grab your purse and
>   shopping list
> No <u>times that are now</u> are <u>times you grab your purse and shopping list</u>
> ───
> No <u>times that are now</u> are <u>times you are going to the store</u> (missing conclusion)

Third order; AEE-2; valid

6. Roughly:

> Where there is smoke, there is fire
> There is no smoke in the basement
> ───
> There is no fire in the basement

Translated:

> All <u>places with smoke</u> are places with fires
> No <u>places that are the basement</u> are <u>places with smoke</u>
> ───
> No <u>places that are the basement</u> are <u>places with fire</u> (missing conclusion)

Third order; AEE-1; invalid; rule five: If either term is distributed in the conclusion, then it must be distributed in the premise in which it appears. (There
is no way to supply a conclusion that would make this enthymeme valid.)

9. Roughly:

> Lend the soldiers a hand
> Buying war bonds will lend them a hand
> ───
> Buy war bonds

Translated:

> All <u>persons who should lend the soldiers a hand</u> are persons who should buy war bonds (missing premise)
>
> All <u>you</u> [implied] are persons who should lend the soldiers a hand
> ___
> All <u>you</u> are persons who should buy war bonds

First order; AAA-1; valid

12.   Roughly:

> There is no law against composing music when one has no ideas whatsoever
>
> Wagner composes music when he has no ideas whatsoever
> ___
> The music of Wagner is perfectly legal

Translated:

> All <u>music composed when one has no ideas whatsoever</u> is something that is perfectly legal
>
> All <u>music of Wagner</u> is music composed when one has no ideas whatsoever (missing premise)
> ___
> All <u>music of Wagner</u> is something that is perfectly legal

Second order; AAA-1; valid (but clearly a joke)

15.   Roughly:

> We have no experience of divine attributes and operations
>
> Our ideas reach no farther than our experience
> ___
> We have no idea of divine attributes and operations

Translated:

> No <u>experiences we have</u> are <u>things about divine attributes and operations</u>
>
> All <u>ideas we have</u> are experiences we have
> ___
> No <u>ideas we have</u> are <u>things about divine attributes and operations</u> (missing conclusion)

Third order; EAE-1; valid

UNIT III

7.1

3. True
6. False
9. True
12. False
15. False

7.2

3. False
6. True
9. False
12. False
15. False

7.3

3. True
6. True
9. False
12. True
15. True

7.4

3. $(A \lor B) \to (C \cdot B)$

A B C	A ∨ B	C · B	(A ∨ B) → (C · B)
T T T	T	T	T
T T F	T	F	F
T F T	T	F	F
T F F	T	F	F
F T T	T	T	T
F T F	T	F	F
F F T	F	F	T
F F F	F	F	T

6. $[D \rightarrow (D \rightarrow E)] \rightarrow E$

D E	D → E	D → (D → E)	[D → (D → E)] → E
T T	T	T	T
T F	F	F	T
F T	T	T	T
F F	T	T	F

9. $J \rightarrow [\sim J \rightarrow (K \vee \sim K)]$

J K	~K	~J	K ∨ ~K	~J → (K ∨ ~K)	J → [~J → (K ∨ ~K)]
T T	F	F	T	T	T
T F	T	F	T	T	T
F T	F	T	T	T	T
F F	T	T	T	T	T

12. $[\sim Q \rightarrow (R \vee \sim Q)] \rightarrow (R \vee Q)$

Q R	~Q	R ∨ ~Q	~Q → (R ∨ ~Q)	R ∨ Q	[~Q → (R ∨ ~Q) → (R ∨ Q)]
T T	F	T	T	T	T
T F	F	F	T	T	T
F T	T	T	T	T	T
F F	T	T	T	F	F

15. $W \leftrightarrow [W \cdot (W \rightarrow X)]$

W X	W → X	W · (W → X)	W ↔ [W · (W → X)]
T T	T	T	T
T F	F	F	F
F T	T	F	T
F F	T	F	T

7.5

3. Substitution instance of c, g; g is the specific form of this statement.
6. Substitution instance of a, f, j; j is the specific form of this statement.
9. Substitution instance of b, k, l; the specific form of this statement is not given. Notice that since *p*, *q*, *r*, and *s* can stand for any statement whatsoever, there is no reason they cannot stand for the *same* statement (in this case "A").
12. Substitution instance of a; the specific form of this statement is not given.
15. Substitution instance of c; the specific form of this statement is not given.

8.1

3. Substitution instance of h; the specific form of this argument is not given.
6. Substitution instance of a; the specific form of this argument is not given.
9. Substitution instance of d; the specific form of this argument is not given.

8.2a

3. A ∨ B
   A
   ∴ ~ B

A B	A ∨ B	A	∴ ~ B
T T	(T) →	(T) →	F x
T F	(T) →	(T) →	T
F T	T	F	F
F F	F	F	T

Invalid

6. L → (M · N)
   ~ N ∨ ~ M
   ∴ ~ L

L M N	M · N	~ N	~ M	L → (M · N)	~ N ∨ ~ M	∴ ~ L
T T T	T	F	F	T	F	F
T T F	F	T	F	F	T	F
T F T	F	F	T	F	T	F
T F F	F	T	T	F	T	F
F T T	T	F	F	T	F	T
F T F	F	T	F	(T) →	(T) →	T
F F T	F	F	T	(T) →	(T) →	T
F F F	F	T	T	(T) →	(T) →	T

Valid

9. S ∨ T
   (S · T) → T
   ~ S
   ∴ T

S T	S · T	S ∨ T	(S · T) → T	~ S	∴ T
T T	T	T	T	F	T
T F	F	T	T	F	F
F T	F	(T) →	(T) →	(T) →	T
F F	F	F	T	T	F

Valid

8.2b

3. If I buy a lamp and a desk, then I will buy a lamp and not a desk. I buy a lamp. So I buy a desk.

$(L \cdot D) \rightarrow (L \cdot \sim D)$

L

$\therefore D$

D L	~D	L · D	L · ~D	$(L \cdot D) \rightarrow (L \cdot \sim D)$	L	$\therefore$ D
T T	F	T	F	F	T	T
T F	F	F	F	T	F	T
F T	T	F	T	T⃝——————T⃝ ——→ F x		
F F	T	F	F	T	F	F

Invalid

6. If Batman is either crazy or good, then he is crazy *and* good. So if Batman is crazy then he is good and if he is good then he is crazy.

$(C \vee G) \rightarrow (C \cdot G)$

$\therefore (C \rightarrow G) \cdot (G \rightarrow C)$

C G	C∨G	C·G	C→G	G→C	$(C \vee G) \rightarrow (C \cdot G)$	$\therefore (C \rightarrow G) \cdot (G \rightarrow C)$
T T	T	T	T	T	T⃝——————————→	T
T F	T	F	F	T	F	F
F T	T	F	T	F	F	F
F F	F	F	T	T	T⃝——————————→	T

Valid

9. If you do well at logic, then you will enjoy this class. If you enjoy this class, then you do well in logic. So you will enjoy this class.

$W \rightarrow E$

$E \rightarrow W$

$\therefore E$

E W	W→E	E→W	$\therefore$ E
T T	T⃝——————T⃝ ——→		T
T F	T	F	T
F T	F	T	F
F F	T⃝——————T⃝ ——→ F x		

Invalid

8.3a

3. C. D.
6. Add.
9. Conj.
12. H. S.
15. C. D.

8.3b

3. 1. G → H
    2. ~ H /∴ ~ G ∨ I
    3. ~ G   1, 2, M. T.
    4. ~ G ∨ I   3, Add.

6. 1. P → Q
    2. R → P
    3. P ∨ R /∴ Q ∨ P
    4. (P → Q) · (R → P)   1, 2, Conj.
    5. Q ∨ P   4, 3, C. D.

9. 1. Y · ~ Z
    2. ~ Z → (Y ↔ Z) /∴ (Y ↔ Z) ∨ (~ Y · ~ Z)
    3. ~ Z   1, Simp.
    4. (Y ↔ Z)   2, 3, M. P.
    5. (Y ↔ Z) ∨ (~ Y · ~ Z)   4, Add.

12. 1. (L → M) · (N → O)
    2. L /∴ M ∨ O
    3. L → M   1, Simp.
    4. M   3, 2, M. P.
    5. M ∨ O   4, Add.

15. 1. (X → Y) → Z
    2. (X → Y) ∨ X
    3. ~ Z /∴ X
    4. ~ (X → Y)   1, 3, M. T.
    5. X   2, 4, D. S.

8.3c

3. 1. (K ∨ J) → H
    2. K /∴ H ∨ I
    3. K ∨ J   2, Add.
    4. H   1, 3, M. P.
    5. H ∨ I   4, Add.

6. 1. $[(Y \leftrightarrow Z) \rightarrow Z] \vee (Y \vee Z)$
    2. $\sim (Y \vee Z)$
    3. $Y \leftrightarrow Z / \therefore Z$
    4. $(Y \leftrightarrow Z) \rightarrow Z$ 1, 2, D. S.
    5. Z 4, 3, M. P.

9. 1. $K \rightarrow L$
    2. $(K \cdot L) \rightarrow [M \rightarrow (O \vee P)]$
    3. K
    4. $\sim (O \vee P) / \therefore \sim M$
    5. $K \rightarrow (K \cdot L)$ 1, Abs.
    6. $K \rightarrow [M \rightarrow (O \vee P)]$ 5, 2, H. S.
    7. $M \rightarrow (O \vee P)$ 6, 3, M. P.
    8. $\sim M$ 7, 4, M. T.

12. 1. $[(\sim A \rightarrow B) \cdot C] \cdot (D \leftrightarrow E)$
    2. $(B \cdot C) \rightarrow E$
    3. $(D \leftrightarrow E) \rightarrow \sim E / \therefore \sim (B \cdot C)$
    4. $(D \leftrightarrow E)$ 1, Simp.
    5. $\sim E$ 3, 4, M. P.
    6. $\sim (B \cdot C)$ 2, 5, M. T.

15. 1. $(Q \cdot R) \rightarrow [\sim (R \leftrightarrow S) \vee T]$
    2. $\sim \sim (R \leftrightarrow S)$
    3. $[(T \cdot \sim S) \rightarrow R] \rightarrow Q$
    4. R
    5. $(T \cdot \sim S) \rightarrow R / \therefore T$
    6. Q 3, 5, M. P.
    7. $Q \cdot R$ 6, 4, Conj.
    8. $\sim (R \leftrightarrow S) \vee T$ 1, 7, M. P.
    9. T 8, 2, D. S.

8.4

3. Dist.
6. Com.
9. Exp.
12. Equiv.
15. Dist.

8.5a

3.   1. G /∴ H → G
       2. G ∨ ~ H   1, Add.
       3. ~ H ∨ G   2, Com.
       4. H → G   3, Impl.

6.   1. (O ∨ P) → Q
       2. P /∴ Q
       3. O ∨ P   2, Add.
       4. Q   1, 3, M. P.

9.   1. X → Y
       2. Y → Z
       3. X ∨ Y /∴ Y ∨ Z
       4. (X → Y) · (Y → Z)   1, 2, Conj.
       5. Y ∨ Z   4, 3, C. D.

12. 1. F → (G · H)
       2. ~ G ∨ ~ H /∴ ~ F
       3. ~ (G · H)   2, DeM.
       4. ~ F   1, 3, M. T.

15. 1. ~ (N → O) /∴ N
       2. ~ (~ N ∨ O)   1, Impl.
       3. ~ ~ N · ~ O   2, DeM.
       4. ~ ~ N   3, Simp.
       5. N   4, D. N.

8.5b

3.   1. F → G /∴ (F · H) → G
       2. ~ F ∨ G   1, Impl.
       3. (~ F ∨ G) ∨ ~ H   2, Add.
       4. ~ F ∨ (G ∨ ~ H)   3, Assoc.
       5. ~ F ∨ (~ H ∨ G)   4, Com.
       6. (~ F ∨ ~ H) ∨ G   5, Assoc.
       7. ~ (F · H) ∨ G   6, DeM.
       8. (F · H) → G   7, Impl.

6. 1. $(O \lor P) \rightarrow Q \;/\therefore\; O \rightarrow Q$
    2. $\sim (O \lor P) \lor Q$ 1, Impl.
    3. $(\sim O \cdot \sim P) \lor Q$ 2, DeM.
    4. $Q \lor (\sim O \cdot \sim P)$ 3, Com.
    5. $(Q \lor \sim O) \cdot (Q \lor \sim P)$ 4, Dist.
    6. $Q \lor \sim O$ 5, Simp.
    7. $\sim O \lor Q$ 6, Com.
    8. $O \rightarrow Q$ 7, Impl.

9. 1. $X \rightarrow Y$
    2. $Z \rightarrow Y \;/\therefore\; (X \lor Z) \rightarrow Y$
    3. $\sim X \lor Y$ 1, Impl.
    4. $\sim Z \lor Y$ 2, Impl.
    5. $Y \lor \sim X$ 3, Com.
    6. $Y \lor \sim Z$ 4, Com.
    7. $(Y \lor \sim X) \cdot (Y \lor \sim Z)$ 5, 6, Conj.
    8. $Y \lor (\sim X \cdot \sim Z)$ 7, Dist.
    9. $(\sim X \cdot \sim Z) \lor Y$ 8, Com.
    10. $\sim (X \lor Z) \lor Y$ 9, DeM.
    11. $(X \lor Z) \rightarrow Y$ 10, Impl.

8.5c

3. 1. $H \rightarrow (I \rightarrow J)$
    2. $K \rightarrow I \;/\therefore\; K \rightarrow (H \rightarrow J)$
    3. $(H \cdot I) \rightarrow J$ 1, Exp.
    4. $(I \cdot H) \rightarrow J$ 3, Com.
    5. $I \rightarrow (H \rightarrow J)$ 4, Exp.
    6. $K \rightarrow (H \rightarrow J)$ 2, 5, H. S.

6. 1. $T \rightarrow U$
    2. $T \rightarrow \sim U$
    3. $V \rightarrow T \;/\therefore\; \sim V$
    4. $\sim U \rightarrow \sim T$ 1, Trans.
    5. $T \rightarrow \sim T$ 2, 4, H. S.
    6. $\sim T \lor \sim T$ 5, Impl.
    7. $\sim T$ 6, Taut.
    8. $\sim V$ 3, 7, M. T.

9. 1. $(C \rightarrow D) \cdot (E \rightarrow F)$
    2. $(\sim C \vee D) \cdot E / \therefore (\sim C \vee D) \cdot F$
    3. $\sim C \vee D$ 2, Simp.
    4. E   2, Simp.
    5. $E \rightarrow F$ 1, Simp.
    6. F   5, 4, M. P.
    7. $(\sim C \vee D) \cdot F$ 3, 6, Conj.

8.6

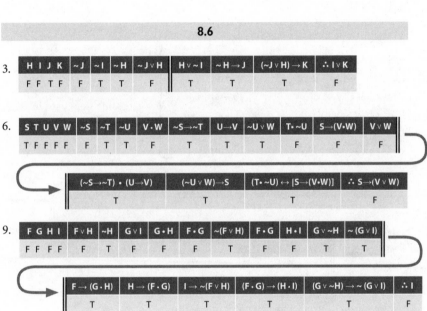

3.

H I J K	~J	~I	~H	~J ∨ H	H ∨ ~I	~H → J	(~J ∨ H) → K	∴ I ∨ K
F F T F	F	T	T	F	T	T	T	F

6.

S T U V W	~S	~T	~U	V · W	~S → ~T	U → V	~U ∨ W	T · ~U	S → (V·W)	V ∨ W
T F F F F	F	T	T	F	T	T	T	F	F	F

(~S → ~T) · (U → V)	(~U ∨ W) → S	(T · ~U) ↔ [S → (V·W)]	∴ S → (V ∨ W)
T	T	T	F

9.

F G H I	F ∨ H	~H	G ∨ I	G · H	F · G	~(F ∨ H)	F · G	H · I	G ∨ ~H	~(G ∨ I)
F F F F	F	T	F	F	F	T	F	F	T	T

F → (G · H)	H → (F · G)	I → ~(F ∨ H)	(F · G) → (H · I)	(G ∨ ~H) → ~(G ∨ I)	∴ I
T	T	T	T	T	F

8.7

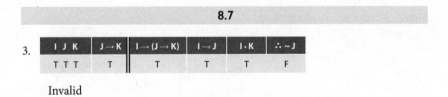

3.

I J K	J → K	I → (J → K)	I → J	I · K	∴ ~J
T T T	T	T	T	T	F

Invalid

6.

S T U V	~T	U · V	S ∨ T	U → ~T	∴ (U · V) → S
F F T T	T	T	?	T	F

It is not possible to find truth values to make the premise true and the conclusion false so we must construct a formal proof of validity.

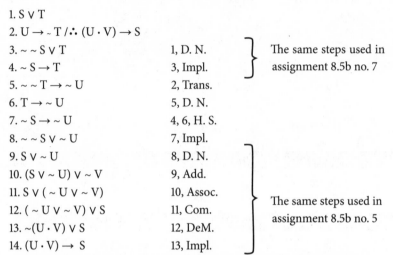

1. S ∨ T
2. U → ~ T /∴ (U · V) → S
3. ~ ~ S ∨ T   1, D. N.   } The same steps used in
4. ~ S → T   3, Impl.   assignment 8.5b no. 7
5. ~ ~ T → ~ U   2, Trans.
6. T → ~ U   5, D. N.
7. ~ S → ~ U   4, 6, H. S.
8. ~ ~ S ∨ ~ U   7, Impl.
9. S ∨ ~ U   8, D. N.
10. (S ∨ ~ U) ∨ ~ V   9, Add.
11. S ∨ (~ U ∨ ~ V)   10, Assoc.   The same steps used in
12. (~ U ∨ ~ V) ∨ S   11, Com.   assignment 8.5b no. 5
13. ~(U · V) ∨ S   12, DeM.
14. (U · V) → S   13, Impl.

9.

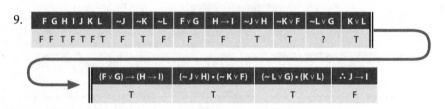

It is not possible to find truth values to make the premise true and the conclusion false so we must construct a formal proof of validity.

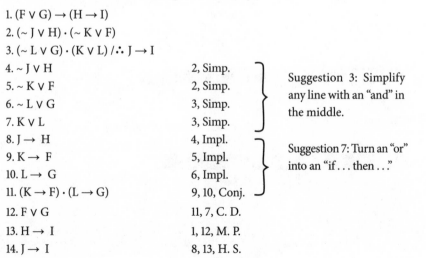

1. (F ∨ G) → (H → I)
2. (~ J ∨ H) · (~ K ∨ F)
3. (~ L ∨ G) · (K ∨ L) /∴ J → I
4. ~ J ∨ H   2, Simp.   } Suggestion 3: Simplify
5. ~ K ∨ F   2, Simp.   any line with an "and" in
6. ~ L ∨ G   3, Simp.   the middle.
7. K ∨ L   3, Simp.
8. J → H   4, Impl.   } Suggestion 7: Turn an "or"
9. K → F   5, Impl.   into an "if . . . then . . ."
10. L → G   6, Impl.
11. (K → F) · (L → G)   9, 10, Conj.
12. F ∨ G   11, 7, C. D.
13. H → I   1, 12, M. P.
14. J → I   8, 13, H. S.

8.8a

3.   (Use letters WGAO)

> If God doesn't want to prevent evil, then God is not all good
> If God isn't able to prevent evil, then God is not omnipotent
> Either God doesn't want to prevent evil or God is not able
> _____
> Either God is not omnipotent or God is not all-good

1. ~ W → ~ G   (Note that you could use W
2. ~ A → ~ O   to stand for "God doesn't
3. ~ W ∨ ~ A /∴ ~ O ∨ ~ G   want to prevent evil," etc.,
4. (~ W → ~ G) · (~ A → ~ O)   1, 2, Conj.   and not have all the "nots.")
5. ~ O ∨ ~ G   4, 3, C. D.

6.   (Use letters FES)

> If there is no first cause, then either there is an endless chain of causes and effects
>   or else some being caused itself
> There is not endless chain of causes and effects
> No being caused itself
> _____
> There is a first cause

1. ~ F → (E ∨ S)
2. ~ E
3. ~ S /∴ F
4. ~ E · ~ S   2,3, Conj.
5. ~ (E ∨ S)   4, DeM.
6. ~ ~ F   1,5, M. T.
7. F   6, D. N.

9.   (Use letters KLCDUH)

> If the Sacramento Kings make it to the NBA Finals, they will lose
> If the Charlotte Hornets make it to the NBA Finals, they will be defeated
> Both the Kings and the Hornets make it to the NBA Finals (note: this will be at
>   some future date)
> Either the Kings will lose or the Hornets will be defeated, but not both
> _____
> The universe will explode in a fiery cataclysm and hell will freeze over

1. K → L
2. C → D
3. K · C
4. (L ∨ D) · ~ (L · D) /∴ U · H
5. K   3, Simp.
6. C   3, Simp.
7. L   1, 5, M. P.
8. D   2, 6, M. P.
9. L · D   7, 8, Conj.
10. ~ (L · D)   4, Simp.
11. (L · D) ∨ (U · H)   9, Add.
12. U · H   11, 10, D. S.

(Valid because of a contradiction)

8.8b

3.   (Use letters EFSH)

Either you enjoy doing these proofs or you find them frustrating

If you enjoy doing these proofs, then you are finding solutions for them

If you find these proofs frustrating, then you are not happy right now

Either you are finding solutions for these proofs or you are not happy right now

1. E ∨ F

2. E → S

3. F → ~ H /∴ S ∨ ~ H

E	F	H	S	~H	E∨F	E→S	F→~H	∴ S∨~H
?	F	T	F	F	?	T	T	F

It is not possible to find truth values to make the premise true and the conclusion false so we must construct a formal proof of validity:

1. E ∨ F
2. E → S
3. F → ~ H /∴ S ∨ ~ H
4. (E → S) · (F → ~ H)   2, 3, Conj.
5. S ∨ ~ H   4, 1, C. D.

Valid

6. (Use letters PGBN)

> Either Socrates's death will be perpetual sleep, or, if the gods are good, then Socrates's death will be an entry into a better life
>
> If Socrates's death will be perpetual sleep, then Socrates has nothing to fear from death
>
> The gods are good
>
> If Socrates's death will be an entry into a better life, then Socrates has nothing to fear from death

---

> Socrates has nothing to fear from death

4. $P \lor (G \to B)$

5. $P \to N$

6. G

7. $B \to N$ /∴ N

B	G	N	P	G→B	P∨(G→B)	P→N	G	B→N	∴N
F	T	F	F	F	?	T	T	T	F

It is not possible to find truth values to make the premise true and the conclusion false so we must construct a formal proof of validity.

1. $P \lor (G \to B)$
2. $P \to N$
3. G
4. $B \to N$ /∴ N
5. $P \lor (\sim G \lor B)$ 1, Impl.
6. $(\sim G \lor B) \lor P$ 5, Com.
7. $\sim G \lor (B \lor P)$ 6, Assoc.
8. $\sim \sim G$ 3, D. N.
9. $B \lor P$ 7, 8, D. S.
10. $(B \to N) \cdot (P \to N)$ 4, 2, Conj.
11. $N \lor N$ 10, 9, C. D.
12. N 11, Taut.

9. (Use letters TWPEFL)

> If I give a test in logic, then people either do well or poorly
>
> If people do well, then I think that I made the test too easy and I am frustrated
>
> If people do poorly, then I think that people didn't learn any logic and I am frustrated

---

> Therefore, if I give a test in logic, then I am frustrated

8. T → (W ∨ P)

9. W → (E · F)

10. P → (~ L · F) / ∴ T → F

E F L P T W	~L	W∨P	E·F	~L·F	T→(W∨P)	W→(E·F)	P→(~L·F)	∴T→F
? F ? ? T F		T	F	F	T	T		F

It is not possible to find truth values to make the premise true and the conclusion false so we must construct a formal proof of validity.

1. T → (W ∨ P)

2. W → (E · F)

3. P → (~ L · F) / ∴ T → F

4. ~ W ∨ (E · F)   2, Impl.   ⎫

5. (~ W ∨ E) · (~ W ∨ F)   4, Dist.   ⎬ The same three steps
                                                          used in assignment 8.5b
6. ~ W ∨ F   5, Simp.   ⎭ no. 4 . . .

7. ~ P ∨ (~ L · F)   3, Impl.   ⎫

8. (~ P ∨ ~ L) · (~ P ∨ F)   7, Dist.   ⎬ . . . and again

9. ~ P ∨ F   8, Simp.   ⎭

10. ~ F ∨ ~ W   6, Com.   ⎫

11. ~ F ∨ ~ P   9, Com.   ⎪

12. (~ F ∨ ~ W) · (~ F ∨ ~ P)   10, 11, Conj.   ⎪

13. F ∨ (~ W · ~ P)   12, Dist.   ⎬ The same seven steps
                                                          used in assignment 8.5b
14. (~ W · ~ P) ∨ F   13, Com.   ⎪ no. 9

15. ~ (W ∨ P) ∨ F   14, DeM.   ⎪

16. (W ∨ P) →F   15, Impl.   ⎭

17. T → F   1, 16, H. S.

Valid

RULES OF INFERENCE (must apply to the *entire* line)

Modus Ponens (M. P.)

$p \rightarrow q$

p

$\therefore q$

Modus Tollens (M. T.)

$p \rightarrow q$

$\sim q$

$\therefore \sim p$

Hypothetical Syllogism (H. S.)

$p \rightarrow q$

$q \rightarrow r$

$\therefore p \rightarrow r$

Disjunctive Syllogism (D. S.)

$p \vee q$ or $p \vee q$

$\sim p$ $\sim q$

$\therefore q$ $\therefore p$

Constructive Dilemma (C. D.)

$(p \rightarrow q) \cdot (r \rightarrow s)$

$p \vee r$

$\therefore q \vee s$

Conjunction (Conj.)

p

q

$\therefore p \cdot q$

Simplification (Simp.)

$p \cdot q$ or $p \cdot q$

$\therefore p$ $\therefore q$

Addition (Add.)

p or p

$\therefore p \vee q$ $\therefore q \vee p$

Absorption (Abs.)

$p \rightarrow q$

$\therefore p \rightarrow (p \cdot q)$

RULES OF REPLACEMENT (can apply to any *part* of a line)	
De MORGAN'S THEOREM (DeM.)	$\sim (p \cdot q) :: (\sim p \vee \sim q)$ $\sim (p \vee q) :: (\sim p \cdot \sim q)$
COMMUTATION (COM.)	$(p \vee q) :: (q \vee p)$ $(p \cdot q) :: (q \cdot p)$
ASSOCIATION (ASSOC.)	$[p \vee (q \vee r)] :: [(p \vee q) \vee r]$ $[(p \cdot (q \cdot r)] :: [(p \cdot q) \cdot r]$
DISTRIBUTION (DIST.)	$[p \vee (q \cdot r)] :: [(p \vee q) \cdot (p \vee r)]$ $[p \cdot (q \vee r)] :: [(p \cdot q) \vee (p \cdot r)]$
DOUBLE NEGATION (D. N.)	$p :: \sim \sim p$
TRANSPOSITION (TRANS.)	$(p \rightarrow q) :: (\sim q \rightarrow \sim p)$
MATERIAL IMPLICATION (IMPL.)	$(p \rightarrow q) :: (\sim p \vee q)$
EXPORTATION (EXP.)	$[(p \cdot q) \rightarrow r] :: [p \rightarrow (q \rightarrow r)]$
TAUTOLOGY (TAUT.)	$p :: p \vee p$ $p :: p \cdot p$
MATERIAL EQUIVALENCE (EQUIV.)	$(p \leftrightarrow q) :: [(p \rightarrow q) \cdot (q \rightarrow p)]$ $(p \leftrightarrow q) :: [(p \cdot q) \vee (\sim p \cdot \sim q)]$

SUBJECT INDEX

Note: Assignments and answers for selected assignments are not indexed

QUESTIONS IN CHRISTIAN PHILOSOPHY

How do we know? What should we do? What is real? What is art?

Philosophy, which means "the love of wisdom," asks such questions in its pursuit of the knowledge and understanding of all facets of life: existence, knowledge, ethics, art, and more. But what does it mean for Christians to pursue wisdom when Scripture affirms that the crucified and risen Christ is "the wisdom of God" (1 Cor 1:24)?

IVP Academic's Questions in Christian Philosophy (QCP) series seeks to help readers in their pursuit of wisdom from a Christian perspective by offering introductory textbooks on the various branches of philosophy. Designed for students with little or no background in the discipline, this series draws on experts in the field and lays a solid foundation for further philosophical reflection in pursuit of divine wisdom.

SERIES EDITORS

- James K. Dew Jr., president and professor of Christian philosophy, New Orleans Baptist Theological Seminary

- W. Paul Franks, associate professor of philosophy, Tyndale University, Toronto

CURRENT AND FORTHCOMING QCP VOLUMES

- James K. Dew Jr. and Mark W. Foreman, *How Do We Know? An Introduction to Epistemology*, 2nd ed.

- Forrest Baird, *How Do We Reason? An Introduction to Logic*

- Dennis P. Bray and David W. McNutt, *What Is Art? An Introduction to Aesthetics*